Journeys to the Spiritual Lands

Journeys to the Spiritual Lands

THE NATURAL HISTORY OF
A WEST INDIAN RELIGION

Wallace W. Zane

New York   Oxford

Oxford University Press

1999

Oxford University Press

Oxford   New York

Athens   Auckland   Bangkok   Bogotá   Buenos Aires   Calcutta
Cape Town   Chennai   Dar es Salaam   Delhi   Florence   Hong Kong   Istanbul
Karachi   Kuala Lumpur   Madrid   Melbourne   Mexico City   Mumbai
Nairobi   Paris   São Paulo   Singapore   Taipei   Tokyo   Toronto   Warsaw

and associated companies in
Berlin   Ibadan

Published by Oxford University Press, Inc.
198 Madison Avenue, New York, New York 10016

Oxford is a registered trademark of Oxford University Press

Library of Congress Cataloging-in-Publication Data
Zane, Wallace W. (Wallace Wayne), 1964–
Journeys to the spiritual lands / Wallace W. Zane.
p.   cm.
Includes bibliographical references and index.
ISBN 0-19-512845-1
1. Spiritual Baptists—Saint Vincent and the Grenadines—Kingstown
Region.   I. Title.
BX9798.S6534K568   1999
286'.5—dc21   98-30455

1 3 5 7 9 8 6 4 2

Printed in the United States of America
on acid-free paper

Acknowledgments

I WOULD LIKE TO NAME THE hundreds of Converted people whom I interviewed. For a number of reasons, all of my respondents must remain anonymous, but I hear their words and see their faces before me as I write. With every word, I have remembered the Converted of St. Vincent and New York who provided me with gracious hospitality and continuous good will. And the assistance came from all of the Converted whose churches I visited, not only those whom I specifically interviewed. Sometimes the clear singing of an individual I did not know helped me to stitch together a hole in the data, or someone acting under the direction of the Holy Spirit in a specific action made many things clear. Sometimes an ordinary member standing at the front of the church to offer "a word to the stranger" put things in a way that clarified many disparate points. My thanks must go to all of the Converted people of St. Vincent and to those Vincentian Converted who live in New York. I am grateful to the people of St. Vincent and the Grenadines, the Vincentians abroad, and other West Indians with whom I had contact in the Caribbean and in the United States.

In the preparation for the fieldwork, the research itself, and the write-up of the findings, several people at the University of California, Los Angeles were most helpful. Peter Hammond was always ready with useful advice. Robert Edgerton not only reminded me of the continuity of the ethnological tradition by matching me story for story, but also provided the example of using wide cultural comparison to find the human context of cultural facts. Douglas Hollan gave me the key question of the research: "What is it like to be you?" Without that, the data would have been of a very different character. Donald Cosentino lent his continual moral support and gave me occasional access to his wide knowledge of culture and folklore on both sides of the African Atlantic.

My preparation for fieldwork began years ago. I owe special thanks to three professors: to A. F. (Sandy) Robertson of the University of California, Santa Barbara, for teaching me how to do fieldwork; to Jérôme Rousseau of McGill University for teaching me that all research is only a part of all possible research; and to the late Roger Keesing of McGill University who introduced me to the literature on colonialism.

During the research in New York, Elizabeth McAlister was a very helpful colleague. In the preparation for the research, and for the duration of the data-gathering and the write-up, many people in California kept me feeling there might really be a home: Lisa Pope, Victoria Sams, Clytie Alexander (and at various times her family—Peter Alexander, Hope, and Julia), Angel Eldridge, Melina Budov, Susan Phillips, Deborah Bird, Lori Frystak-Eschler, Sarah Sullivan. Kay Parker handled my mail and sent me many good thoughts. More than everyone else, my thanks must go to Ellen Elphand and Rebel Clair, my urim and thummim, without whom I would have seen nothing at all.

Part of chapter 11 appeared as "Spiritual Baptists of New York City" in *Religion, Diaspora, and Cultural Identity: A Reader in the Anglophone Caribbean*, J. Pulis, ed., Amsterdam: Gordon and Breach, 1999.

Contents

ONE • Introduction 3

TWO • A Shouting 17

Part I   Spiritual Work

THREE • Spiritual Workers 31

FOUR • Music 52

FIVE • A Banning 66

Part II   Spiritual Experience

SIX • Pilgrim Travelers 79

SEVEN • Mourning 107

Part III   Vincentian Context

EIGHT • Work and Travel 121

NINE • Converted Cosmology 139

TEN • Comparative History of
the Converted Religion   149

ELEVEN • Going to Brooklyn   164

TWELVE • Conclusion   176

Glossary   179

Appendix: Converted Ritual Classifications   189

Notes   205

References   217

Index   235

Journeys to the Spiritual Lands

Introduction

I WAS A LITTLE NERVOUS AT MY first Converted church service. I sat on the unpainted bench trying to adjust to the humid weight of the tropical air while the congregation said the opening prayers. Presently the pastor gestured to me and invited me to introduce myself to the church. As I stood, he stopped me and said, "Would one of the sisters . . . ?" A song in polyphonous harmony sprang from the congregation, "All the Way from Africaland, Coming to Hear them Singing, All the Way from Africaland, Coming to Hear them Sing." The song continued for five minutes while two older women danced with me at the front of the church. I was later told, "That is a greeting song. We don't have one for America. So we give you that."

Journeys to the Spiritual Lands

This book is about a people and a religion called "the Converted" on the Caribbean island of St. Vincent. Also known as Spiritual Baptists, Believers, the Penitent, and by a number of other names, they occupy a special place in Vincentian society and are noted for their distinctive dress, their beautiful music, and their dramatic rituals. Converted people dedicate themselves to a life of service to God and to their fellow Vincentians. Much of that service takes place in a spiritual world unseen by ordinary people.

Colonial experience is reproduced in a spiritual world in which tens of thousands of Christian believers—the Converted—travel and conduct spiritual work. Converted religion is a sort of shamanistic Christianity that emerges as a distinct expression of the culture and history of the Caribbean as it is found on St. Vincent. In its combination of shamanic technique and Christian ideology, the religion is dramatically new to anthropology. Historical and comparative data show that Converted religion is not merely opportunistic syncretism, but an invention of colonialism in its local idiom. The present study has three aims: (1) to describe the spiritual work and travels of the Converted; (2) to demonstrate that the experiences of the Converted in the spiritual world are derived from the local context; and (3) to explain how Vincentian culture and Converted religion are each a part of the other. The main body of the text is divided into three sections that emphasize those ideas.

Spiritual Baptists are widespread in the Eastern Caribbean. The Converted (that is, Vincentian Spiritual Baptists, formerly called Shakers) make up a minimum of 10% of the population of St. Vincent. It is a Christian religion similar to Pentecostalism in theology and practice. In addition, African influences are strong as well as elements taken from the physical setting of St. Vincent and its status as a British colony. The most distinguishing characteristic of Converted religion is the emphasis on spiritual travel on a regular basis for all adherents to the religion. All, also, are required to do spiritual work as a result of this travel.

Converted cosmology is completely a Vincentian cosmology derived from Christianity and the colonial context. It is not African, not European, but something produced out of the peculiarly Caribbean circumstances that make St. Vincent what it is. For one example among the curious many, *The Pilgrim's Progress* is used as a sacred text that serves as a template or guidebook to the spiritual realm in which the Converted travel. But they are not limited to Bunyan's imagination. The Converted also travel in Biblical lands as well as to the sources of British colonial labor: Africa, India, and China. Though the religion is not syncretic in philosophy (it is exclusively and totally Christian), it may be considered so in the manner in which it expresses the Christian philosophy.

The latter half of the fieldwork on which this book is based was undertaken among Vincentian Converted in Brooklyn, New York. I went to Brooklyn because I hoped to document how the religion had changed with the people who took it with them in migration from St. Vincent. In fact, it had changed little. The colonial structure of the religion is its essence; for that to change, the religion itself would become something different. Data from Brooklyn are included in the description of Converted religion in general. Patterns of difference and similarity between Vincentian Converted practice in St. Vincent and Brooklyn are described in a separate chapter. The colonial nature of the religion and the colonial influences to which it responds are as present in Brooklyn as in St. Vincent.

The Research Setting

St. Vincent and the Grenadines is a nation composed of 32 islands and cays in the Caribbean Windward Islands. The island of St. Vincent, referred to locally as "the mainland," is 18 miles long by 11 miles wide and had a population of 106,499 people in 1991. Sometimes the locals call the island "Hairoun," its Carib name. It means "the blessed isle."

St. Vincent may indeed be the "most beautiful of the Caribee islands" (Martin 1937:212). The whole aspect presents the lushest of tropical settings. Kingstown, with its natural harbor, sharply rising mountains in the center of the island, deeply cut valleys, striking volcano, and black sand beaches stretching into the raging Atlantic on the windward coast and into the calm Caribbean on the leeward coast, all add to the effect. More impressive than everything else is the verdure. A local saying claims, "If you plant a nail in St. Vincent, it will grow."

St. Vincent was one of the last Caribbean islands to be colonized by Europeans. The aboriginal Caribs existed there in sufficient force to hold off European incursions until the eighteenth century. In the early seventeenth century, the Black Caribs emerged on the island—a population composed of the descendants of Caribs and African maroons from other islands (and several shipwrecks)—who quickly came to outnumber the original (or Red) Caribs.

European vessels had been watering and victualing on St. Vincent since the 1500s, and eventually some Frenchmen settled on St. Vincent as guests of the Caribs and Black Caribs. In 1748, St. Vincent and three other of the Windward Islands were declared neutral between England and France and were left to the Caribs. However, in 1763, the Treaty of Paris granted St. Vincent to the British, who quickly set up plantations with large numbers of slaves. Many of the Frenchmen remained and Vincentians today may have French as well as English names. The Carib lands in the northern part of the island had been excluded from expropriation by the British, but the promise of profitable sugar cultivation led to encroachment by planters and eventually to two Carib wars. After the Second Carib War (1794–1796), the entire population of up to 5,000 Black Caribs was ordered removed to Central America, where they remain today (in Belize, Guatemala, Nicaragua, and Honduras) as the Garifuna. A remnant of the Red Caribs was left. Their descendants make up the more than 3,000 Caribs who currently live on St. Vincent.

Despite the supposed removal of all the Black Caribs to Honduras, small groups of both Black Caribs as well as Red Caribs remained on the island. They cannot be ruled out as one of the sources of Converted religion.[1] In 1876, Ober (1880) spent several months in St. Vincent. His encounters with Caribs at that late date record many of the practices that are found today among the Black Caribs of Central America, but no longer in St. Vincent.

Gullick wrote in 1971 that the Shaker (Converted) religion was "mainly confined to the few remaining Carib Indian settlements" on St. Vincent (Gullick 1971:7). But he did not see much connection between the aboriginal religion and the Converted. Instead, he felt it was ironic that Amerindians should adhere to a religion described as "African." The Caribs on St. Vincent today are as culturally Vincentian as anyone else on the island.[2] Converted religion is a religion that appeals to poor Vincentians because it developed out of the experience of poor people on St. Vincent. The Caribs are the poorest people on the island, and it makes sense that Converted religion should be "the chief Carib sect" (Gullick 1985:19).

Although slavery had probably already existed in some form among the Caribs, it certainly came to St. Vincent with the French settlers around 1720. By the time the English took over the island, some accounts indicate that the slaves of the French outnumbered both the Red and the Black Caribs. In 1764, there were 1,300 Frenchmen and 3,400 African slaves, whereas there were only 3,000 to 5,000 Caribs. By 1831, not 70 years later, there were still only 1,300 Europeans on the island, but the number of African slaves had increased to 22,589 (Madden 1835:54; Boucher 1992:106). The Red Caribs had been reduced to a few hundred. Slavery and its effects, as elsewhere in the Caribbean, have been the main social force in Vincentian society—in 1831 as well as in the 1990s.

The population in 1991 was 106,499, with over 82,000 describing themselves as "African/Negro/Black" (77.1%); 3,341 as "Amerindian/Carib" (3.1%); 1,477 as "East Indian" (1.4%); 511 as "Portuguese" (0.5%); 982 as "White" (0.9%); 17,501 as "Mixed" (16.4%); and 140 describing themselves as "Other" (St. Vincent 1993: 28). Most of my respondents who were listed in the census as "Mixed" identified closer with Black Vincentians than with other Vincentians. They said, "If you born in St. Vincent, we figure you have some African blood."[3]

The categories listed in the census provide a sort of history lesson of the island. The Caribs derive from the remnant that was not deported at the end of the Carib wars. The Blacks represent descendants of slaves. The East Indians and Portuguese were indentured after emancipation to make up for labor shortages. The Whites were also brought in to make up a labor shortfall (only a few are from planter families). Most of the Whites in the census are descendants of those who came from Barbados in the 1860s as laborers. They actually have a lower social and economic status than most of the Blacks on the island.[4]

The population I worked with was rather homogeneous—poor Black people living close to the capital. I did notice the class-based stratification discussed by Rubenstein (1976; 1987; 1991), Fraser (1975), and V. Young (1990; 1991; 1993), but my contact was mainly with poor people. The complex layers of stratification identified by Rubenstein, Fraser, and Young seemed to have little impact on the people I studied (the poor majority), because everyone who was not poor was placed by them in the same class as, for instance, the Prime Minister. In other words, to my respondents, one was poor or one was everyone else. To illustrate, when I was on the island, unemployment was 52% and the employed were overrepresented by the middle class.

As elsewhere in the Caribbean, the plantation in St. Vincent is the symbol of privilege and exploitation. As late as 1954, plantations in St. Vincent were fighting the local legislature to continue to employ child laborers (Lewis 1968:152). A peasantry supporting itself (incompletely) by the land employs 24,000 people working for themselves on small plots of land (Mintz 1985:144). Nonetheless, plantations remain. In St. Vincent, 40 farms control 54 percent of the land, whereas most farms are of only one to five acres.

The current pattern of land distribution and use began during slavery and as an adjunct to it (Marshall 1991). All locally grown vegetables are still called "provision" as they were by the planters during slavery. The same food prescribed by Collins (1803:93–94) for slaves nearly 200 years ago is the same as most Vincentians eat today: yams, Indian corn, plantains, beans, peas, tannies or eddoes, flour, salt-fish, herring, beef, pork, rice, breadfruit, cassava, and farine (cassava flour). Staples of the twentieth century he did not mention are pineapples, guavas, mangos, peanuts, and chicken.

Fishing, through highly visible to the tourist, does not make a significant contribution to the subsistence of most Vincentians. Poor Vincentians view fish and other meat as "relish," often a rarity (Rubenstein 1987:167). However, whaling has a special cultural significance to Vincentians. St. Vincent is one of the last whaling nations on Earth. The primary whale caught is the pilot whale, called "blackfish." All whales are hunted, but only pilot whales and killer whales were caught while I was in St. Vincent. Iaconetti (1994) reports that Bequia has been granted aboriginal whaling status by the International Whaling Commission; however, the status of St. Vincent is uncertain (*Searchlight*, St. Vincent, June 9, 1995).[5]

In St. Vincent, a feeling of a lack of local control is prevalent and seems to have increased in the last several years. Grossman (1993) shows that importation of food has risen with the emphasis on banana export; land that could be used to grow subsistence is used for income-production. The entire banana industry, in turn, is heavily dependent on financial aid from Great Britain (Grossman 1994:168). The next most important sector of the national economy, tourism, is also at risk: An international group has threatened to lead a boycott on tourism to St. Vincent because of the practice of whaling (*Searchlight*, St. Vincent, June 9, 1995). In the 1995 Carnival, "ground provision" and "blackfish" were two symbols of Vincentian resistance to U.S. hegemony in calypsos—"No, Uncle Sam, we will not give up blackfish," and "Ground provision is our security." Ground provision and whaling are Vincentian; bananas and tourism are a function of external control.

The region-wide pattern of a decline of the importance of agriculture and a rise in reliance on tourism and emigration is expressed in St. Vincent. *The 1994 World Almanac* (1993:305) indicated, "The entire economic life of St. Vincent is dependent upon agriculture and tourism." That is not strictly true, but it reflects the gross figures regularly available. Remittances from abroad form a significant portion of the national income.[6] High prestige is placed on emigration, and St. Vincent is included among the "migration-oriented societies" (Rubenstein 1987:197). Given the reliance on remittances by the local economy, family members on the island have a positive association with emigrated members. Additionally, kin networks in metropoles ("mother-countries" of colonial powers) are important for assisting members in St. Vincent to emigrate as well.

St. Vincent is classically dependent and underdeveloped. The island is largely agricultural. Bananas and arrowroot are the main export crops, and some local vegetables are exported to Trinidad. Food staples must be imported—all of the sugar, rice, wheat, and nearly all of the chicken. During my last month on the island there was a chicken shortage, because the regular shipment of chicken parts from the United States had failed a health inspection and been dumped.

Tourism is not a big factor in St. Vincent itself (most of the arrivals are in the Grenadines). The tourists that (poor) Vincentians do meet reinforce the conception of St. Vincent as a site of economic and cultural subordination. These feelings of inferiority often surface as violence (cf. Hadley 1973). The tourist commission of St. Vincent reported that the high incidence of hostility and outright violence toward tourists was a threat to tourist-derived income (*The Vincentian*, August 4, 1995; cf. Kurlansky 1992:25, for neighboring St. Lucia). Violence against foreigners is a significant indicator of the sort of frustration that, for many Vincentians, is moderated by Converted religion. Although I often felt hostility from Vincentian men and women, I never did from Converted of any age or sex. For non-Converted Vincentians confronted with their own powerlessness, violence against a momentarily powerless tourist may be a means to even the balance of power. For the Converted faced with impenetrable oppressive structures, their religion serves the same purpose. Both the spontaneous violent acts of "road boys" and the deliberate rituals of the Converted mediate the situation of the poor Vincentian individual with the (neo-) colonial world system.

Colonialism, Religion, and Ritual

Much of this book deals with the idea of colonialism and its relationship to Converted religion. Although this work is not intended specifically as a study in colonialism, it could be viewed as such, and the following paragraphs are included to give the reader an orientation to where I stand on this complex and fascinating topic. I conclude this section with a discussion of previous research on Caribbean religions and on the Spiritual Baptists.

Colonialism is problematic when it is used to apply to present-day situations. Fifty years ago, most of the current nations of the world were colonies. Today, actual colonies are almost extinct. However, the means by which colonial powers exerted authority still function. For the most part, these amount to extra-local control over significant elements (political, economic, social, military, etc.) of otherwise sovereign territories, a condition easily observable in formerly colonized countries. "Colonialism" in the text will refer to the "ways" of colonialism. For the purposes of this study, neocolonialism, postcolonialism, and other terms descriptive of continuing inequality in relations between controller and controlled on an international level are all subsumed by me under "the ways of colonialism" or simply "colonialism." Although colonialism seems to have ended, its methods persist. St. Vincent ceased to be a colony in 1979, but colonial processes continue to operate. For example, before the end of slavery, the sugar trade and its subsidies were controlled from England. The legislative assembly of St. Vincent continually lobbied the crown for assistance. In the 1990s, the economics of the single prime earner, the subsidized banana trade, are determined by England (and to some extent by the United States and the European Union). The government of St. Vincent, though independent, continually lobbies the metropoles for assistance.

One influential approach to colonialism pays attention to the creation and contestation of boundaries between the colonizer and the colonized "other."[7] The identification of a debased other is essential for control of that other. In the Caribbean, the African has been the censured alter. Converted religion was persecuted and eventually made illegal in St. Vincent in 1912 because of its "traits of African barbarism" (Fraser 1995, April 20). It was only when an astute Vincentian politician, 53 years later, identified himself with Converted religion because it was a Vincentian rather than a foreign institution that a bill was finally passed to legalize the religion. However, the colonial attitudes prevailing in 1912 still operate among the elite and much of the rest of the population, and Converted religion is widely despised in St. Vincent (but not without some fearful respect).

Other significant work on colonialism addresses the encroachment of the dominant powers and the overt and covert efforts at resistance by local people. South Asia, the other most important area in the British colonial world (along with the West Indies) is the source of much of this research. The aim of the Subaltern Studies Group, for instance, was to draw out from the colonial records the hidden histories of suppressed groups (e.g., Guha 1987; Spivak 1988). Prakash's (1992) critique of the *Subaltern Studies* effort argues that the analytical structures of subaltern analysis are still the structures of the colonizing histories that the Subaltern Studies Group tries to address. This is important for my thesis, because it shows that even intentional breaks from the dominant ideology may yet be structured by that ideology. Like the unintentional Vincentian response to colonialism in the form of Converted religion, the subaltern studies operate in a constrained dialectic established by the controlling entity.

The same thing happens elsewhere. Beckett's (1993) description of a native history of the world displays dramatically the internalization of colonial structures among colonized peoples. Walter Newton, an Australian aborigine, tells the history of the world; he combines selections from the Bible, local aboriginal histories, and colonial political notions in his uncritical presentation of world history. That world, as Beckett shows, is Australia; Newton's experience includes nothing else. The Converted do exactly the same thing. In the same way that Newton's history of the world is an expression of his lived experience as a colonized subject, the cosmology and practice of Converted religion is likewise a colonial product.

In my thinking on the subject, I have been most influenced by those studies that portray local populations as effecting ritual amelioration of their subordinate position in colonial (and neocolonial) circumstances.[8] Rituals are performances that stand for something else—a memory, a spiritual reality, or a change in status. When oppressed people are unable to better their situation by political or military means, they often use performative mechanisms to enact the termination, or reversal, of their oppression. Dirks (1987), in his study of Christmas in the British West Indies, shows that such rituals often led to insurrection. Many aspects of Converted religion can be traced to these annual rituals of inversion and license. The temporary ritual of reversal became permanently enacted in the institution of Converted religion.

This study shows the cosmology of the Converted to be a response to colonial structures. Converted religion was not built on a native substrate. Like all West Indian societies, St. Vincent (and Converted religion) is the product of a recent historical event: The advent of Europeans in the Americas and the effects of their colonial policies. British colonial society is reproduced in the spiritual world; the spiritual world reflects not only British organizational structures, but recognition of the many cultures—African, Indian, Chinese, North American—that make up the colonial experience. Colonialism has not strictly ended in St. Vincent. As a member of the Commonwealth of Nations, St. Vincent and the Grenadines still must honor the Queen of England as its queen by celebrating her birthday and acknowledging her sovereignty at sessions of the Legislative Council. To further emphasize that Vincentians do not have the final say over their lives, the Queen maintains a Governor General in the island and court decisions may be appealed to the Crown in England. Of course, these ritual vestiges of colonialism have less real impact than the economic hegemony of the numerous recently emerged metropoles of the world free market, for example, New York, Tokyo, London.

In the rich body of literature that has developed on religions of the African diaspora, the African origins of most of the expressive elements of those religions are emphasized.[9] In a recent article, Besson and Chevannes (1996:223) contend that "any attempt to polarize the debate around Caribbean culture into an African continuity versus creole creativity position is misplaced." Nonetheless, that has been the way the discussion of Caribbean culture—and Caribbean religion in particular—has been framed (especially by Herskovits 1958; and his students, e.g., Simpson and Hammond 1957; but also by others—e.g., Thompson 1984; Murphy 1994). Certainly both continuity and creativity are happening with the Converted. However, the Converted are a dramatic example of the latter, to the point of obscuring African elements in the religion. Indeed, following this approach, the Spiritual Baptists of St. Vincent are cited for their lack of African traits (Bourguignon 1970; Pollack-Eltz 1993:21);. As Besson and Chevannes point out, the dynamism inherent in the continuity of African traits appears to obviate the question; the historical and environmental factors should be the focus. That does not mean the African elements are not there, only that they are situated in Caribbean culture as other traits are. Converted religion does appear to be African-derived, as its adherents claim. It also seems to be completely Christian as the Converted say. It is also shamanistic in style and practice.[10]

It is not a problem to find African religions in the Caribbean. We should expect to find them. For instance, it is probably true that spirit possession religions in the Caribbean derive their spirit possession from African sources (Simpson and Hammond 1957). Yet, when we find spirit possession with identical movements, sounds, and local exegetics in many different places in the world, we are led to ask questions about the nature of spirit possession in general and not just African spirit possession. Consequently, particularly because the African origins of most aspects of Caribbean religions have been celebrated to the obscuration of elements common to many diverse cultures, most of the comparative examples I use are from cultures that are not strongly influenced by Africa. I want to show that the context of Converted religion is larger than its historical derivation. The African origins are important, but they are not the whole story. This study, therefore, shows a religion that, though expressing African influence, appears to be a local creation embodying selections from all available cultural materials—European and African as well as those that arise from human biology and human ways of living in the world.

Spiritual Baptists have been of interest to anthropologists since the publication of Herskovits and Herskovits' (1947) *Trinidad Village*. Most of the research on Spiritual Baptists has been done in Trinidad, with shorter studies on the religion in Grenada, Tobago, and Barbados.[11] Previous research on the Vincentian Spiritual Baptist, whose traditions are different from those on other islands, consisted of a two-month visit in 1966 (Henney 1968), supplemented by one other short visit in 1970 (Henney 1971; 1974; 1980). The present work represents the first anthropological study of the religion in St. Vincent based on traditional long-term fieldwork. Rather than seeking to explain the spiritual experience as hallucination derived from sensory overload (Ward and Beaubrun 1979) or sensory deprivation (Henney 1974; Sargant 1974), this study takes the experience as a starting point. With this approach, Converted cosmology is clearly laid out and the nature of the religion as a response to colonialism is easily seen.

In the postmodern world, the discrete boundaries of primitive and modern have come undone. Anthropologists "look at a world in which all the cultures are flowing together in most curious ways, and symbols have become world travelers" (Anderson 1995:72). The Converted is one such case. The explanation I give in these pages is one that addresses the international and intercultural flow of symbols, whose selection and combination are predicated on long-standing structures and processes.

Methods

The findings I report are based on data gathered during 14 months of fieldwork among the Vincentian Converted in St. Vincent (April–September 1995) and Brooklyn (October 1995–June 1996). I visited 17 churches in St. Vincent and had contact with many others. I went to meetings in private homes and yards, and in the market square in Kingstown, and attended several baptisms at different beaches. In Brooklyn, I attended four of the five Vincentian churches there at the time of my study (the number and makeup of the churches in Brooklyn changes frequently). In the 14 months of fieldwork, I attended over 150 Vincentian Converted meetings. I also attended a Spiritual Baptist convention in Grenada with delegations present from Trinidad, St. Vincent, the United States, England, and Canada. In Brooklyn, I visited several Trinidadian and Grenadian Spiritual Baptist churches and one Jamaican Spiritual Baptist church.

I selected the Kingstown area in St. Vincent for its easy access to several villages in the surrounding hills. My method beyond that may be described as both comprehensive and accidental. I visited every Converted church within walking distance of my residence. I chose three churches in three adjacent villages as the ones on which I would concentrate most of my attention. Church schedules vary by church (usually several meetings a week) and I was able to attend most of the important rituals that occurred during my fieldwork in each of the three churches. In Brooklyn, I also selected three churches to be the main ones I would attend and made visits to the others. Converted churches, both in St. Vincent and in Brooklyn, have a tradition of visiting each other as congregations. In this activity, I was able to travel with the regular churches I attended and to visit many others. More than half of my time during the fieldwork was spent among Vincentian emigrés in New York. However, the religion, even in New York, remains firmly grounded in the island of St. Vincent.

While I was careful to be attentive to all aspects of Vincentian culture, I found that most of the ethnographic work had been done already. No fewer than 16 anthropologists have made extensive studies of St. Vincent and the Grenadines.[12] This was a tremendous benefit to my research, because I was able to concentrate on the small focus with which I had come.

I did not go to the field expecting to find travels in spiritual lands. They had not been described as other than hallucinations in the previous literature. However, my aim was to get an understanding of Spiritual Baptist experience. My constant question was, "What is it like to be a Spiritual Baptist?" The answer often involved travels in the spiritual lands. Although I did find some respondents to be especially easy to talk to, or to have particularly clear ways of explaining Converted phenomena, I did not rely on a few key informants. I talked to hundreds of Converted and conducted interviews with scores of them.[13]

While I outline the colonial restraints on the Converted worldview, there is room in their world for invention. Like Hollan and Wellencamp (1994:215), I recognize "the anthropological subjects as actors, actively and creatively engaged in the construction of meaning, rather than as passive recipients of a cultural tradition." While actively creating meaning, the Converted also receive a cultural tradition, one that has been constructed by the Converted who came before them; people build a ritual house, but they must use materials around them to do so. The focus of the present study is on that construction in a larger sense, in the identification of norms of that experience, but acknowledging that the experience of individuals "whether shared or idiosyncratic, may clash with cultural expectations as well as be consistent with them" (ibid:214).

The Researcher in the Research

One day in St. Vincent, I met a Spiritual Baptist woman on the road. When I told her I was writing a book about the Spiritual Baptists, she said, "I hope you do not write too many bad things about us." I was surprised to find that her reaction was common. At a church service the evening before, after I had introduced myself to the congregation, the *pointer* admonished the people, "This man is writing a book. Is this what you want him to say about you, that you sat down and did not sing?" A pointer in another church on another night said to the congregation, "Look this man here. A writer! From California! Don't think he going to see you do something wrong and he isn't going to write it down." My presence in the church services was always noted. I learned that if I was expected at a church service, the members behaved in the way they felt was most proper. This turned out to be a good thing because I could compare the services where I was expected with those where I was unexpected. It allowed me to learn what was considered important behavior to the Converted themselves. It also made me very aware of the effect of my own presence in the fieldsite.

In Eliade's book *Ordeal by Labyrinth* (1982:121), he and Claude Rocquet talk about the Western researcher's encounter with non-Western religion. Rocquet says, "So one has to hold on to one's own identity and also to maintain one's reason against the terrible forces of the irrational?" Eliade replies, "[T]he power of the irrational is certainly lurking there." It seems to me that the power of the irrational is strong for those who have not accommodated it, or conquered it, in their personal life. Bastide, for instance, found it necessary to be initiated into Candomblé (including possession) in order to understand the religion (Price in Bastide 1978:vii–xii). Many researchers in spirit-possession religions find it useful or compelling to join, or initiate into, the religions they study—including the Spiritual Baptists (e.g., Houk 1995:81; Goldwasser 1996:162).

At this point I need to situate myself in the research. In my teen years, I was a Pentecostal street preacher and a chaplain to a (nonaccredited) Christian school. I had the complete Holy Spirit possession experience and taught it to others. For fully ten years prior to the research, I had been (and still am) a sturdy apostate. The irrational was not lurking when I went to the field. It had been addressed and dismissed. The irrational holds appeal to me only as a resource for immense creativity. I did have to deal with the evangelical concerns of my respondents. I did not say that I was not a Christian unless asked and Christianity was usually assumed. I struggled with that for a good part of the research as I felt that anything less than full disclosure might approach dishonesty. When I realized that my prayers in church, said when requested out of respect for the Converted, and my singing and dancing in church, done for the genuine pleasure of it, convinced Converted that I was "really a spiritual person, no matter what" I said, I stopped telling the Converted that I was not a Christian. I did tell those Converted whom I got to know fairly well of my apostasy. Most of them did not believe me anyway. I never became comfortable being mistaken for a Christian. However, as the Converted are said to be able to see into the hearts of men and several told me, "You at peace" (that is, they could see that I did not have a psychological need for conversion), I eventually stopped trying to make everyone sure exactly where I stood on matters of belief.

Academically, I must confess to a (somewhat postmodern) positivism in my dealing with the data. My primary research assumption is that the purpose and test of knowledge is prediction. If it predicts, it is useful knowledge. I do find the poststructuralist, deconstructionist, and textualist inquiries to be energizing critiques of anthropology. My avoidance of direct engagement with them in this work reflects my view that there is a reality—a predictability—that, though not exact in social science, may be close enough to provide a good idea of what to expect. That is, useful knowledge is there—we use it every day—and we know it is useful because our predictions of what it will be are fulfilled. I mean this in the most practical manner: the sun rises in the morning; it sets at dusk; we go about our daily lives.

I am not in the camp of Olivier de Sardan (1990), who says that deconstructionism and textualism are fashions that will and should pass. He claims that in the former the ethnologist becomes his own hero, while in the latter, she cannot say anything for herself. It is my view that deconstructionism, textualism, and the other postmodern critiques are essential to the making of a sharper analytical knife. In the meantime, the old tool, though worn, may, with careful use and a little polishing, still cut cleanly.

Despite the claim to an adjusted positivism, I am an "ironist" in Rorty's (1995: 100) sense of the term. That is, I can never take things too seriously, because I am always aware of the contingency of language (and experience). It was precisely that sense of irony that allowed me to approach a religion that a round dozen other anthropologists had considered and to see in it not only what the others had seen, but also (approximately) what the participants in the religion said they could see. Rorty opposes irony to common sense. When the Converted said that they went to Africa while the whole time they lay on the floor in a little room, I did not emphasize hyperventilation and hallucination like the common sensualists. Instead I said, Why not? and, Tell me how.

The Structure of the Text

The three distinctive features of Converted religion—the shamanistic work, the experience in the spiritual world, and its colonial nature—are all closely related. The text is divided into three parts. The first details the spiritual work of the Converted. The second part describes the experiences of the Converted in the spiritual world and shows them to arise from the local context. The third part situates the religion, explaining it as a consequence of Vincentian culture—socially and historically—and comparing Converted religion with shamanism and other religious styles. Chapters of vivid description of typical events alternate with those of comparative analysis. Shifting points of view from experience to close examination is intended to enable the reader to get the feel of the religion as well as the "why" of the religion.

The Introduction is in two chapters. This one sets the stage and the next puts the reader in the action. The next chapter of the Introduction, chapter 2, describes a *shouting*, which is usually the first way that ordinary Vincentians are exposed to the Converted. All of the important features of the religion are exhibited at a shouting; the rest of the text can be seen as an explanation of each of those elements.

In Part One, I concentrate on the spiritual work of the Converted. Chapter 3 discusses the types of work the Converted do, the tools they use, and the types of tasks and titles assigned to different Converted workers. Chapter 4 examines the main spiritual tool of Converted religion, its music. Music is used to enter into and travel in the spiritual world. It is used to accomplish actions, both in the spiritual lands and in the physical realm. Chapter 5 describes a *banning*, an important ritual where the concept of work is most articulated and most easily observed. The banning requires joint effort by numerous Converted workers. The purpose of the ritual is to prepare one or more Converted people for extended travels in the spiritual world.

Part Two takes a close look at Converted travels and actions in the spiritual lands. In chapter 6, I describe the spiritual lands and the beings who inhabit them. Chapter 7 details the process of *mourning*—the days-long ritual of prayer, isolation, and spiritual journeying.

Having established the main characteristics of the religion in Parts One and Two, I contextualize the religion in Part Three, showing how Converted religion is a product of Vincentian history and society. Part Three contains material that is usually placed at the beginning of an anthropological monograph rather than toward the end. Because the meaning of the religion is found in its historical and cultural matrix, I felt it was important to lay out just what it is that is being explained (Converted cosmology) before saying why and how it got to be what it is. Chapter 8 discusses Converted religion in reference to shamanism and describes a wake performed by the Converted. The wake is an important way that the religion is integrated into and serves the rest of Vincentian society. Chapter 9 identifies elements in the common experience of Vincentians as sources for specific Converted traits. In chapter 10, I outline the history of the religion in St. Vincent and compare it with religions elsewhere. Converted religion is shown to be resilient in the face of persecution because it speaks to the people of St. Vincent in their own terms.

Chapter 11 looks at the religion in Brooklyn, at the pressures for change outside of St. Vincent, and at the response of the Converted to those influences. The self-definition required of the Converted in the foreign land (New York), one that is not necessary in St. Vincent where the Converted are so much a part of the local culture, provides a concise summary of the religion. Chapter 12 reviews the main points and suggests areas for future research.

"The Converted," "Converted people," and "Converted religion," are terms referring to the religion identified in legal documents in St. Vincent as Spiritual Baptists, and formerly as Shakers, Christian Pilgrims, Pilgrim Baptists, or Wesleyan Baptists. In the text, I alternate between the three terms most commonly used in St. Vincent—Converted, Spiritual Baptists, and Baptists. I refer to the people I studied as "respondents" rather than "informants," because all information I received from individuals in the field came in response to direct or implied questions. With the exception of historical figures, all names and identifying information of individuals have been changed. General statements of practice or belief reflect the view reported most often by my respondents or what I observed most often in churches I visited. While norms can be identified, the revelatory nature of the religion leads to a wide range of variety in practice.

All unattributed quotes are from my fieldnotes and were said by one or more Converted. Converted terms are italicized the first time they are used and may be found in the glossary. Quotations around a word or a phrase are not to indicate that

I think it is specious, but to denote that while I heard it from one or more Vincentians, it is not necessarily a term in general use. It should be noted that Vincentians have a unique accent and that many of them speak in *dialect* (or *dialek*), the Vincentian dialect. When I quote Vincentians, I spell the words the way that Vincentians spell them. For instance, although the word "there" is pronounced by most Vincentians as "dey," they spell it "there." However, I do not add words that were not said (e.g., the copula). I feel that the use of phoneticized orthography in writing Vincentian speech unnecessarily exoticizes the Vincentians. Their pronunciation departs no more from the written form than that of standard English. Many elements in the Vincentian Spiritual Baptist tradition are not customarily written, and for those I asked a number of Baptists to suggest a spelling and I have used the spelling indicated by the majority.

When referring to ethnic identification, the words *White* and *Black* are capitalized. In the text, I tend to use the words White and Black to refer, respectively, to people of European descent, and to people of African descent, because that reflects the usage of the Vincentians with whom I had contact. Although there is some debate as to which words should be used by anthropologists and how they should be spelled (e.g., Houk 1993), I use "White" and "Black" as proper nouns (or as adjectives derived from proper nouns) and capitalize them as such.

All quotes from the Bible are from the King James Version, the translation used by the Converted. I have removed the italics that the translators of that version use to indicate words and phrases not found in the original Hebrew and Greek. I capitalize the word *God* to refer to the Christian god, as Converted and other Christians use the term. Uncapitalized, *god* refers to an unspecified deity.

Throughout the text, I use the term "ritual experience." By this I mean all experience that is mediated or represented by ritual, not necessarily the ritual alone. Therefore, experiences in the spiritual world, which may take place in a ritual setting or in an ordinary dream, are all ritual experiences. The way of experiencing the spiritual world is established by ritual even when the ritual does not precipitate the experience (e.g., in a dream). Thus, ritual experience is in the perception of the experience, the performance of the rituals, as well as in the use of ritual goods and ideas apart from the ritual setting. Lakoff and Johnson (1980:234) say of rituals: "The real-world objects stand for entities in the world as defined by the conceptual system of the religion. The coherent structure of the ritual is commonly taken as paralleling some aspect of reality as it is seen through the religion." Both sides of the metonymy are included in my idea of ritual experience.

In the introduction to his history of religion, LaBarre (1972:4) suggests that the best one can hope for in understanding someone else's worldview is to see the same thing the teller sees when he points to it. As that is the aim of the Vincentian Converted (pointing out to others a richness in experience of life—ritual and eternal), good pointing is also my goal.

TWO

A Shouting

IMAGINE, IF YOU WILL, that the sky is dark like deep sea velvet, that the hill is steep like a water slide, that the legion crickets' chirp chirp is testing your ability to think your own thoughts, that the inky shadows in shrubs and trees are hiding men and monsters to challenge your way. If you were a Vincentian, this could be any night of any day of any year. This is a Vincentian night. On sundry evenings, you might also hear, as the clock ticks over to nine o'clock, in any part of the island, a ringing of bells and a singing vibrating from the hills that defeat all other sounds. You would know from friends and neighbors and by the vanloads of arriving visitors in Converted uniform that it is a *shouting*. If you live nearby, within a quarter mile or so, you might as well go watch.

Color and sound and bright catchy movement gleams from the windows and doors of the little church, about the same size as your own little house. You would likely know most of the people in the church, and as you approach, standing outside the windows with friends you have known all your life, other nonbelievers, you will hear sometime appeals to "those outside" to come into the joy of the Lord. There is something compelling about the way these folks represent that joy. As you arrive, they are "jumping spirit," "working *doption*." The congregation is singing an abruptly vigorous tune—no words, just the tune with polyrhythmic clapping, hummed and shouted melodies sitting on top of each other and rolling through the church like ocean waves. Seven or eight in the congregation are shoulder to shoulder, bouncing, eyes closed, beating the earth with one foot in time, breathing heavy in time, their cleaned and pressed uniforms shaking in time. The rest are urging them on—driving them on with the tune. As one "outside," all you know, perhaps, is that they have caught a spirit. Others outside mock them, imitating the movements, turning them into a sort of Calypso dance—the word "Soca Baptists" is ejected. Derision of the Spiritual Baptists, of the Converted, is normal behavior: These are the backward people, the poor people, backsliders, and sinners, dressing up like they are better than anyone else, when they are sinners like any Vincentian. They should be mocked, your neighbor might say. If you ask what is really happening, the Converted will say you have to come inside and taste the sweetness of God to find out. The sweetness mocked by pelvis grinding, outside, in the dark; the sweetness that drives the Converted to give up a life of sameness and safety with fellows and friends and accept one of strangeness and scorn. To accept a life of music and heavy breathing, beating doption. The doption ends in a release of whoops, adjusting of clothing, and a moment of catching breath.

Presently, a woman or man, elaborately blindfolded, shifting from foot to foot in time to the beating, hotly burning candles in each hand, wax dripping on fingers and clothes, emerges. This is the *mourner*, the *pilgrim* returned from the journey. The ritual continues for some time yet, doption and songs interrupting the prescribed elements, giving of gifts to the pilgrim, *washing, anointing*, prayers of many kinds. The time comes for the mourner to speak. She begins softly by thanking God and her *pointing parents*. The pilgrim is hoarse. For days she has not spoken above a whisper, lying in *the room*, blindfolds on, searching her soul for sin, praying to God. She says, "On my pilgrim journey, I found myself. . . ." This is the shouting.

※　※　※

"I found myself in Africa," she might say, or in India, or in the very church she is standing in, or in a ship on the ocean, or on an island, or anywhere that the Spirit of God determines to take her.

"On my pilgrim journey," she might say, "I found myself on a road. I heard this song." She sings a tune with words (or without words). All the Converted sing with her. They may dance if the *Spirit* moves or if the pilgrim demonstrates a dance that she learned in the spiritual world. Every song and every dance and every doption encountered by the shouter is performed by the congregation as the pilgrim recounts her journeys. The shouting is more than a recounting of a remarkable experience. The shouting is a performance for the pleasure of the Holy Spirit and for the joy of those who have come. Everyone must sing their best, dance their best, following the current of the Spirit. Seldom are events in the Spirit unaccompanied by song.

"I met a gentleman," she may report, "The gentleman says . . ." The gentleman may say anything, but if he speaks, he has a message. He may give the pilgrim a message to deliver to the congregation, to nonbelievers outside the door, to a church in another part of the island, to a specific individual. He may admonish. He may predict. He may bestow gifts. It is usually a good idea to listen to what the gentleman says.

"I entered a room," she might say, "In the room was a golden crown. I picked it up."

"I found myself in a hospital, taking care of children."

"I saw a building and went inside. It was a school."

"I saw a belt dancing in front of me."

"A snake barred my path."

"I was writing with a pencil."

"I saw my pointing father in the distance, on a hill."

"I was locked up."

"A beautiful woman with long hair talked to me. Everywhere I went she was there."

"They were all sewing and I sat down at a machine and started to sew."

"Number two was stuck in a hole and I pulled him out."

"I used my *pass* to go into the cave."

After any of these come Hallelujahs and Amens from the congregation, dancing, and singing, evidence of great joy. No perfunctory performance here. Hearts are bursting with happiness.

✴ ✴ ✴

Why? What does it mean to say that one went here or there, that one met one or another person, that one did one or another activity? The pilgrim always says, "On my pilgrim journey I found myself [in a location]." Is this merely ritual language? How could she go anywhere if she never left the *mourning room*? She stayed there praying, for possibly 3 or 7 or 12 or more days.

The shouting, like much of Converted religion, is the formalized expression of direct experience. Contrasting forces are at work here. The ineffable is forced into words. The formless is put into form. The form is both a trope for the formless and an organizer of the experience. Each song, each dance, each formalized report of a journey is a reminder, an actual transporting of the Converted in attendance into the same inexpressible Spirit they experienced in the mourning room. The beautiful songs, the dances, the soul-thrilling liturgy are part of and stand in for one's spiritual experiences. Transcendent unspeakable emotion is not the only thing happening in the Spirit. The events the Converted mourners report are real to them. The visions and journeys are a gift from God, who allows them to see and experience things no one else does. That is why they are willing to endure persecution from friends and family, intensifying the stigma by wearing distinct clothes, by behaving in distinct ways. By following the tradition that God has revealed, a blessing will occur. Tradition and revelation have equal importance. Revelation, though, comes in ways that confirm the tradition.

Taken from various shoutings, each of the quotes above is an indication of an important genre of event in the Spirit. The gentleman is usually Jesus. But, if he does not say his name and the pilgrim does not ask, it cannot be said for certain. Those who have deep spiritual knowledge will know. If a journey with a gentleman is reported at a shouting, most likely it was Jesus, or some good spiritual person. On the other hand, it might be someone in the audience.

The shouter has to be careful what she (or he) says. Names are often avoided out of respect for the people mentioned. No one wants their name to be called in any way that may possibly reflect badly on them (many of the visions and journeys do reveal hidden sins of people in the congregation). In addition, caution must be taken regarding unscrupulous people who might take advantage of special knowledge learned at the shouting. The shouter must be "wise as a serpent and harmless as a dove." The *pointer* will usually censor those journeys that would lead to confusion. The five or six or seven hours set aside for a shouting are not long enough to report all of the journeys of most pilgrims. Only the best—or most instructive—will be given at the shouting. The rest the pilgrim can tell to individuals later. Some the pilgrim must never tell.

Usually more-experienced mourners go to places like Africa, India, to the bottom of the sea. Less-experienced mourners tend to have spiritual experiences that reflect their day-to-day life. They find themselves around St. Vincent, in a ship or boat on the sea, in a van or truck, sometimes flying through clouds, all experiences yet wonderful and new to them. These have the quality of a super-real dream and sometimes not of a dream at all, but of the spirit journey only. The pilgrim is aware of the journey during these, cognizant of her purpose in the Spirit, in St. Vincent or in more exotic places.

In most cases, the pilgrims (like shamans) must descend and ascend before going on to the full scope of the spirit world. In practice, the order is not rigid because God can take one anywhere and show one anything he wants to at any time. God can make you a pointer the first time you mourn, the Baptists always say. But usually things take time and practice and strong-willed dedication. They ascend Holy Mt. Zion. Many, if not most, first-time mourners find themselves going up a hill—the Christian road, the road to Heaven. One of the usual early experiences in the Spirit during mourning is the descent into the cemetery, or into the Valley of Dry Bones, a place of death and rejuvenation where skeletons can come alive. In each of these places, there is something vital to learn. Just what it is varies from *spiritual school* to spiritual school.

Danger can be found in the Spirit, too—from spiritual beings, from Satan. From time to time, Satan may tempt one or try to fool one by posing as one's pointer. The pointer is there to assist the pilgrim in the Spirit, always watching, always aware of the trouble. Many Converted report meeting their pointer at indecisive moments on their journey. One's *password*, given in secret by the pointer and always kept secret by the pilgrim, can be used in dangerous or uncertain circumstances. But most of the danger in the spiritual world comes from benign spiritual persons barring access to areas of experience and knowledge the pilgrim is not yet prepared to encounter. One may be taken hostage by an Indian tribe, one may be arrested and placed in jail, one may be bitten by a snake, chased by a dog, or get stuck in a hole in the ocean. Sometimes the way out is for the pointer to go in the Spirit and find the pilgrim and bring him back. Sometimes the pointer must intercede with the spiritual beings on behalf of the pilgrim. But the pointer must know them already, must know the language and songs of that country in which the pilgrim has become lost. Sometimes the pointer need only sing the right song for the pilgrim to come back, without traveling in the Spirit at all. Sometimes the Holy Spirit brings the pilgrim back to himself. Sometimes the pilgrim uses the knowledge he learned to get out by himself. The purpose of the journeys, after all, is learning. Going to mourn is going to school.

The purpose of the learning is going to work. The mourner gets a job in the Spirit and tools and clothes associated with that job. It is a privilege to be chosen for any spiritual job. Each office is called a *gift*. In response to, What is your gift?, one may hear, I'm a *nurse*, or I'm a *watchman*, or I'm a *warrior*. Or one may get no answer. Those with *spiritual eyes* to see can tell one's gift. To some, it is seen as presumption, as bragging, to say what it is. One can usually tell, however, as the gifts are also known as *spiritual names*. In church, one is addressed as Nurse A——— or Warrior B——— or Shepherd C———, and so forth. One can tell sometimes by the clothes that a Converted person wears—*spiritual clothes*, they are called, though anyone can see them with "natural" eyes. They are spiritual clothes because they were given in the Spirit. Once given in the Spirit, they are made physically by a seamstress and then worn in church—in daily life by the most devout. In the shouting, if one were to report, "I found myself in a hospital taking care of children," the congregation would assume that she has been given the spiritual gift of "nurse." She still would not say her spiritual gift without confirmation. A common way of doing this is for the pointer to say to the congregation, "What does she look like?" Those who have eyes to see (and the rest of those who regularly attend) shout, "A nurse!" They can see it spiritually before the pointer announces it (and the rest know from experience).

As one deepens in one's spiritual experience, she may gain the association of a particular saint, who works along with her, teaching and assisting in the spirit world. Usually male saints work with males and female saints with females, but not exclusively. The shouter is unlikely to reveal publicly the name of a helping saint—provided she knows. To attain useful knowledge, the pilgrim is admonished to ask, ask, ask of beings met in the Spirit. Some are good at it and ask the identity of everyone they meet, ask where they are, ask for advice. But, as the Converted say, "So carnal, so spiritual." If one is not very good at asking questions in normal life, one will not be good at it in the Spirit. Needless to say, the facility increases with time and practice.

A further genre of spiritual experience reported during a shouting is the learning of practical tasks. Converted individuals are very excited about this in private conversation. They know it is theoretically (or doctrinally) possible for God to teach one, spiritually, to read, to sew, or to cook, but they never thought it would happen to them. Most regular mourners acquire some practical skill in this fashion, or have enhanced a skill they already have, each of which may be used for church work (e.g., reading the Bible, sewing spiritual clothes, cooking food for church functions). But the skill is intended for the general edification of the individual and many use the skills gained in this way to find or enhance their secular work.

God can do all of the things reported in a shouting. The Converted say that God does do all of those things. And there is more that is not reported.

✻   ✻   ✻

Of course, the one "outside," leaning on the window, enjoying the music, or attracted by the prospect of a spectacle, would not know all of this. Probably very little of it. What is acknowledged is that the Spiritual Baptists are in touch with unusually powerful unseen forces. They have powers—good or bad—but powers still. Many non-Converted told me they would not associate with somebody if they knew that person to be a Converted. The Converted understand this. Because of their spiritual style of singing (quite un-church-like compared with the established churches), because of their uninhibited spiritual dancing, because of their acknowledgment of sin as a fact of life, not to be hidden in shame, but acknowledged for God's forgiveness (in contrast to the hidden sins of the other churches), because they celebrate their difference with biblical pride—because of all this they are ridiculed, hated, despised. And all by those who share the identity of Christian. Many Converted accept the burden of persecution with fortitude. Some hide their faith.

Absorption of local prejudice is the first way most Vincentians learn about Spiritual Baptists. In addition, most Vincentians have some family relation who is a Baptist. Non-Converted may observe the Converted, from afar, giving an "*open air mission*" in the Market Square, or at a cross-roads in the country. But where most Vincentians really begin to learn something about the Baptists is outside, in the dark, at a shouting.

✻   ✻   ✻

Let me describe one shouting I observed in August of 1995. It is a baptismal shouting, the first experience in the mourning room for the pilgrim, only three days instead of the usual minimum of seven. Rather than saying, "On my pilgrim journey . . .", the correct form here is, "On my baptismal journey . . ."

✻   ✻   ✻

The sun is setting as I walk up the steep hill toward the church. The sky spreads orange and saffron in streaks over the hills to the West. The capital, Kingstown, lies below. The great boundary of the sea, as always, stretches out beyond. I am the first to arrive. Soon, there will be no seats. Soon, the chirp of the crickets will be overpowered by raucous holy singing. Soon, the Spirit will descend. Right now, the church is suffused with a yellow light. I enter and sit to the side. Listening.

I hear dogs and children and an occasional truck grinding up the curves of narrow roads. From the mourning room, an annex to the small church, the pilgrim and her nurse are conversing in low tones. Are they talking about spiritual journeys? Right ways of living? That will come soon enough. Right now they are discussing food and events at the baptism earlier today. The nurse comes into the church building, looking for water. A slight embarrassment. She knows I overheard. She and the pilgrim should be in prayer until the start of the service this evening. The shouting.

Visitors are expected. A fan has been installed in the rafters—an unusual luxury in any Converted church. It will be removed after the service. Now it is for the benefit of the guests. Fresh flowers, *crotons, dragon* plants, and candles are installed at the altar and around the *center pole.* Dimming light catches the charming paintings and scriptural exhortations found on the walls, as in most Converted churches. Spiritual *flags* representing themes and places in the Spirit, bright colors arranged in the corners and at the pole, fade as the light fades. The brief tropical dusk descends abruptly. The pastor's ten-year-old son comes to sweep the church. He turns on the harsh fluorescent light that illuminates most night-time services here. It does not interfere with the work of the Spirit.

Responding with the schooled politeness of all West Indians, the boy is still delighted that I am talking to him. My presence is an influence in the church service and I am constantly aware of it. My presence, as well, does not interfere with the work of the Spirit.

⚒   ⚒   ⚒

Now the church is full. No seat available on the backless benches, many people standing. Visiting congregations ("courts" in the stylized Converted ritual language) with their large hand-held church bells ringing had approached the building from the road below and were greeted in return with a ringing of the bell of the host church. They were seated, and those who were thirsty had been given drink, those hungry had been given food.

The pastor arrives. The visiting pointers and leaders are seated on the altar dais. The beautiful preliminary ritual performed at every Converted gathering completed, we all shift in our seats, leaning forward in anticipation of the highlight of the evening: the report of the pilgrim traveler on her journeys in the Spirit world.

Non-Converted peer through the open windows, leaning, sometimes mocking, but as intently interested as everyone else. The pilgrim has come back with knowledge revealed directly by the Spirit of God. Everybody wants to know. Not of the least interest is the possibility that she might have some direct knowledge of the future of any individual, Converted or non-Converted. Everybody wants to know. Not the only reason non-Converted would be hovering around the edges, in the dark. One is the very beautiful and compelling music of the Converted, for which everyone has praise, even if they hate all else about the Converted. Another is that

time. After the song, she resumes the account. She says, "Pointer Clary stepped out from behind the pole and held out the dress [the one from the first journey] and said, 'I told you you would have needed it.' " This is a powerful journey, calling her to work. Some in the congregation arise, catching Spirit, beating doption. The doption gets heavy, strong, potent. The ground shakes with the stamping of the feet. Another chorus is sung by those of us not beating doption, "Lay Down Your Weary Head and Rest." Another church mother dances with Number One. The song over, she resumes telling the journey. She says, "Pointer Clary handed me the dress. He said, 'I should give you three more lashes.' " Laughter from the congregation. One loud "Amen!" She says, "The pastor sat down and I came back to myself."

The pointer tells her to give only one more. She says, "I was going up a road." She heard the song, "Oh the Road, the Lonesome Road." Another Converted favorite. A young church shepherd dances with Number One. Others are dancing. Some start up again with doption. The pointer calls out, "Coming down now . . . Take it easy . . . Sit and wrap . . . Behave yourself." Much of the congregation wants to continue, but this has been a long shouting. People are hungry and tired. It is time to finish. The pointer tells Number One to finish the journey. Number One says, "I kept walking on the road to a corner" and there on the corner was her very pointer meeting her on the way.

She says, "Before I take my seat, I'd like for you all to join me as I bring this song, 'When Peace Like a River.' " We all sing one verse. She says, "I say a peace and a pleasant good night." The account of her journeys (the ones she is allowed to tell) has taken 45 minutes.

The pointer has one more thing to say before we end. He says, "As I cut the first *band*, a direction came to me, I should sign the band this way so that I could meet someone on the way."

The service ends immediately after these remarks with a doxology in which we all join. Number One pushes up her blindfolds slightly but does not take them off. Her ritual is not completely over. She will go home but will not remove the bands for nine days. After the service, we all sit in the church benches, we are all served food by the host church and we all eat heartily.

※   ※   ※

What do these journeys mean? Has she really been there? Why is everyone overjoyed at all she recounts? This is more than a story. More than a mechanical ritual. Something happened to Number One. All the Converted know because it happened to them, too. Every element that she reports has wide cultural meaning. I will describe here disparate elements as they came up in the shouting. They will be made clear in later chapters.

In the first journey, she says she met a man who looked like Pointer Clary. Although she knew quite well what Pointer Clary looked like, as part of the ritualized language she cannot say with certainty that it was him because the spiritual person did not say that he was Pointer Clary. Everyone assumes, though, that it was him. The dress given to her in this way is a usual manner to receive one's spiritual clothing. The dress given is a sign of submission to the choices of the Spirit and to spiritual work. That she refuses is a common reaction for Spiritual Baptists. That she gets lashes is a common reaction for the Spirit.

In the second journey, Sister Tina may have been there in the Spirit, even if Sister Tina may not remember it herself. At a shouting, all are expected to perform positive actions they are described as doing in the Spirit. That is why Sister Tina gets up and counts out "One! Two!" to Number One. By the power of the song and by the doption (but all through the power of the Holy Spirit), people are transported to the Valley, one of the key locations in the spiritual world. Number One did not go there on this trip, but because she heard the song, the Spirit is indicating that she will be taken there the next time she goes into the mourning room.

Every shouting I attended in St. Vincent had at least one episode reported of something happening in a Vincentian reality. When she says she found herself in the middle of a road, she is both in St. Vincent and in the Spirit; St. Vincent is a part of the spiritual world. She reports, "How I got there, I don't know." This sort of reality testing is very common in spirit journeys, setting the journey apart from normal dreams where reality testing is uncommon. It is not merely the prelucidity found in some ordinary dreams, because the consciousness between the wide-awake church setting, one's outside life, and the journey, is unitary. For the most part, pilgrims are aware they are on a journey throughout the events in the Spirit. That is why they can ask themselves how they got wherever they are.

The song, "Our Father Who Art in Heaven" is the Lord's Prayer, a prayer said repeatedly (in some spiritual schools constantly—almost as a mantra) in the mourning room. That would be especially true in this case, where the time in the mourning room is the short three-day period preceding a baptism. The dancing with the pilgrim is a sign of tenderness and support.

The fifth journey is a fine example of the theme of spiritual work and disobedience and the role of spiritual beings in carrying out the will of the Holy Spirit. This particular journey is also a good story. Note that even though the first and fifth are separate journeys, a common consciousness prevails. Her refusal to accept the garment (and the work associated with it) in the first journey comes back to her later in the mourning room experience. This sort of episodic scenario is common in spirit journeys. That is one reason why the pilgrim refers to the whole experience as "on my journey" as well as each episode as a separate journey. Consciousness shifts between individual journeys, but the entire mourning room experience is a single journey in the Spirit.

The collective experience in the Spirit is a theme that amazes both outsiders and the Converted. Not every Converted is without doubt, especially when they are just beginning. Much of the spirit journey feels internal, like a dream. But to meet one's pointer on the way, and to have the pointer later confirm the encounter, is a persuasive faith-building event, throwing the experience definitively outward, into a world of collective experience. Of the dozens of people I asked, nearly everyone reported some emphatically convincing moment when they found their pointer in the spirit world, or when they returned from a journey to find the pointer describing specific events and items just experienced in the Spirit. The pointer is there to help, both in the Spirit and in person. The cloth bands tied over the pilgrim's eyes by the pointer are written on with words and symbols of directed spiritual power. In this case, the pointer placed the symbols specifically to effect the outcome of Number One's last reported journey.

✹   ✹   ✹

The shouting is an exterior expression. Expressive elements in Converted religion are artistically radiant and enticingly beautiful. That is why people come to watch. Converted religion is, equally or more, an interior religion. Converted repeatedly admonish each other to "go deeper." After the shouting, the resolve of the pilgrim is tested. She must go on to do her spiritual work.

PART I

Spiritual

Work

THREE

Spiritual Workers

T HE WORK OF THE CONVERTED IS frequently an attractive performative spectacle. If prophets, shamans, and priests are "impresarios of the gods" (LaBarre 1972:161), few are doing a better job than the Spiritual Baptists. Almost any Converted ritual will draw spectators, but one rarely sees interested loungers fighting for a good window position at Anglican, Catholic, or even Pentecostal events. The visually, kinetically, aurally rich religion of the Converted is attractive in ways that no other religions in St. Vincent are. While it may be a performance, it is nonetheless work. To be a Converted person in St. Vincent is to be a spiritual worker.

This chapter details the types of work the Converted do, the types of workers found in Converted churches, and the tools of the Spirit that the Converted use to conduct their spiritual work. The most important tool, the music of the Converted, is considered in the next chapter. The actual technique of traveling in the Spirit, where knowledge to conduct the spiritual work is obtained and often used, is examined in chapter 6.

Spiritual Work

The work that the Converted do is both the intensely mystical experiential otherworld *knowing* and *doing* of the shaman and the society-affirming liturgical ritual of the communal church (Wallace 1966).[1] Converted ritual helps individual Spiritual Baptists make sense of their temporal world (the churchly) and allows a ritual subversion of the temporal world (the shamanic). I will enumerate these techniques momentarily. First, I want to introduce how this work is conceptualized by the Converted themselves.

The Converted constantly say about their spiritual work, "We are working out our own salvation" (referring to Phillipians 2:12). Some add that if they do their work well, they will hasten the return of Jesus Christ and the era of heavenly eternal life (and the end of earthly problems). The Converted (the Spiritual Baptists) are a Christian religion like other Christian religions. Like Roman Catholics, Anglicans, Pentecostals, Apostolics, and Seventh Day Adventists—all denominations to whom the Converted compare themselves—they see themselves as working for the salvation of the world. Like other Christians, the Converted must battle wicked spiritual forces and the sinful nature of man to do so. The difference lies in technique and recruitment. To be a member of one of the other religions in St. Vincent, one is either baptized as an infant into the religion and raised as a member of that denomination or recruited from one's christening religion to the other denomination (more usual in denominations relatively new to St. Vincent like the Pentecostals, Apostolics, or Jehovah's Witnesses). To become a Converted, one must receive a call. Not merely a call to salvation, but a call to service.

Converted describe their work as "doing the will of God." Their means of knowing the will of God are more diverse than those of other denominations in St. Vincent. For the Converted, these include the Bible (like all the others) and other scriptures, direct revelation (like many of the newer denominations), and direct experience of seeing the unseen and hearing the unheard in the world of spirits (unique to themselves). Doing God's work includes visible ritual like that of the other denominations (baptisms, marriages, burials, preaching) as well as a large portion of spiritual and ritual work not found in any of the other denominations. The latter include public rituals surrounding the private experience of *mourning* (that is, the *banning* preceding and the shouting following), private healing rituals and dream interpretation for individuals (Converted and non-Converted), and individual work in the spiritual world itself.

Every ritual action by the Converted is justified by reference to the Bible. In the tremendously Christian population of St. Vincent, Biblical knowledge is highly valued. People in every strata of society read the Bible at work, on public transport, at picnics, and in any moment of free time. But the Converted may have a better grasp than most. Mormon missionaries in St. Vincent told me that of all the denominations, Spiritual Baptists were the most difficult to proselytize because of their knowledge and effective use of Biblical passages. Converted interactions with the Mormons are not merely disinterested rejections, but spirited rebuffs powered by verse after verse from the Bible.

One characteristic separating the Spiritual Baptists from other Christians is the condition that every member is required to do the spiritual work. In other Christian denominations the clergy carry on the work of the church, sometimes assisted by a small number of distinguished laity. Among the Converted, the ministers do have greater responsibility than the rest of the congregation, but everyone has a specific ritual task. I must add "in principle," because a lot of pulpit time is spent on decrying the fact that many of the spiritual people do not do their spiritual work.

In relation to other churches in St. Vincent, the Converted see themselves as apart from other Christians in that they do work in the spiritual realm, whereas others do not. In recent years, Southern Baptists have established a presence in St. Vincent. Among Vincentians, the Converted are commonly known as Baptists. Walking with some Converted one day, I asked them as we passed one of the Southern Baptist churches to explain the relationship between the two types of Baptists. The reply: "They carry the name, but they don't do the work." The work is the reason the Converted are called to be Converted. The purpose of the work is to achieve salvation by following the dictates of the Holy Spirit.

The Spirit

Spirit is the central concept in Converted religion (and perhaps all African American religion; see J. Murphy 1994). Enabling all work is the Spirit. Like most deeply felt words, this one is potently polysemous. The term "Spirit" refers to three things: (1) the Holy Spirit of God (in a trinity with the Father and the Son); (2) one's spiritual self; and (3) the spiritual realm in which the Baptists work.[2] The word "spirit" can also mean any spiritual being. The first three meanings can all be conflated, and they are, mystically, into a single meaning. The last meaning is almost always separate and inferior, frequently indicated by the indefinite article. "A" spirit may be a bad thing, but "Spirit" or "the" Spirit is always a good thing. The Converted say of "inferior" religions: "When they think it's *the* Spirit, it's really *a* spirit." The Spiritual Baptists themselves are elevated by connection to the Spirit: "Contrasting with the simplicity, and often poverty of the physical setting of this worship, is the richness in concept of identification of the worshipper with 'the Spirit,' with 'Glory,' with the 'Holy Ghos' " (Herskovits and Herskovits 1947:192). A window into the richness of the Spirit is provided in chapter 6.

Events in the Spirit have direct and real consequences in the physical world. The Spirit, being numinous and everlasting, has predominance over the world, which is temporary and corruptible. Daily contrast between the carnal or the natural and the Spirit in Converted discourse draws out this distinction. Natural and carnal are both terms for one's physical existence and life. The terms "natural" and "carnal" as used in the King James Version of the Bible mean simply "fleshly" or "physical" (I Corinthians 2:14–15; 9:10–11). The Converted spend so much time in the spirit world, and the spirit world has so much influence on their carnal life, that I was forced every day to ask whether reported events occurred in the Spirit or in the physical and whether people referred to were carnal people or people met in the Spirit. The emphasis in Converted religion is on becoming more spiritual and less carnal.

Another way the Spirit has ascendancy is in the presence in Converted religion of a dual hierarchy of offices. Spiritual hierarchy is present in every church, but in Converted churches that are "registered" (that belong to one of the two government-recognized Spiritual Baptist denominations) a second, secular, hierarchy operates. The latter consists of individuals who by display of merit are placed in positions of authority and responsibility by the church officials and gain a measure of temporal authority as well. For instance, in the secular hierarchy—deacons, pastors, canons, and bishops—each of the ministers is allowed by the State to exercise some form of authority, such as christening and/or marrying. The spiritual hierarchy, however, has greater importance, and a pointer, the highest grade of spiritual office, has more ritual authority than any office in the secular hierarchy. They are not mutually exclusive. While few in the church have a part in the secular hierarchy, everyone has a spiritual rank. Those who have attained official status in one of the organized denominations usually are rather high up in the spiritual hierarchy as well. Every canon and every bishop is also a pointer (as are most of the pastors).

Spirit is invisible, but reactions to the Spirit can be observed. For the individual Converted person, sensations and perceptions from the spiritual world require managing and channeling. Work in the church setting helps to do just that.

Types of Work

Everything visible in the church service has significance and origin in the Spirit. All work that one does, the form of every ritual, every implement, and every item of spiritual clothing must be experienced first in the Spirit (that is, the non-visible) before it can be utilized and performed physically.

"Performance" is the word used by the Baptists themselves. The church rituals, including the basic liturgy of the evening service used at all church meetings, are performances for the Holy Spirit. They are also performances for the church members themselves. After one of the first services I attended in St. Vincent, the minister asked me, "How did you like our performance?" The minister may implore the members to sing better so they will enjoy the service better or so that non-Converted looking on from the outside will witness their fervor. Penalties for poor performance do not come from the minister, but from the Spirit. The idea of ritual performance is an academic construct (Turner 1969; Grimes 1990), but the Converted use it in exactly the same way.

The number of rituals performed by most Christian denominations rarely approaches the seven (sacraments) of the Catholic Church. Most Protestant churches accept only Baptism and Communion as sacraments—that is, as rituals implemented by Christ on Earth and regarded as "necessary to salvation" (*Book of Common Prayer* 1948:581). Every ritual performed by the Converted is by the command of God, making them of a different order from the Works of Supererogation (those unnecessary to salvation), as most of them would be classed by priests in the Established (Anglican) Church. Each Converted ritual is necessary to salvation and, by definition, a sacrament instituted by God.

A list of Converted rituals must include at least these 30 to 40 items: anointing, banning, baptism, blowing, candlelighting, christening of a baby, christening of a church, christening of a house, consecration, communion, crowning, fasting, funeral, house blessing ("cleaning" of a house), laying of cornerstone for a church, marching, missions (to specific places or churches), mourning, nine days, open air missions, repentance (baptismal candidacy), rising, robing, sealing, shouting, signing of bands, spiritual baths, Sunday morning worship and/or evening praise, taking a proof, thanksgiving, wakes (nine night, forty days, and one year), washing.[3] Along with these, the tasks associated with the dozens of different spiritual offices must be considered. Some churches have more rituals yet. New rituals may be added by revelation from the Spirit and then included in the repertoire of an individual congregation or performed only once.

In addition to these physical activities are those that take place only in the Spirit that only those with spiritual eyes are able to observe. Many of the activities in the Spirit are as formulaic as the physical rituals, but they can vary extensively according to spiritual school or church. Rituals that occur entirely in the Spirit are considered work as much as any of the above-named rituals.

Converted ritual comprises both public and private events. The former are centered on reaffirming the tenets of the believing community; the others are private rituals of healing and consultation of the sort normally associated with shamanism. Besides conducting rituals in the church services, pointers and congregations perform rituals by request as a service to individuals (Converted and non-Converted) in the larger community. A third sort of work concerns secular tasks (and trades) learned in the Spirit and used either in the church setting or for the livelihood of the Converted individual so instructed (this remarkable form of Converted work is dealt with in chapter 6). I discuss here three representative rituals of communal importance to the Converted: *baptism, mourning,* and *wakes* (but see chapters 2, 5, 7, and 8 for detailed depiction of other key rituals). I also consider the healing functions of pointers in private consultation.

Balandier (1970:112, emphasis original) writes of a cultivation festival in New Caledonia, "By offering to the eye a sort of résumé of society as a whole, it makes it possible to capture an *enacted* social system, corresponding to its theoretical formulation. . . ." The baptismal cycle in Converted religion provides such an enactment of the theoretical foundation of Converted being. To become a Converted is to be baptized by immersion as an adult (or cognizant older child). Historically, the Converted were the only ones in St. Vincent to baptize their members in this manner. Commonly called "Baptists," the Converted refer to the infant baptism practiced by other churches as "christening." Baptism by full immersion in water is the only type of baptism they acknowledge as such. With the arrival in the island of other denominations that also baptize by immersion (Seventh Day Adventists in the early part of the century and Pentecostals in the 1960s and 1970s), the Converted accentuate mourning as the ritual that sets them apart. The name "Spiritual Baptist" highlights both aspects.

Being baptized as a Converted is not a simple or speedy event. The process normally takes months (though it may be as short as three days in an emergency). Dedication to one's calling and one's experience of the grace of God are tested. A

Vincentian receives a call from the Holy Spirit to become a Converted in a dream or as the result of conviction that persistent misfortunes are God's way of influencing one to turn to him. Frequently the call of the Spirit is resisted. Punishment by God for such an action can lead to the need for an emergency baptism to avoid supernaturally caused sickness or death. Non-Converted who come to pointers or other Converted for private consultation sometimes learn that the solution to their problem is baptism.

With some variation from church to church, the baptismal cycle consists of these segments: *sealing, repentance,* (baptismal) *banning,* (baptismal) mourning, *rising,* baptism (or *immersion*), (baptismal) *shouting.* Sealing is the public ceremony whereby one comes forward in church to "accept Christ." The candidate is prayed for and "sealed" by the pointer (chalk symbols with mystical power are drawn on the candidate's head, hands, shoulders, chest, back, and feet). Next begins a liminal period of repentance, lasting from several weeks to several months. The candidate spends every church service (usually several a week) sitting on the *mercy seat* with eyes closed if a male, eyes covered by the *headtie* if a female, palms up in a begging stance, praying for forgiveness, feet marching in place whether seated or standing, preparing to "walk the heavenly road" on one's baptismal spirit journey. Banning is the ritual by which one is blindfolded with numerous cloth bands sealed with pointing *seals,* placed in the mourning room and "pointed on" to the Spirit. The baptismal journey takes place for three days, usually from Thursday night to Sunday morning. This is the introduction of the candidate to the work of the Spirit and to experiences in the spirit world. During the baptismal mourning, the pilgrim normally receives a *spiritual gift* (that is, an office), but not always. The third night in the room is *rising night,* when the candidate is symbolically raised from the dead. The following morning the candidate is led, still blindfolded, to the water, where the bands are lifted just long enough for her to observe the witnesses to her action; she is then immersed and led back to the room. That evening, clothes changed, new blindfold bands placed on her head, she gives her shouting (see chapter 2).

The baptism rituals provide the candidate with a complete view of the religion and her place in it. She is taught that the locus of power is in the Spirit of God (who can choose anyone) and in her *pointing parents* (who guide her into the Spirit and into membership in the church). All of the workers of the church come into play during this time. Besides the various mothers, teachers, and nurses that attend to the candidate directly, every member of the church is expected to give "words of consolation" and "a message of salvation" (that is, to preach) during the church services for the duration of the candidacy. The candidate is shown that she must rely on the church for spiritual guidance, especially as she is introduced to the amazing psychic phenomena of the Converted as a result of following the instructions she is given. The process of getting baptized, from sealing to shouting, allows the individual to taste direct knowledge (that is, mystical experience), to enact death and rebirth, to join the hope of heaven and confirm it by personal experience of the spiritual world, and to relate the experience to onlookers (believing and unbelieving).

As powerful as baptism is, mourning is the defining ritual of Spiritual Baptist practice (see chapter 7). It is by mourning, by setting aside as many days as the Spirit requires in prayer and fasting, by seeking out the will of God, by pouring out one's heart—all fears, sins, and joys—to God that one partakes of the work of the Converted church. Mourning may precede or follow baptism. Both are required. One pastor explained, "Mourning is a must; baptism is a must must must." Some do not mourn without a specific spiritual call, but one prominent preacher affirmed: "From the day you first accepted Jesus you were called to mourn." Mourning is the work of the Converted. To be trained to save souls, one must mourn. To be trained in ritual tasks, one must mourn. To work out one's own salvation, one must mourn.

Mourning is not only a ritual tradition, but also a biblical precept. Jesus said, "Blessed are they that mourn" (Matthew 5:4), and he did it himself by withdrawing into the wilderness for 40 days (Matthew 4). It is a sacrament instituted by Christ but not originating with him. Ezekiel, David, and Daniel all mourned. Converted acknowledge that they are "not as good as Jesus" who mourned for 40 days or as Daniel who mourned for 21. In St. Vincent, most Converted mourn for 11–14 days. In Brooklyn, for 7 days. Bands are placed over their eyes (Ezekiel 3:24–25). They lie on their right sides or pray on their knees for the entire time, waiting for God to take them into the Spirit. The word "mourning" in the Spiritual Baptist churches has the same meaning as elsewhere. It is an expression of grief. In response to why the ritual is called mourning, the Converted reply, "You mourn for your sins." One Converted told me that in mourning, "everything in your life comes before you, everything good, and everything bad." When the sins are remembered, real sorrow, real mourning, is felt. When the sins are confessed and forgiven, then the journeys begin.

Mourning is going to school. It is an educational experience. "Welcome to St. Margaret's College" is the sign greeting visitors to one mourning room in St. Vincent. Converted are perpetual students. Their task is to study in the Spirit so that they will be prepared to do work in the Spirit.

Converted work is not restricted to fellow believers. Non-Converted utilize the skills of the Converted as a resource in both public and private ways. Converted are the psychological specialists of St. Vincent. If the medical doctors cannot bring healing, the Converted will be sought. If bad luck follows one, the Converted will be sought. If disturbing dreams pester any Vincentian, it is a sign to seek out the Converted.

Wakes (or *memorials*) are a service that the Converted provide to the larger community (see chapter 8). When any Vincentian dies, the Converted are called to perform a wake in the house of the deceased on one of the traditional wake nights (usually *nine night* or *forty days*). Regardless of the denomination of the deceased, the Converted are called. I was told that in recent years, Pentecostals and Apostolics may perform a wake for families of those denominations, but that "most people use the Baptists." Converted feel that as people privileged by God to do spiritual work, they must provide the service. They do it for nothing more than a nominal gift in kind. The wake is a shamanic performance in the usual sense, with the Converted doing the activity and the family and friends of the deceased looking on without participating. In fact, the wake is little more than the common Converted praise service. But it is enough. The powers of the Converted accomplish the task. The spirit is put to rest.

The private work the Converted do for the community is mostly performed by pointers. Clients may be non-Converted or Converted, though Converted are more likely to seek solution to their problems by mourning. Some pointers who I regularly visited (especially pointers particularly noted for their effectiveness at combating illness or warding off misfortune) often had a line of people waiting for consultation. The most common physical action prescribed or performed on behalf of these clients is a *spiritual bath*. Some pointers bathe the individual themselves; some give bathing instructions to the person seeking help. Pointers, like other Converted, are expected to continue to mourn and to learn. In mourning, they may receive additional gifts such as *doctor* (cf. Simpson 1966). The techniques are taught in the Spirit. A *bush doctor* prescribes baths using various plants and leaves, a *chemical doctor* utilizes baths whose ingredients include common perfumes and vegetable oils. The physical effectiveness of the plants and chemicals used is of little import—the problems the pointers treat are spiritual.

Dream interpretation is another significant task the Converted perform for the community at large. Converted starting out "on their Christian path" all know to consult their pointer about vivid or disturbing dreams. More-experienced Converted are likely to be able to interpret the dream on their own. Almost any Converted can be approached regarding a dream. In St. Vincent and in Brooklyn, low-ranking Converted told me that they are sought out by their friends and acquaintances for advice on dreams. Difficult interpretations are referred to those "higher up in the Spirit." For pointers, dream interpretation is a daily occupation. In St. Vincent, dreams carry great weight, and many in the population are afraid of any sort of dream. Disturbing dreams are a sign to seek out a Converted person. Dreams of Converted people or of oneself in Converted dress are a call to be baptized or to mourn.

Types of Workers

In Spiritual Baptist churches, every member has a role to play. All are spiritual workers. Herskovits and Herskovits (1947:193) report that in mourning are received " 'gifts' which define for each humble worshipper in supernatural terms a specific task, or series of tasks in the fabric of church organization."

In St. Vincent, I asked a high-ranking church official what he thought I should emphasize when writing up the data. The first two things he mentioned were *spiritual names* and *uniforms*. Spiritual names are so called because once given by the

Spirit, the gift becomes a title affixed to one's name. One is thereby called, for instance, Pointer James or Nurse Candice. These gifts have the effect of spiritual offices, the precise function of which varies by church.

The division of labor represented by spiritual names attracts the immediate attention of the ethnographer as well. The list is not set or stable (for either hierarchy or type of work) and varies from island to island, church to church, and, in understanding of the roles, by individual. However, general patterns do hold. By every count, the number of tasks required in the church is large.[4] The longest list I was able to obtain from a single Converted individual had 20 offices.

Combining all of my collected lists and checking with Converted individuals to find a consensus, the types of spiritual offices, properly called spiritual gifts (from I Corinthians 12:4, and Ephesians 4:11) or spiritual names look like this: (male): bell ringer, cross bearer, shepherd, messenger, watchman, surveyor, captain, diver, prover, assistant leader, leader, assistant pointer, teacher, pointer, doctor, inspector; (female): florist, water carrier, flag waver, bell ringer, trumpet blower, surveyor, diver, assistant nurse, nurse, nurse matron, African warrior, leadress, shepherdess, assistant mother, pointing mother, inspector.[5] These are the ones on which everyone (or nearly everyone) agreed. There was some discrepancy in the explanations of what each role entails. Converted who receive any of these spiritual gifts are normally addressed by their spiritual names in the church setting (e.g., Nurse Ford, Pointer David). Most of the gifts listed above may have the term "crowned" affixed to them, as in crowned watchman, or crowned shepherd, designating a specific method of obtaining the gift in the Spirit (in bestowing the gift, the Spirit or a spirit places a crown on the individual). Additionally, many of the spiritual names may be prefixed or suffixed by "king" or "queen," though terms of address do not include these additions. Similarly, a pointer with the gift of doctor is addressed as pointer, not doctor.

Converted practice, being an oral and spiritual tradition, bolstered by new revelations, the meaning ascribed to the gifts is subject to alteration and to variation. One *teacher* informed me that there are both "king shepherd" and "shepherd king," and that the latter is higher in the Spirit. I was unable to verify shepherd king from other respondents, though most of them deferred to his knowledge as a teacher.

Each gift is a duplication of some task in the Spirit, frequently the result of schooling in the Spirit. In the spiritual cities to which the Converted travel are schools they may attend. The gift or work may be learned in a classroom in one of the schools or may be given instantaneously with no conscious spiritual instruction. For many gifts, the responsibility of the gift is bestowed on the individual and then she or he learns the task from others who already do that work. Some gifts (like *pointer* or *doctor*) must be learned entirely in the Spirit.

God is not restricted to a list. While in St. Vincent, I met several individuals who told me of gifts they had received in the Spirit that they said they had never before heard in church. One of these was the spiritual name "Knight Commander." Although he had not heard the name before, the Spirit detailed for the Converted man the responsibilities associated with that status. Trinidadian and Grenadian Spiritual Baptists I encountered had numerous additional spiritual gifts, often with hierarchical orderings and tasks quite different from the Vincentian tradition.

Other gifts do not carry a spiritual name. Among these is the status of musician. Every Converted is expected to be a (spiritual) musician, and it would be superfluous to refer to someone as "Musician so and so," when everyone is expected to utilize one or another instrument in a spiritual sense (that is, singing the sounds of the instrument). Occasionally, I did meet someone whose spiritual gift was "soldier," but as every Converted is expected to be a "soldier for the Lord," it is not used as a term of address. I must add that no one questions such a gift. If God specifically gives one the gift of soldier, it is respected like any other spiritual status.[6] Most Converted agree that once one has been given a spiritual gift, it is never lost. For instance, if one is a *bell ringer* and later becomes a pointer, one is still responsible to ring the bell when appropriate. Some few contend that the higher gift supersedes the lower. Only a small portion of those in any congregation have no spiritual gift, but even they are expected to assist in the spiritual work—by singing the appropriate songs, reading certain Bible passages, or by doing whatever small task the pointer may assign them.

The spiritual names (gifts, offices, tasks, roles) are a reproduction of secular world order in the spiritual context. They provide the Converted with a measure of prestige and respectability they are unable to receive in the "natural" world. The spiritual work is an inversion of the "natural" order of society. The Converted, typically, are drawn from the segment of Vincentian society that is the most illiterate, the most poor, the most at the mercy of others in power. In St. Vincent, where schooling must be paid for by the student or the student's family, many poor children do not go to school. Admission to nursing school, to the police academy, to every position respected by society is by influence more than merit, and the poor and unconnected remain ever powerless. Spirit possession religions are often cited as a means of compensation for poverty and powerlessness (e.g., Henney 1974; Lewis 1989). By direct identification with a deity, societal relations are subverted in favor of those poor who adhere to the spirit possession religion. Few do it more explicitly than the Converted. The order of the secular world, with policemen and soldiers and teachers and captains and doctors and nurses—all people who must be obeyed—is inverted. The Spiritual Baptists become by name and title police *inspectors*, corporally punishing *teachers, captains* of ships—all positions unavailable to them in the "natural" world. The horrors of slavery, the horror of the memory of slavery, the difficulties of colonial oppression, are effaced symbolically in Converted religion by the seizure of control of those very same oppressive structures.

Other peoples impressed by the inequalities of colonialism have attempted similar solutions. Most outstanding are the "cargo cults" of Melanesia (Worsely 1957), who similarly reproduce the dominant power structure as under their control. Although cargo cults are spiritually sanctioned seizures of the structures of oppression like the Converted, cargo cults utilize the symbols of colonial power as additions to a native substrate; that is, they rest on "non-Western assumptions about reality" (Errington 1974). The Converted, in contrast, accept the European premise of Christianity as the root of their ideology.

An intriguing case of ritual inversion is that of the Rose and Marguerite societies of St. Lucia, an island 30 miles from St. Vincent (Crowley 1958; Midgett 1977; Guibault 1985, 1987). These societies sponsor secular dances and *grand fêtes* in a reproduction of the dominant sector of colonial society. Offices in the Rose and Marguerite societies include king, queen, magistrate, policeman, soldier, doctor, and so on. Archaic dances such as the quadrille and belair (or steps from them) that are performed by the St. Lucian societies are found in the Converted churches of St. Vincent but not at secular events. Societies of the Rose and Marguerite type were widespread in the English and French colonies in the nineteenth century, and one must wonder what influence they might have had on the development of Converted religion at the same time. Spiritual Baptists do not have a noticeable presence on St. Lucia, and it is possible that the role provided by the Converted in St. Vincent is filled in St. Lucia by the Rose and Marguerite societies, making the added burdens of Converted life less attractive to St. Lucians, who already have a ritual means of inverting oppressive structures.

One difference between the St. Lucian and Vincentian cases is that offices in Converted religion are acquired by travel in a spiritual realm—a decidedly shamanic style of recruitment. The figure in Converted religion most embodying the characteristics of a shaman is the pointer. If there is a focal person in the church setting, it is the pointer. He (or she, in the case of a *pointing mother*) is the one who conducts healing sessions on behalf of clients, Converted or non-Converted. It is he who is the master of travel in the spiritual world. He is the teacher to all of his spiritual children. Every ritual in the church setting, every task performed, and every journey the members take are occasions for instruction of the members by the pointer. Every Converted who is not a pointer or a pointing mother acts as an apprentice shaman, assisting the pointer and learning from him. Each is expected to strive for more responsibility, more knowledge of, and in, the Spirit. The Converted of each church are all learning from their pointer—their teacher. Pollock (1992:59) notes of Culina shamans: "Not every shaman has the same knowledge. . . . Of course, all apprentices seek to go as far as possible with their knowledge, but they do not all have the same opportunities, abilities, or strength." The Converted perceive spiritual knowledge in the same way.

In the ritual performance, all Converted act. Each has a ritual role. However, the types of gifts (or shamans) that are available in a church varies. Who gets what is determined by God, not by the ritual needs of the church, and a church may have an imbalance. If there are too many of a certain office (as, for instance, often happens with *nurses*), the pointer will sometimes call out when that job is required in a ritual, "Whose turn is it?" While God is the owner of the church, the pointer is the manager. I heard more than one pointer say, "It is not easy running a church."

The pointer is father, teacher, doctor, and drill sergeant to those in his church. He is responsible for all of the nonphysical needs of his spiritual children—teaching, healing, discipline. Representing that authority and responsibility is the pointer's belt. The belt is held in the pointer's hand during services or worn on the outside of the garment, ready to come off when needed for discipline.

In the sense that all in a church are under the tutelage of the pointer, they are also apprentice shamans. Each baptized member of the church has been required to mourn and undertake a baptismal journey through the spiritual lands (wherever the Spirit has seen fit to take them). As a result of personal knowledge gained on these journeys, the Converted person undertakes her own work, albeit in the context of the work of the group. In this way, the Converted spiritual gifts represent different shamanic grades or various "kinds of shamanic specialists" (Langdon 1992:14). Members of Converted churches fit the descriptions of those training in shamanic work as well as those who do shamanic work in their own right.

For the Converted, power comes from the Spirit and operates on three axes: gift (name, office), spiritual city (spiritual location), saint (one's spiritual helper). Each Converted has a specific task or tasks, a certain spiritual location or locations on which she is most knowledgeable and to which she is said to "belong," and a saint or saints to help her with her spiritual work and who will usually accompany the Converted individual on many of her journeys through the spirit world. At each mourning, any one or each of these axes may be augmented or altered according to the will of the Spirit, the actions of the mourner and her pointer in the Spirit, and the intensity with which the mourner prays. Embodying and organizing each of these are the songs utilized by the Converted for specific spiritual effects.

Spiritual Baptists take St. Paul's advice personally, "Study to shew thyself approved unto God, a workman that needeth not to be ashamed" (II Timothy 2:15). The Converted study by "going to school": mourning to acquire spiritual knowledge. The object of the knowledge is spiritual work.

Tools of Workers

Work that takes place in the church service is accomplished by three modes (but all by the action of the Spirit): use of the eyes, use of the voice, and use of the hands. Each employs the Spirit in a specific way. All are essential and neither has precedence over the other.

Spiritual eyes are a major feature of Converted religion. Although pointers are able to see into the Spirit when watching mourners on their pilgrim journey through the spiritual lands, the concept of spiritual eyes is different from the journey itself. Spiritual eyes, given to many but not all Converted, differ from the journey in that one's consciousness and presence are completely in the physical world. Spiritual eyes are a means of seeing actions, items, and people in the Spirit (another trait common in shamanism—see Noll 1985:446). Baptists are said to be able to see into one's soul. Some pointers are feared "because they have eyes" to see sin in the lives of Converted and non-Converted alike. Baptists also are able to see items in the Spirit. One woman in Brooklyn, recently baptized as a Converted, reported being in a market purchasing candles for a thanksgiving ritual she was giving in her home.

She was not certain what color to get, but then a yellow candle appeared before her eyes. She said that she was astonished, but told herself, "When these Baptists say they see things, they know what they are talking about." In principle, what can be seen with spiritual eyes is unlimited. In practice, what is reported as seen follows some conventional patterns.

Three things commonly "seen" in the church setting are sin, spiritual implements, and spirits. Sin leaves a residue. Most often it appears on one's clothing. Those who curse outside of church without repentance may be called out by the pointer, who will report that he can see every foul word that was uttered written on the member's clothing. Those who steal may come to church with, for instance, the stains of the stolen fruit smeared (spiritually) all over the dress. These two types of seeing of sin were reported on numerous occasions while I was in St. Vincent. A pointer, or a prover, or anyone "deep in the Spirit" or "high up in the Spirit" can also see what is in one's heart. This is called *proving*. Sometimes sin seen by proving is reported as a blackness in the heart, and sometimes the person proving "just knows" what the sin is, sometimes both simultaneously. Provers and many pointers can also tell one's history ("reading" one's soul), and many non-Converted reported to me in amazement their encounters with Baptists who told them things about their lives no one else could have known.

Spiritual implements (to be detailed) may be seen by any Converted with "eyes to see." By this means, one never need announce one's spiritual name, as the pointer and others deep in the Spirit should be able to see the tools accompanying each gift. A pointer may be seen with a pencil, a surveyor with a surveying rod, a captain with the captain's wheel. Interestingly, these are not necessarily held by the person, but may be seen hovering about them. There is never confusion as to what is "natural" and what is spiritual. The two have different qualities, though at times spiritual accoutrements are as vivid or more so than natural items. Physical elements in the church, such as the center pole or the bell, have a spiritual component. If left unguarded (spiritually) they may be stolen spiritually, with the consequence that the power of those items is greatly diminished. An individual inattentive to an item in his or her spiritual toolkit (e.g., a key, a crown, a sword) may drop it. It may be seen by others and picked up for their own use. Often, the item will be returned after a spiritual fight between the two. The spiritual fight takes place in the church and has the aspect of the hands held as swords with thrusts and parries, and also, as the hands held as firearms and the reports delivered with the mouth ("bim!," "bam!"). Often the willingness to fight is enough, and the spiritual item is returned quickly. All but a few of the 50 or so fights that I witnessed were didactic in nature (and I knew only one to be a conflict over spiritual implements), the pointer initiating the fight to test the spiritual vigilance of the member. Those who have eyes to see can see all of this. The rest must rely on physical cues and on explanations of the participants. Spiritual fighting is discussed in more detail in chapter 6.

Spirits are sometimes present in the church. Again, these are only seen by those with spiritual eyes. The others in the congregation may be cued by sudden activity on the part of those higher in the Spirit who busy themselves with welcoming the spirits by waving flags and ringing bells as they would greet members from any visiting physical church as well as pouring water (a representation of spiritual force) as they do with individual spirits and groups of spirits and the Holy Spirit. The spirits who do come (only after the presence of the Holy Spirit is felt) are usually in response to or in conjunction with music from their part of the spiritual world. Therefore, African spirits may come when the congregation is singing songs ascribed to Africa, Indian spirits may come when the tune is an Indian one, and so forth.

Use of the voice is the second important manner in which the spiritual work is performed. Music in the Converted church is vocal, not instrumental. It is used not only to set mood, but for spiritual action. Mostly it is to invite the Spirit to come and abide with the congregation for the time of the service. Specific songs have specific powers (see chapter 4). The pointer "has to know all of the songs," and one's status in the spiritual hierarchy corresponds to one's range of knowledge and skill with Converted music. When talking about spiritual work, music cannot be divorced from anything else in the Spiritual Baptist tool kit.

Speaking in church is indispensable (though singing or humming of some type is normatively expected to continue through all speaking). Words are a commodity. They are valued and exchanged.

On my first Sunday with the Converted, the church I had visited in the morning invited me to go with them to a different church in the evening. The occasion was described as going "to give encouragement to an old teacher." At the church far up the Windward coast, several congregations and their leaders had assembled. The ancient pointer of the church called himself an "old soldier," who had been "in the field" a long time. Nearly blind and unable to stand without assistance, but dressed in full Converted regalia, he sat while 10–15 pointers (whose pointer he had been) stood up to give him words. The venerable one, facing the congregation with the other pointers behind him, called out each of his spiritual children by name: "My son James, give me words. I gave you words. Now, I want words." For five hours his children obliged.

The acquisition of words is valuable for instruction as well as encouragement. In preparation for mourning and baptism, those in the congregation are invited to "give the pilgrim a word" and to offer "words of consolation and a message of salvation." The form of the words is, more than anything, quotations from inspired sources (the Bible, *The Pilgrim's Progress*, and lyrics from hymns). The congregation generally recites the quotation along with the speaker. The fact that the words are mostly known emphasizes the performative nature of the speaking and that all are working together. Also, all work together with words in the reciting of the liturgy— most of which is said aloud by all. In reading Bible passages, likewise, the congregation reads the words aloud. During sermons, prayers, and the public telling of visions, important dreams, and important spiritual journeys, the congregation uses its voice for encouragement of the speaker (calling out responses at lacunae in the speaking).

Use of the hands is requisite for spiritual work. The Baptists daily cite Psalm 24, which states that only those with "clean hands and a pure heart" can stand.

When one's hands are anointed at the banning, a common exhortation informs that the hands are being anointed so the pilgrim can "do the work of the Lord." When Converted pray for their pointers they frequently refer to "the hands that signed the bands." Many Converted viewed my constant writing of fieldnotes as my own spiritual work. On one occasion when my hands were washed and anointed, the pointing mother doing so told me, "I am going to wash your hands as you writing everything with your hands that you may be able to write the notes of the Lord."

Handshakes are an essential part of Converted religion. Sometimes I wanted to call it "the handshaking religion," because handshakes are required at numerous periods throughout the service. The handshakes take several forms and some non-Converted call them "secret handshakes." In fact they are not. They are more elaborate than the handshakes used in everyday commerce in the West Indies or North America, but the elaborateness is a way to gauge the spiritual character of the individual with whom one is shaking hands. If one is not practiced in the form—or cannot spiritually anticipate the form—one's spiritual status is evaluated as unprepared for meeting God in the service.

In the church service, the most visible use of hands is in the manipulation of ritual goods. Ritual goods are essential to the spiritual work done by the Converted. That much of the paraphernalia of the Converted is invisible matters little. Everything visible in the Converted church setting is a representation of something in the Spirit. Space limitations prohibit me detailing all of the spiritual and physical paraphernalia of the Converted; I note below the most important tools used in ritual work.

First we must start with the church building itself. The church has four corners and a center post, even as the world has four directions and the universe has Christ at its center.[7] The center pole has many uses and many meanings (though some Converted may only recognize a single meaning). Conflating many explanations I received, the pole represents the center of one's heart; it represents the pole on which Christ predicted he would be metaphorically lifted up (John 3:14; Numbers 21:8); it represents the flagpole in the center of every city in the spiritual lands; it is the ship's wheel spinning to send the Converted to the Spirit. Around the pole are various items representing different sorts of spiritual power (e.g., glasses of water, candles, calabashes, the bell, flowers and plants). In church buildings without a center pole, the space is marked off with chalk. The center represents the Spirit. The center is the emotional heart of the church.

The altar is the liturgical heart of the church. Benches in church are arranged so that the congregation faces the altar. Prayers are said facing the altar. At the altar, the leader opens the service, reciting the liturgy. From the altar, the pointer directs the service and dispenses the Eucharistic elements at communion. The church collection is blessed at the altar, as are children during christening. The altar represents the order of the church. In most churches, only the male leaders are allowed on the altar (which is the altar table along with its dais).

In every church, an empty space between the altar and the center pole acts as a proscenium, where the action of the church occurs. In the (unnamed) open space, speakers address the congregation, bands are placed on the pilgrim, robings and crownings and other investitures take place, special songs are offered, and congregational dancing and doption occur. All of these are the spiritual work of the church. Performance pleasing to God requires a balance between the emotion represented by the center pole and the order represented by the altar. Order and Spirit work together.

At the beginning of every Converted meeting, whether in a church, in an "open air" setting (crossroads, market square), or in someone's house for a blessing or a wake, the ground must be consecrated. Consecration ("surveying" in some churches) is the establishment of the sanctity of space. It is the signal that the work of the church has begun. In St. Vincent, the more than 70 consecrations I observed nearly always had the following form. The congregation sings a hymn, usually "Peace Be On This House Bestowed." The pointer blesses a glass of water containing a white flower (usually a white rose) or a sprig of a plant known as "evergreen" by making the sign of the cross with a candle, dripping wax into the glass, and ringing a bell over the glass. Two women approach the altar carrying candles that they light from the pointer's candle. The pointer hands the glass of water to one woman, the bell to the other. At each corner, proceeding in the form of a cross (usually beginning with the east corner), the bell is rung three times, a brief silent prayer is said, and the bell ringer curtsies. The woman with the glass comes directly afterward to each corner, spilling a few drops of water three times or sprinkling the water on the ground by using the flower as an aspergillum, saying a silent prayer, and curtsying. The women repeat the pattern at each door, then while circling the pole and at each corner of the altar. Ending at the altar, the women shake hands as a sign of friendship and each takes a sip of the consecrating water. Verses of the hymn are repeated for as long as the consecration lasts.[8] In the consecration, attention is given to both the altar and to the center pole, but not to the space between them. It is not the space between the center and the altar that is important in the church setting, but the interaction between the established liturgy and the unpredictable Spirit represented by that space.

In each corner of most churches, one finds a candle, a flag, and sometimes also a *calabash*, glass, or *goblet* filled with water. The flags in the corners are placed there at direction by the Spirit, usually in a dream or vision. Flags hang, too, from the rafters of most churches (ceilings are rare and impractical in the tropics). When a Converted has a vision of a flag in a certain location in a church, it is a sign to make that flag or have it made and place it where it was seen in the vision. Vincentian churches typically have 20–30 flags placed around the interior of the building. When the flags are taken down for cleaning or to repaint the church, care is taken to replace the flags in their proper locations. Most flags represent a spiritual city or other location, but they may refer to anything God chooses. Many flags have a simple legend (e.g., "God is love"), some are simply a field of a single color, and some have rather complex symbols embroidered on them.

Converted churches are usually painted with bright colors on the inside. Quotations from the Bible and from hymns are painted on the walls of most churches.

Some churches have painted scenes from the Bible. Others have pointers' seals drawn or painted on the walls. Most churches have all three, as well as plaques or framed prints with quotations, biblical scenes, and depictions of Christ. Prints of the Sacred Heart of Christ are especially common—visually representing the sort of spiritual *seeing* the Converted are able to practice. Every church has a calendar prominently displayed for temporally organizing the busy ritual schedule of every Converted church. The calendar must be available in the church because the rituals required of the Converted are responsive to the Spirit as well as to the changing needs of the congregation and the community. (Wakes, like deaths, are not planned in advance.)

At the altar or in a corner are one or several staffs, rods, and crosses used in rituals that require processions. These are all made of wood and are usually around six feet tall. The rod is used by the watchman, who may hold it as he stands at the door in normal services. The crooked staff is the tool of the shepherd of the church, who may, in addition to processions, hold it as he sits in church and spiritually guides his sheep. The cross is an important element in banning and in robing.

At either the pole or the altar or both one sees these items: candle, Bible, bell, water. Sometimes to these four are added the *lota* (or *luther*), the calabash, and the goblet. In St. Vincent, candles are usually the white eight-inch, ten-hour candles (that end up burning quicker) used by many Vincentians for light in their homes. In Brooklyn, a wide assortment of candles are used for different occasions. The Bible is nearly always the King James (Authorized) Version. The bell is the sort sometimes known as an English hand bell—a large hand-held brass bell with a wooden handle and a six-inch mouth. The water is usually in an ordinary transparent drinking glass and contains a white flower or a green leaf. The lota (or luther) is a brass vase of (East) Indian origin, containing water, yellow and white flowers (the colors of the spiritual city of India) or yellow croton leaves, and a candle.[9] The calabash is the fruit of the calabash tree, used as a container for water and food in many Vincentian households. In church it is filled with water, flowers, and a candle and represents Africa. When African songs are sung, those who belong to Africa, or who happen to be there in the Spirit when the song is sung, may dance with the calabash balanced on the top of the head. The goblet is a terra cotta vase about 12–18 inches tall with circular handles at its narrow neck. I saw no goblets in St. Vincent, but they are present in every Vincentian church I visited in Brooklyn, where they represent the spiritual city of China. Other elements that reflect a Trinidadian influence are described in later chapters.

The candle represents the Bible, and both represent Jesus Christ as "the Word" (John 1:1). Sometimes the words "Bible" and "candle" are used interchangeably; one Converted chorus begins alternatively, "When I put my Bible in front of my door" or "When I put my candle in front of my door." The candle symbolizes both Christ as the "light of the world" (John 8:12) and the Bible as "a lamp unto my feet" (Psalm 119:105). Every person speaking in church and every person leading prayers must hold a Bible or a candle to represent it. Speakers returning to their seats hand the lighted candle to the next speaker. Candles must be used in every service. They are the largest weekly expense in most churches and offerings of candles as well as money are sometimes placed in the collection plate. Extensive use of candles is made in mourning. At a shouting, nearly all in the congregation bring gifts of candles to place at the feet of the pilgrim. Some of these are taken home by the pilgrim to use in prayers at home; at least half stay in the church to replenish the supply. One of the most joyous, though rare, events in Converted ritual is a *candlelighting* ceremony, where hundreds of candles are burned at once.

The bell and the water are connected to the Spirit. The bell rung and the water spilled at the consecration are an invitation to the Holy Spirit. When spirits from various spiritual lands come to the church service, those who recognize them will welcome them into the church by ringing the bell and spilling water along a path from the door to the center pole. Spirits are welcomed slightly differently according to where they are from. For instance, African spirits are welcomed by spilling water from the calabash. Flags from the spiritual city to which the visiting spirits belong may be waved; songs from those cities may be sung; the language from those cities may be called out. The bell is used also in blessing the church collection, water to be used in ritual, or the bands for mourning. It can be rung at any time in the service as various Converted hear the bell spiritually and are impelled to ring it physically.

Plants of many kinds decorate Converted churches. They are not only to provide a pleasant atmosphere (though they are explicitly for that as well). All plants are symbolic of life, most specifically of the everlasting life given by God after death. Converted call themselves "tender plants" as the Messiah was called "tender plant" (Isaiah 53:2). Flowers represent Christ as the "sweet smelling savior." White flowers represent the purity the Converted should have in their hearts. Leaves of the Sago palm (*Cycas revoluta*) have spiritual significance, reflecting Christ's entry into Jerusalem on Palm Sunday as well as worship of him. When baptismal candidates are not seated on the special bench known as the *mercy seat*, either a candle or a sago palm leaf is placed on the seat to indicate its sacred status. Those Converted who "belong" to the spiritual city of Israel sometimes wear a cycad (sago) leaf in their headtie. The colorful leaves of the croton (*Croton spp.*) represent the different aspects of the Spirit (and sometimes Africa). Most powerful of all is the plant known as the *dragon* (*Dracaena spp.*)—its pointed, reddish, sword-like leaves represent both Africa and the Spiritual Baptists themselves. The dragon was imported from West Africa. In Vincentian cemeteries, it is customary to plant flowers or shrubs on the graves of loved ones. The dragon is planted only on Converted graves.

Every item in the church signifies a spiritual reality beyond St. Vincent. Each item represents a lesson to be learned by the Converted. Each item represents power.

The people in the church carry on their person items symbolic of spiritual tools they possess. The most important of these are the Spiritual Baptist uniforms. The Converted uniform is important not only because it sets the Converted apart visually, but because the uniform is heavy with symbols, containing information about the person's work, the spiritual city to which she belongs, her spiritual tools, and individual revelation. The uniform, as we saw in the last chapter, is presented to the pilgrim by the Spirit, usually agented by a spirit. The Spiritual Baptist uniform consists for the women of the *headtie*, the dress, the apron, and *cords, sashes,* and/ or a belt as given in the Spirit. For men, the uniform is the *headwrap*, the *gown*, and sashes, cords, and/or a belt as given by the Spirit. Men or women may carry additional items in their hands or affix them to their clothing as part of their spiritual uniform. Converted in spiritual uniform looked very much like what I had always imagined a pirate should be (see Driver 1991:66, who felt the same about Vodou houngans).

Women must have their head covered in church (I Corinthians 11:13) and, according to some, all the time. Men are not required to do so unless they receive direction from the Spirit. When men do wear a headdress, the top of the head is generally left uncovered. This sort of head covering is a headwrap. Women wear headties, which cover the top (or "mount") of the head. A headtie is usually a piece of cloth 18 to 24 inches wide and 6 to 12 feet long, composed of one or two colors. Considerable variety appears in the actual style of tying the headdresses, from simple wrapping with the ends tucked in at the sides to elaborate knotting. The men's headwraps range from a strip around the forehead to wide turbans of many colors of cloth. One's style is usually revealed in a vision or in a spiritual journey. Colors of the headdresses and other clothes may represent spiritual cities or the saints with which the individual works, but which color goes with which city or saint varies.

Spiritual garments for men usually are in the form of gowns worn over their usual clothing. Gowns are long or short cassocks, sometimes elaborately pleated and of various colors. Gowns may have no collar or have a wide mantle covering the shoulders and may be straight or flared on the lower portion. Ministers (deacons, deaconesses, pastors, bishops) frequently wear a surplice over their gowns or other clothes. Men are just as likely to wear no special spiritual clothing. Women wear a dress that comes to mid-calf or lower (trousers are not worn by women in church). Typically, the dress has a wide round collar that lies on the shoulders. An apron, usually with pockets, is tied around the waist and falls to the hemline. The apron, as in secular life, signifies preparedness for work. Both men and women normally own a number of garments of different colors and perhaps different designs depending on their experiences in the Spirit. Inspectors have a chevron affixed to their sleeve and dress in khaki-colored garments. The apron of nurses may have a bib held in place with safety pins, as with nurses in the (Vincentian) secular world.

Sashes and cords have widely different meanings depending on the church. Usually they are also bestowed by the Spirit. Sometimes sashes and cords have a military meaning, sometimes they represent some responsibility (like that of shepherd) or a spiritual city (by the color of the cord or sash). Belts are worn only by those in a teaching capacity in the church (pointers, teachers, mothers).

Sticks (or *rods*) of various descriptions are part of the spiritual uniform of a number of spiritual gifts. All of these sticks are roughly the same—18–24 inches long and made of wattle or guava wood approximately one-half inch wide. Teachers and pointers carry sticks. Inspectors carry them as a sign of office. Surveyors require them to survey the ground. One surveyor in St. Vincent carried an aluminum tube of the same proportions as the usual wooden ones. Flag wavers bring their sticks to church; the flags are carefully folded and carried separately. At church, the flag is attached to the stick and the flag waver is able to wave her flag.

One pointer of my acquaintance said that every item one acquires in the Spirit must be represented in one's uniform. I pointed out that this would be impractical even for him because of the large number of items I knew him to possess spiritually. He admitted that although it was expected, few people did it. Nonetheless, many Converted people do have small wooden swords or wooden keys hanging from their belts or cords. These stand in for spiritual swords and keys (often described as golden). One church mother had a small wooden representation of a rifle. I saw no other gifts symbolized in this fashion.

Pointers' tools are used to teach others so that those others can do their own spiritual work. A pointer usually acquires his tools all at once. The set of tools essential to the pointer are the belt, Bible, water, bell, and candle. These are what is required to run a church. As the pointer gains spiritual children (that is, points mourners), the usual pattern is for him to establish his own church. In Converted terms, the Bible is "the chart and compass" (that is, the map and the method to find one's way in the Spirit), the water is "peace," the candle is "the light of the world," the bell is "the signal," and the belt is "submission." The purpose of the belt is to discipline one's spiritual children by beating them, just as teachers in secular schools do to their students.[10]

Besides the spiritual implements needed to run a church, the pointer must have a pencil. The pointer actually uses chalk in the church, but in the Spirit it is usually described as a "pencil." With the pencil, the pointer must know what to write. These are spiritual *seals* written on the bands used to blindfold the pilgrim in the banning in preparation for mourning. The seals are the most powerful knowledge owned by the pointer. Misuse of the symbols can lead to madness and death. To avoid those consequences (or because they are sworn to secrecy in the Spirit), most pointers are reluctant to disclose the meanings of their seals. Seals are discussed in more detail in chapter 6.

According to the Converted, more important than all of these tools is what they consider the "Word of God," the Bible. They constantly urge each other to read and study the Bible more and more. Besides the Bible, they perceive as inspired the words in the hymnals and John Bunyan's *The Pilgrim's Progress*. When I asked if the hymns and *The Pilgrim's Progress* were the word of God, I always received an affirmative answer, but no one equated them in importance to the Bible itself. In practice, however, quotes from either the hymns or from Bunyan were frequently attributed to the Bible. Knowledge of all three is required for spiritual work in many churches, but some do not use *The Pilgrim's Progress*. One pointer, in describing how hard he worked to gain the scriptural knowledge needed to be an effective pointer, told me, "See that mango tree over there? That was my college. I was always sitting there studying hymn books and the Bible."

All Converted work is seen by them as doing the will of the Spirit. That is what Converted work is and "work" is the word used for all of their activities. It is most frequently heard in reference to the performance of rituals, but it refers equally to efforts (especially the pointer's) in the spiritual world. The intense identification with work in a spiritual realm sets the Converted apart from other Christians. The Christian ends of that work set the Converted apart from others who practice shamanistic techniques.

FOUR

Music

ONE NIGHT I WAITED FOR TWO hours for service to begin at a church near my house in St. Vincent. After chatting with the leader for some of that time, and when it became apparent he would not get more than the two or three others already sitting in the benches, I asked him if he was still going to hold church. He replied, "It is very important to sing." We had church. One night when too many members were out of tune, a pointer implored the congregation to sing better, indicating me and saying, "What do you want him to write about you?" Singing is the most important daily event for the Spiritual Baptists. Not only do they take singing very seriously, but they know they are good at it, sometimes jibing as they pass other churches, "They don't sound sweet like us." The performance of the music is the measure of its efficacy. If it sounds good, it is working.

This chapter considers Converted music as a spiritual tool that draws its power from the spiritual world and its form from the Vincentian context. Music is the most important item in the Converted repertoire of ritual tools. One requirement for the office of pointer is that he "know all the songs."

Other Vincentians may denigrate the Baptists for many things, but I found no one who could say a bad word about Spiritual Baptist music. Even when they hated the Converted, they still liked the music. The great beauty that I, the Vincentians, and the Converted themselves perceive cannot be communicated in print. The emotive feel of the music will have to be left aside. However, there is beauty in the way music organizes Converted ritual and Converted experience. That property of the music is what I will try to communicate.

Converted music is a spatial as well as a temporal experience. The music sends the pilgrim out and brings her back, it lifts her and sets her down, it "keeps her spinning," and helps her to be "rooted and grounded." It is able to do this because music itself "moves vertically and horizontally, slowly and rapidly . . . strolls and runs, jumps and walks, climbs and descends" (Schoen 1948:402). Converted songs are *ships*, *roads*, and *keys*. The music imparts mood to the individual and the congregation; it communicates with the Spirit of God and is the means that the Spirit communicates with the Converted. Converted songs are an invitation and a greeting. They are praise of God and joyful expressions of togetherness. As with Spiritual Baptists elsewhere, Converted theology is constructed and played out in sacred music in the ritual setting (Glazier 1997). The music, by structuring inner time and space, allows the Converted to share an event outside of time, though bracketed by it. The experience of the Converted is regulated by a musical *entrainement*. Just as two clocks set together tend gradually to beat in time, the rhythmic, harmonic, melodic ordering of Converted ritual trammels and channels the meaning the Converted derive from their ritual experiences.[1]

In church services, songs may be initiated by individuals. However, when "a current" of the Spirit is flowing through the church, when the members are singing in unison, and when the Holy Spirit has accepted the invitation to be in the midst, music is not generated by the Converted, but comes from the ground. The Converted leaders and others who are in tune can feel the music running through the ground and know which song to sing next. *The Spirit*, it will be remembered, is not only the Holy Spirit of God, but also the entire spiritual world. Music is part of that world. The "current" of the Spirit that comes through the ground is the music itself. Music in Converted religion is an actor in its own right. It moves, it spins, it has causal force.

Kinds of Music

All Converted music is vocal. All Converted music, then, consists of songs. Singing in church is talking to God. It is interaction with the Spirit. As one Converted leader explained to me, "The songs are ways of gaining access to the spirit world." Singing is normatively required at all times in the church service. Different parts of the service take different songs, but they are all songs. When Converted specify types of song, they make reference to these terms: *choruses, hymns, humming, chanting, hailings, prayers,* and *sankeys* (or *song keys*).

In my first few days in St. Vincent, I sat down with a Converted pastor, explained that I wanted to write about what it was like to be a Baptist and asked him to help me come up with a list of topics that might become chapters in the write-up of the research. His first word was, "Choruses." I was skeptical, but later came to see that an examination of Spiritual Baptist choruses is essential to understanding Spiritual Baptist experience. Choruses are tickets to various places and experiences. They are easy to learn and remember. By singing them, the Converted hitch on for the ride. Through the words and tunes of the choruses all are able to enter metaphorically into different spiritual lands. Some, by singing them, empirically enter those spiritual realms. The titles of the choruses are clues: "Go Down in the Valley," "Canaan Land," "Beulahland," "We Are Marching Onward to Zion," "Over in Zion, There Is Music in the Air," etc. Other choruses attend actions in the church service or set a certain mood. For example, "Be Still and Know That I Am God" quiets the congregation and "Greet Somebody in Jesus' Name" is used during the greeting ritual.

Choruses are short musical pieces of about 15 seconds in length, seldom exceeding 30 seconds. They are always repeated several times. When the mood is appropriate they may be sung 50 or 60 times (like the ones sung by Jamaican Revivalists [Chevannes 1978:8]). Choruses may be quick and light, slow and solemn, or any combination of tempos and moods. They may be called on at any time to enliven a service, to change a mood, or to effect some spiritual work. Frequently, they have a very Pentecostal flavor. They are often borrowed from the Pentecostals as well. One of the benefits of visiting other churches in the island is learning choruses that might not be known in one's own church.

Hymns are the multistanza songs found in hymn books. Usually, these are taken from the *Methodist Hymn Book* (1954), but not exclusively. Some hymns sung by the Converted are only found in the Anglican hymnal, *Hymns Ancient and Modern* (1916). My respondents stressed that any hymnal is acceptable. Other hymnals commonly used by Converted in St. Vincent are *Redemption Songs, Sacred Songs and Solos* and *Hymns of Faith* (the official hymnal of the Spiritual Baptist Archdiocese). All of these hymnals contain only the words, no scores. Hymns, like choruses, also may be lively or solemn and may be used for dancing or prayer. Their more complicated lyrics are less responsive to quick changes in mood than are choruses. However, the tune has the spiritual force. The lyrics do, too, but far less. The lyrics of hymns as well as choruses are often dispensed with, especially in moments of deep spiritual drama, and the tunes themselves are hummed.

Sankeys play only a small role in Converted ritual. Since they are acknowledged by Converted as a special category, and as they are widespread in the Caribbean and have been since the 1880s, they deserve mention. Sankeys (also called song keys), as used in Converted practice, are not merely the songs compiled by Ira Sankey (n.d.) in *Sacred Songs and Solos* (most of the songs in that book are in other hymnals as well). For most Converted, a sankey refers to one of a select group of solos sung in church (but not the only solos).

Humming is a style of singing without words. The Converted term "hum" does not refer to singing with the lips closed, or even to murmuring, but merely singing without words, that is, singing the tune alone. Besides devolving into humming, some hymns are introduced by humming only. The vocalizations in the wordless singing of tunes are often "bam" and "beem" (contrasting with the North American "la dee da"). "Bam" and "beem" are the sounds of a drum beating; however, being vocal, they are subject to melodic modulation. In non-Converted Vincentian practice, humming vocalizations are similar to the Anglo–American model (that is, "la dee da"). In Converted humming, dramatic overlayering takes place, emphasizing the presence of the Spirit in the congregation.

Chanting is low singing. Some Converted use "chanting" only in the sense of singing while someone is speaking in church. Others say that one can chant at home as well. Chanting is never chanted; it is always the melodic singing of any one of the usual Converted songs. Usually it is a humming, but may be singing with words. Chanting is meditative and is used by Converted to "go through" into the Spirit. Chanting is also used to "keep the current moving" while someone is speaking. Chanting may well up into a louder song or a chorus. Loud singing is seldom a problem to the speaker. It is more important that she say what she has to say than it is that she is heard. Most often, though, the chanting is soft enough that she is heard. Usually the speaker will continue talking during the chanting. Sometimes she will join in the singing as well, going back to what she was saying after a few moments.

Converted prayers do not have to be sung, but in church they usually are. During mourning or in a dream or vision, many are given a tune by the Spirit to use in praying. In practice, some just copy their fellows. A single congregation tends to have only a few prayer tunes and the range varies by congregation. Prayer tunes are among the most beautiful tunes in the Spiritual Baptist repertoire. A prayer that is sung is called a *sing prayer* or, seldom, a *centurion*. The Converted say that if one sings while praying, "you pray twice." Non-Vincentian Spiritual Baptist churches I visited place far less emphasis on sung prayers. Vincentians in Brooklyn told me that they are noted among other Spiritual Baptists for the beautiful singing of their prayers.

Hailing is singing of a different order; hailings are special sung vocalizations. They are used for calling people at a distance—that is, spirits. Hailings are used in approaching a spiritual city in the Spirit; they are also used to liven or deepen the spiritual response of the congregation. Sometimes they are prayers, the words of the hailing being a name of one the person praying wants the Spirit to pay special attention to (e.g., "Sister Violet-O, Sister Violet-O, Sister Violet-O, Oh-oh-oh"). Frequently, the words to hailings are in languages associated with certain spiritual cities (e.g., a hailing for the spiritual city of India goes, *"Rashiminah-hey, Rashiminah-hey, Rashiminahey-O-O-O"*). The hailing may also merely be the (standardized) welling, melodic calling out of the name of the spiritual city (e.g. "Israel Israel-O, Israel Israel-O, Israel Israel-O, Ai-ay-ay"). They seldom last more than 15–20 seconds. In every case, hailings are always sung.

Another type of song present in Converted churches is not differentiated by them with a term. However, they are responded to in a special way. These are songs from the spiritual lands themselves (in contrast to choruses that may carry one *to* specific spiritual lands). For instance, what is called by them an *African song*, an *Indian song*, *Chinese song*, etc. These songs are sung by the congregation when members are traveling in those lands. They may be initiated by the individuals traveling there or by those who can feel the song coming through the ground. Songs of spiritual cities have no words apart from some that may be in the language of that city, but the tunes are instantly recognizable by all present as pertaining to the city. The songs of spiritual cities almost always impel dancing of the style of that city.

Performance of Music

Converted life is about pleasing God. Good ritual performance is a primary way of accomplishing that. Good performance of music is essential. Musical instruments are not allowed in most Spiritual Baptist churches in St. Vincent. Occasionally I saw a "shak–shak" (gourd shaker) or a tambourine, but most people would not consider taking an instrument to church.[2] In a few churches, a conch shell is blown at times of spiritual intensity. It is called the "trumpet" or sometimes the "horn," but most churches do not have one. Percussion is obtained by clapping, or beating one's hands or stick on a nearby bench or Bible, or stamping on the ground.[3] Physical musical instruments are unnecessary. The glory of the Converted is their vocality.

God gives each Spiritual Baptist a musical instrument in the Spirit. When the mourner returns from her spiritual journey, the pointer may test her ability as a "musician." She then must perform the instrument God gave her. All of these instruments are invisible. One pastor, taking note of the use of physical instruments in a non-Converted church said to his congregation, "We don't need a guitar; we have our guitar in our heart." In church, each sings his instrument during the humming (especially in the most dramatic humming). The Converted simulate the instrument or "play" it with their mouth. When "the Spirit is moving," when "the service is sweet," and when the performance is at its best, members of the congregation hold and move their hands as if they are playing the instruments while they "play" them vocally. Different instruments that respondents identified for me were: guitar, keyboard, piano, organ, trumpet, drum. I observed each of these, as well as several of what were apparently some kind of woodwind (saxophone, clarinet, or perhaps flute). The drum is the most common. Listening one night to several men singing a skillful "bam-ba-bam-ba-bam-beem-beem," a nurse leaned over and whispered in my ear, "Those are African drums." With the other instruments added in polyrhythmic harmony, as well as voices, the effect is unexpectedly beautiful. McDaniel (1995:47) described Trinidadian Spiritual Baptist music as consisting of "overlayered, superimposed 'sheets of sound'."

Men who lead the singing in church have developed a peculiar style. It is a rhythmic deep-throated time-keeping (similar to the South African style featured in Paul Simon's *Graceland* album) combined with a vocal overtoning (overtone singing). The male Converted singers simultaneously produce a tone from the throat as well as produce a higher tone focused in the mouth. When done right, it sounds as if two people are singing rather than one.[4] Herskovits and Herskovits (1947:222) may have been referring to this in Trinidad when they wrote, "[The hymn] almost disappeared in the 'ram-bam-i-bam-bam' of the full-throated song leader." I tried to learn the technique during the 14 months I was in the field. While I was able to get closer and closer, I never did master it (to the amusement of my respondents). Many, and maybe most, men are unable to produce the distinctive sounds. I never heard a woman make them. When several men who have the ability lead the singing together, the church resounds with the vibrations. Overtone singing is very rare as a cultural style and is practiced in only a few places in the world, notably among the Tuva pastoralists, but also in Mongolia and in some Tibetan monasteries (Smith, Stevens, and Tomlinson 1967; Alekseev, Kirgiz, and Levin 1990). Overtone singing is not restricted to Asia; it has also been described among Basque singers (Bloothooft et al. 1992:1827). Like most of the cultural materials of the Converted, I suggest that overtone singing is a human capability that should not be seen as deriving from a specific cultural source. It is part of what marks the Converted as unique in St. Vincent and part of what makes their music attractive to other Vincentians.

The features of African music listed by Manuel (1995:7–8), collective participation, emphasis on rhythm, polyrhythm, and call and response, are all present in Converted music. Yet, while the music may be African in much of its performance style, European forms have as much prevalence as African in Converted music.

An important part of Converted ritual performance is "calling out the hymn" (hymn-lining), formerly common in the eighteenth and nineteenth centuries in Anglo-American churches, but largely abandoned (Pitts 1991). Bilby (in Manuel 1995:150) reports that it remained in Caribbean churches because, while a European tradition, hymn-lining was "fully compatible with the antiphonal style of music making brought by enslaved Africans." Some Converted are good at it and consider calling out the hymn as part of their spiritual gift. Even those who do not do it regularly may be told by a leader or mother to call out the hymn if they happen to be holding a hymn book and the regular leader is not present. A man who has the spiritual gift of *leader* normally does not need a hymnal. He has all of the words memorized and calls them out at regular rests in the music.

Herskovits and Herskovits (1947:210) wrote about song performance of Spiritual Baptists in Trinidad that "the manner of singing emphasizes a certain lugubrious quality by means of drawn notes and slurs from one tone to another, rendered at full voice, and with a kind of paradoxical enthusiasm by the singers." A queering rubato, exciting coloratura, and smoothing legato are techniques skillfully practiced in St. Vincent in elaborating the tunes ascribed to the hymns. Most astonishing, given the lack of instruments in the church and the lack of musical scoring in the hymnals, is the long preservation of original tunes in reference to key church hymns. For the Wesleyan hymns, most of the original tunes used in the eighteenth century are sung for the same hymns in Converted churches (Stevenson 1883).

Uses of Songs

One thing that impressed me in St. Vincent as different from my Euro-American background was that Vincentians sing all the time, out loud, anywhere, as the mood takes them. There is no embarrassment about singing. Vincentians sing in the market square, walking down the road, while resting on a porch, or in a lull in a conversation. The song may be of any type, from the latest soca or reggae tune to a Jimmy Swaggart gospel song or an Anglican hymn. Church songs do not have to mean church, though they may. Converted walking together to church and especially when going to visit another church sing choruses and hymns.

Songs do have practical "natural" uses in church. Set songs confer changes or stages in the liturgy. Songs may be sung by the congregation to welcome an individual; I was greeted at my first Spiritual Baptist service with the chorus, "All the Way from Africaland, Coming to Hear Them Singing." Special solos may be sung in honor of an individual at a thanksgiving. These tend to be sankeys or gospel songs popularized by American gospel singers on the radio—almost always of the style known as White Gospel or Country Gospel. It was quite odd to hear West Indians singing with an American Country twang.

One of the most important "natural" uses of songs in the church is for organizing speaking in church. All who speak in church are required to "come with a hymn" or a chorus. So many people speak in Spiritual Baptist services (in some services all are required to speak) that separation is needed between the speakers. The songs allow each speaker to set her own tone as well as to keep the musical current flowing. The custom also prevents more than one person at a time from going to the front of the church, presenting a more orderly performance to the congregation and to the Spirit. If two or more speakers start songs together, the one who is able to make her song prevail with the congregation is able to speak—usually the one with the strongest voice or who is willing to sing loudest. The other sits down and waits for another chance. The dozens of occasions where I witnessed this happen were accompanied with good humor on the part of the contenders and the audience.[5]

As with everything in the Converted world, the spiritual side of music is (theologically) more important than the physical or "natural." Music communicates from and to the Spirit. In the same way that for the Malaysian Temiar, "The dense, tropical forest is visually opaque but acoustically transparent" (Roseman 1984:435), so with the Spirit of the Converted. Music is a physical action that penetrates the spiritual world. It has substance there. By coming from the bodies of the Converted themselves, it carries those same bodies (or the sensual perception of those same bodies) into the spiritual world.

When by *doption* or *gazing* or *dying away*, an individual Converted is in a spiritual land, the singing of a song by the congregation may send her further into that land. When a pilgrim gets lost in some part of the Spirit, a hailing by the pointer is likely to bring him back. Songs sung by the congregation or the pointer may persuade hostile inhabitants of a spiritual city to release a pilgrim who may be held hostage there. Most important of all, singing is pleasing to God.

The Spiritual Baptist service "comprises multiple symbols in sound, color, and gesture" (McDaniel 1995:56, fn 2). The pointer is the manager of those symbols for the congregation. As the chief spiritual practitioner (or the practitioner-teacher) of the church, the pointer must know the meanings of the different tunes. He—or she, in the case of a pointing mother—must know which songs are appropriate for specific spiritual actions.

Three spiritual offices have charge of the music in a Converted church. These are the *pointer*, the *leader*, and the *captain*. The pointer sets the general tone for the service or may send the service in a certain direction if he needs to. Usually he lets the leader and the captain do what they feel is necessary. The leader (or leadress) opens the service and selects hymns in addition to the ones required in the liturgy. He may conduct all of the set liturgy himself. He also begins choruses and calls out lines to hymns throughout the service. His job is to enliven the congregation. One leader told me that "it is a hard job keeping up the rejoicing." The captain takes over the singing when the congregation or significant numbers in it enter the spiritual lands. His job is navigating the church from spiritual city to spiritual city. He is assisted by the leader and vice versa. Both the liturgical "natural" singing of the leader and the spiritual traveling singing of the captain are assisted by everyone in the congregation. Anyone may take the role of captain or leader temporarily on the direction of the Spirit or the pointer. While anyone who is moved by the Spirit may introduce a chorus, the pointer usually takes over this role during important rituals. Some choruses are standard, and everyone expects them (such as, "Light Your Light, Angels Watching Over Me" when candles are lit at a thanksgiving). The pointer may introduce a chorus to lend spiritual force to a particular point of ritual.

In Converted religion, the tune is both the vehicle and the path into the spiritual world. It is both the "road" and the "ship" to the spiritual lands, as well as the "key" to open the gate to certain spiritual locales. Roseman (1984:426) notes of a shamanic culture similar to the Spiritual Baptists, "There is no Temiar word for 'song;' the spirit-guide's 'musical gift' is referred to as the 'path,' or 'way.'" Hill (1992:183) describes the Wakuénai shaman as journeying *in* his songs. The Spiritual Baptist pointer has to know all of the *songs*, which are themselves paths into and out of the spirit world. Songs are a source of power. Although the words are often important, they are adjustable. The words are important for education and understanding, but the tune is what does the spiritual work. Up to half of the singing in church is without words. The tune is the focus of performance. However, as we shall see, it is the meaning the Converted give to the tune that really counts.

What is important to the Converted, and for the study of shamanic singing, is "not merely sound structures *per se*, but the cultural logics informing those structures, the metaphors and theoretical concepts which render sounds meaningful to performers and listeners, and the strategies of sound in use" (Roseman 1984:435). As Glazier (1983:45) and Parks (1981:79) indicate for Trinidadian Spiritual Baptists, music at different parts of the service and in different rituals place the worshipper in the proper mental disposition for effective spiritual work. The subjective nature of the meaning of music drives the work of the music. Intervals in music, motifs, and melodies "also do what speech does: they connote, denote, and emote. They express ideas, describe situations, and create moods" (Schoen 1948:402). Music enables the Converted, and everyone, to identify with a feeling and to live that feeling (404).

Dances

African musical practice implies physical movement with no separation between music and dancing (Lincoln and Mamiya 1990:353). After several months with the Converted, I began to take that style for granted. When I visited a Methodist church in St. Vincent one day, I was startled by the immobile singing style of the worshippers. Movement is the order for singing in the Spiritual Baptist churches, but a distinction is made between moving to the music and dancing.

Like most things in Converted life, dances are divided into those that take place primarily in the "natural" and those that take place primarily in the Spirit (but moving the physical body). The former are lexically unmarked; the latter are sometimes referred to as "spiritual dancing." Both have their part in the ritual order of the church.

Dancing in a Converted church may be done by a single person but is usually done in pairs or with several people dancing in pairs. A person honored at a thanksgiving, a pilgrim being "pointed on" at a banning, or someone who is known to need cheering up in general will be "danced with." The focal individual is handed off after a few bars from partner to partner until the song is finished. Not all songs are dancing songs, but some songs almost always inspire immediate dancing (e.g., the Wesleyan hymn, "Talk With Us Lord, Thyself Reveal"). A song may be a waltz (e.g., the chorus, "Oh Yes, Oh Yes, Oh Yes, Oh Yes, The Water is High Over Me"), and the dance that accompanies that song is also a waltz. The commonest dance seen in Vincentian Spiritual Baptist churches is a two-step shuffle, partners holding hands, the couple proceeding four steps forward, four steps back, and after several of these moves, spinning so that places are switched. With this and all Converted dances, couples may be male-male, male-female, or female-female. Other dancing involving couples has bits of the quadrille, the belair, and other figure dances.

We can see in the dancing, as in the spiritual offices, a sacralization of the secular world order. Dances of elite society, the waltz and the quadrille, are performed in Converted churches although they are not done outside of church. This contrasts with the condition on the neighboring islands, where the quadrille, lancers, and belair are still equated with a secular context (see Crowley 1958, for St. Lucia; Steele 1996, for Grenada), though in Montserrat, these dance styles have been incorporated into a religious performance (Dobbin 1986). For the Jombee dance of Montserrat, the appropriation of European dances in a ritual context as a prelude to "trance dancing" may be a similar sacralization of secular colonial power symbols to legitimize and emphasize spiritual power over secular. The St. Lucian society fêtes do display an African element by the rhythmic dancing to the chanted name of the society (Dalphinis 1985:31). The St. Lucian dances have a ritual aspect, though secular. Guibault (1985) suggests that the slave musicians present at the European dances of the eighteenth century are the source of elaborate dances, such as the quadrille in the Rose and Marguerite societies, which are, like Converted religion, a ritual reproduction of the dominant society. A similar occurrence may account for the presence of many of the same dance steps in the Converted churches.

Normal (or unmarked) dancing in the church contrasts with spiritual dancing (or, more accurately, dancing associated with specific spiritual cities). These dances will be discussed in more detail in Chapter 6. Here I want to note some features comparable to dancing on other islands. While most spiritual cities have a specific type of dance that may be performed in the church setting, two cities stand out for the frequency with which their dances appear: Africa and India. Dances from both break out spontaneously as soon as the proper tune is sung. For both, the individuals may be either in the Spirit (mentally), or in "the physical" during the dancing. To do the spiritual dancing, each participant must "belong" to the city that the dance represents (that is, have traveled there during mourning and learned the dance from the inhabitants of that place).

The Indian dance has some fluid movement, but is characterized by a hunched posture and a patting of the feet. A vocalization during the dance is often a whooping while patting the lips with the palm of an open hand. The Indian dance looked very much to me like the standardized war dance of Hollywood films about the American West. The Converted also conceive of Indians in the spiritual city of India as being of the same type they see in American films and on television. Indians, like those from South Asia, are also believed to live in the spiritual city of India, but my respondents had less contact with them than with the other sort. I had supposed this condition was a response to American hegemony in visual media, and it may be. However, Steele (1996:36) reports that a "Wild Indian" dance existed in Grenada in the nineteenth century. Its description is different from the Indian dance of the Spiritual Baptists, but the intent is the same: imitation of Amerindians. I believe there is no direct connection in this dance with the Amerindian Caribs who still inhabit St. Vincent.[6] The Indians whose dance the Converted perform are described as living in a desert (in the spiritual lands).

The African dances all feature extremely fluid movements—rolling of the hips, careful stepping (the *piqué* in ballet), pointing of toes—as well as seductive interaction with others—sidelong glances, inviting smiles, and pulling on the cords or sashes around the waists of those dancing with them or those merely watching. All, however, even those not dancing, sing the song. One of the African dances involves the dancer placing the church calabash (filled with water, flowers, and a lighted candle) on her or his head and dancing with it balanced without hands. Another dance (and one usually performed while in the Spirit) occasions a hitching up of the skirt (or gown for the men), sometimes to quite revealing heights, while rolling the pelvis. The African dances in Converted churches appear identical to one described by Steele (1996) as extinct in Grenada: "the pique," which was performed in a secular context. Steele also writes that the pique was known as a "Nation Dance" in which African origins were celebrated. Dances in Revival churches described by Chevannes also appear to be similar to the Converted African dances. Revival dances involve balancing, "spinning, headwork, footwork, and far greater use of the limbs and whole body than is permissible in secular dances"; some involve "movements of an unmistakably sexual nature" (Chevannes 1978:7).

It is clear that the dances of the Converted have both European and African antecedents. The current meaning of the dances establishes a sacred connection between the dancers in the normal dancing as well as with the inhabitants of the spiritual cities in the spiritual dancing. Both kinds of dances are an exultation in spiritual joy; both are intimately connected to the music associated with each dance.

Where Songs Come From

From the examples I have given of African and Indian dancing, one should not conclude that the European forms are more liturgical and the African forms are more spiritual.[7] Not only do the Converted not view it that way, but tunes and styles that I identify as of European influence are as spiritual and conducive to trance (that is, "going through" into the Spirit) as any other.

Music in hymns comes from the hymn writers. They, in turn, were inspired by God. Choruses and the tunes associated with them are taken from Pentecostals, Apostolics, Catholics, Seventh Day Adventists, or anyone else who has a good tune. God can use for his work any tune he sees fit. The Converted may use any worthy tune to praise him. However, some tunes to hymns and choruses do come from the Spirit. The meaning of tunes to individuals also comes from the Spirit. Hailings and the songs of spiritual cities all originate in the Spirit, as do the beats to doptions. This is all from the Converted point of view. Many of the most spiritual tunes are, in fact, shared with secular songs; some of those contain deep meaning in their European contexts.

Music may come to the Converted person in a dream. This is common throughout the world in secular and sacred settings (Mayhew 1953; Roseman 1984:415; (Kalweit 1988:149; Tunes may be heard during doption, or in meditation. But songs are always encountered in the spiritual world during mourning. Any being—a saint, a dog, a tree, a stone, or a disembodied voice—may give one a tune in the Spirit. Tunes so acquired, whether completely new or well known, become special songs for the individual and may be used to accomplish spiritual actions. They also happen to elicit a strong spiritual reaction when they are heard in church. With almost any hymn or chorus, individual Converted in different parts of the church jolt or "shake" with the Spirit in reaction to hearing one of the songs they received in the Spirit.

Hymns are taken from the hymnals, from the *Methodist Hymn Book* more than any others. Common hymns used by Converted are the same as those popular in many parts of the world. For instance, the Converted liturgical greeting song, "And Are We Yet Alive," by Charles Wesley, is popular with several African American Methodist denominations and had been used to open the English Methodist conference since the eighteenth century (Stevenson 1883:303; Spencer 1992:56). Hymns display a conservatism of form. Glazier (1997) found that some Trinidadian Spiritual

Baptist hymns contain stanzas that have not been sung in other churches for over 150 years. Tunes, as well, tend to be ones from long ago. For instance, in St. Vincent, the Wesleyan hymn "Jesu Lover of My Soul," is most commonly sung to the tune "Refuge," as it had been in England at least since the nineteenth century (Stevenson 1883:121).[8]

If the Converted are to be linked with any other denomination, it would be much more accurate to call them a shade of Methodist than a schism from the Baptists (as do McDaniel [1995], Hackshaw [1992], and many Trinidadians). Despite calling themselves "Baptists," the Converted follow the Methodist "Order of Morning Prayer," itself a version of the Anglican service, in both morning and evening services, in some churches in entirety (unlike the Methodists). While the hymn book used may be any one available, the hymns selected are overwhelmingly those that appear in the *Methodist Hymn Book* (1954). The nearly universal consecration hymn, in St. Vincent or Trinidad, is Charles Wesley's "Peace Be on this House Bestowed." This selection is not available in the hymn books currently in use in St. Vincent and must have been remembered from a time prior to the 1933 edition of the *Methodist Hymn Book* on which the 1954 revision is based. It is not outrageous in Christian practice that the hymns are used by the Converted as canonical scripture. Berger (1995) demonstrates how the Methodist hymnal acts as a theology-ratifying "Methodist Manifesto": a theology that is largely accepted by the Converted (although the Converted cosmos is larger). The popularity of the Methodist hymns, with the Spiritual Baptists and others, may stem from the ability of the Wesleys to borrow compelling phrases, ideas, and images from all available literary sources (Bett 1946). The Converted themselves do the same—and, like the Wesleys, without attribution to authors. To the Converted, the derivation is not important, but the experiential truth of the image.

The sources of Converted choruses disclose the same condition; any chorus that speaks to or about Converted experience is welcome in church. Many Spiritual Baptists take pride in being the first to introduce a particular chorus to their church or their part of the island. Sources of choruses are discussed in the same way that the weather is discussed. One girl told me, after she and her mother had introduced a new chorus to their church, "We went to the Pentecostal church, and we thiefed it." Unlike hymns, choruses are readily modified in both tune and words. Visiting churches often stumble over the first few lines of a chorus that in their own church may be sung differently.

Converted music, like everything else in the religion, reflects daily Vincentian context: historical, political, social. Not only are the symbols from the larger Vincentian context combined for spiritual use, but they are recombined in a way that emphasizes the predominance of the spiritual, where the Converted are powerful, over the natural, where they are relatively powerless. This is most obvious in the songs emanating from the spiritual world—that is, hailings and songs of the spiritual cities.

Hailings, the sung vocalizations calling to spirits or the Spirit, are common in church. They may be sung at high points in the service (when approaching a spiritual city), at low points in a service (to enliven the praise of the congregation), or in prayers. Hailings bear structural similarity to African American slave "field hollers" (Courlander 1992; 1996:506–510) and may be related to that genre. Vincentian slaves were plantation workers in tall cane and may have used "field hollers" for communication. In the mountainous geography of St. Vincent today, people call out to friends or workers on opposite hillsides of the steep valleys in a standardized musical call that sounds similar to some of the spiritual hailings. Converted see the two as quite different things, but when I pointed out the similarity, some did say they may be related. Like all of the Caribbean islands, St. Vincent was and is a maritime society. As well, the Converted church is perceived by them as a ship. Spiritual hailings may be related to the sort of hailing used at the approach of ships.[9]

Many of the hailings sound familiar to me. I have only been able to identify the tune of one. It is *Taps*, the "lights out" bugle call, to which millions of soldiers have been sent off into slumber and dreams for hundreds of years. It is also well known as a military funeral song. The tune is slow and evocative. Yet, it has been interpreted by the Baptists into their own meanings. To the Converted, it is a general hailing for use in almost any spiritual situation.

Songs of the spiritual cities may reflect similar transpositions. One of the songs associated with China is the tune to "Auld Lang Syne." The words, however, are in the spiritual language of that city: "*Chong chong chong chong chong chong chong ... Saw, saw, saw, saw, saw. . . .*" As Jonathan Hill tells us (1993:160), "Musical sounds are not separated from mythic meanings but directly embody primary sources and relations of power." One can imagine that the tune used by colonial masters to celebrate the change of calendar, and hopes for a better year ahead, may have been taken by those with no hope of a better future and used by them to represent a world where they could be the masters of change. The answer may not be accessible, though. When I suggested to the pointer who sang that song at a banning that it (Auld Lang Syne) was a famous tune, he said, "Yes, it is from China." On the other hand, to the Converted, it is not a contradiction that one tune is shared by two contexts. The Spirit is God's domain. He may do there whatever he pleases.

Colonial Natures

Manuel (1995:12) lists as the European genres of music most influential on the development of local Caribbean music, "Sailor's chanteys, church hymns, military marches, and social dances like the quadrille, mazurka, waltz, and contradance." All of these we find in Converted ritual performance. A Vincentian police report of 1905 indicated that Converted rejoicing consisted of songs set to "dance music" that inspired shaking and jumping in an "awful manner" (Fraser 1995, April 20). The European is combined with an African aesthetic to create the much admired music of the Spiritual Baptists (cf. Bilby 1985:97 Thornton 1992:228, fn89).

The use of European music may be a way of fighting back against oppression. Music and dance in the Caribbean has been interpreted as a means of resistance (Entiope 1987; Desch 1994). I think we cannot discount the possibility that the tunes and dances I have identified as of European origin might just be good tunes and good dance steps selected for euphony and graceful movement. However, the evidence leans at least as much to resistance as to aesthetics.

Everywhere people must make sense out of the fact that much of their life is not in their control. Music, like the forces that spin fate, is invisible and can communicate with the unseen. In all cultures, music is used to speak with the deities and to hear from them. Lincoln and Mamiya (1990:348) write that African American gospel singing is one way that "black people 'Africanized' Christianity in America as they sought to find meaning in the turn of events that made them involuntary residents in a strange and hostile land." Converted music demonstrates an attempt (and a success) to make meaning out of the entire social landscape.

Although it appears to be unconscious on their part, the incorporation into church services of military tunes, popular music, and dances of colonial gentility is a brilliant move. Converted music, like other parts of Converted religion, is a sacralization of the secular in a ritual inversion that subverts European notions of sacredness and order. Sacredness and order are not in the hands of Europeans, but in the hands of their servants. They are Converted people who convert all they touch into a more sensible meaning. Not only are the symbols of colonial propriety taken in by the Converted, but they are turned on their head.

Unlike the seldom performed Jombee dance of Montserrat, or the once-a-year fêtes of the Rose and Marguerite societies of St. Lucia, the Converted of St. Vincent exercise a permanent restatement of power relations. The Converted must endure more by wearing their uniforms regularly, by being ridiculed regularly. But the psychic rewards may be greater; they also get to experience their ritually heightened status regularly.

According to Hill (1993:160), "History is not just a set of past events recounted in narrative forms but a dynamic process of en-chanting and singing-into-being the imagery of mythic power and transformation." Like the Wakuénai, the Converted "have not only preserved the memory of Western colonial power but en-chanted it into the musical reproduction of their social relations" (159).

A Banning

"YOU MAY NOT BE ALLOWED to see the banning." "Only people who have mourned are allowed in the mourning room." "They might not want you to see it." I was told these things many times. The secrets of the religion become visible at a banning. The sacredness is most intense at a banning. The sense of important work is strongest at a banning.

The *banning*, the *placing of the bands* on the pilgrim's head, the *pointing*, the *pointing down*, the *pointing on*, the *sending on*, the *putting down* or the *laying down* of the pilgrim are terms for the same thing. Each pointer does his banning somewhat differently. One's pointing skills come from the Spirit, and God may direct one to do a certain action in a particular way. Each banning has several essential parts: *giving a word* to the pilgrim (encouragement or instruction), the *proofs*, the *washing*, the *anointing*, the *sealing*, the placing on of the *bands*, and the laying down of the pilgrim. The order varies among the different pointers, but almost all bannings have these elements. Most of the description that follows is from a banning I attended in St. Vincent in June of 1995.

Opening the Service

The church is on a steep hill by the shore. The sound of the crashing waves is loud from the beach below. The ground is moist from a recent rain. The night is thick and close.

It is Friday night. Six people are in the church when I arrive at 7:50. They are chatting among themselves. They wonder if the banning will start soon. One church mother said, "If they band before 12, they come up Sunday morning. If after 12, they come up Monday morning." The *rising* ritual takes place after all or part of three days in the mourning room. Most pointers try to place the bands on the mourners by midnight so that the rising will take place a day sooner.

Two women come in who are wearing bands under their headties. The bands are pushed up so they do not blindfold the women. The women have recently finished mourning. They are in their *nine days*—that is, their mourning ended within the last nine days and they are "still partly in the spiritual world." They are still receiving visions and they travel to the spiritual world in their dreams. They must come to church every time a service is held during their nine days, to "turn thanks" to God.

While sitting there without much activity, I am again enchanted by the simple paintings and decorations of the church. On one wall is a painting of three mountains: Mount Zion, Mt. Moriah, and Mt. Ararat. Spiritual seals are painted above the altar. All around are painted verses from hymns and from the Bible. Over the door, black letters read, "Welcome to St. Stephen's Spiritual Baptist Church." A clock on the wall ticks off the minutes to midnight.

Leader Timothy arrives shortly and opens the service. He greets the congregation and opens with a hymn. The general confession is recited. The opening hymns are sung, the church is consecrated, the three evening Bible lessons are read. The *foundation lesson*, the one that is to set the tone for the service is taken tonight from Ezekiel 37. It is the account of the Valley of Dry Bones, an important location in the Converted spiritual world. Then the opening prayers are sung. The leader prays first, then the captain. The two who are in their nine days pray next—like the others, on their knees, with a lighted candle in the right hand, improvising words to prayer tunes they have been given in the Spirit.

At 9:12, 32 people are in the church, five of them men. We sing the hymn "Trust and Obey." At 9:13, Pointer Jeffries comes in with a heap of bands on an open Bible. The bands are covered with a red cloth. The pointer wears a crimson gown and a black headwrap tied in a boat-shaped turban style. The church leaders and mothers go up and shake the pointer's hand with the distinctive Spiritual Baptist handshakes.

The prayers end with the recitation of the twenty-third Psalm in which all join. Then everyone recites Psalm 121. Those who have been praying go around the church and shake everyone's hand while we sing the hymn, "How Sweet the Name of Jesus Sounds."

Then the hymn, "And Are We Yet Alive." This is the greeting hymn during which everyone in the church shakes hands with everyone else. Converted people shake hands a lot. The greeting signifies the end of the opening. The opening liturgy has lasted just over one hour.

Two pilgrims, a man and a woman, are brought in by a nurse. They are wearing old, but comfortable clothes. They will be wearing these same clothes, without washing them, without taking them off, for up to 14 days. They sit with eyes closed. The headtie of the woman is loosened. Throughout the service, either sitting or standing, the pilgrims keep time with their feet, marching. They have already begun to journey.

At 9:30, the pointer *seals* the bench reserved for mourners with different seals for each pilgrim. The pointer rings the bell over each spot and sets the pilgrims in front of their seats. The mourners are given lighted candles to hold, one in each hand.

Words to the Pilgrims

Pointer Jeffries says, "Those of you who are supposed to give the pilgrims a word, you can do it now because of the time." Mother Carol gives a word. She approaches the front of the church with a hymn, as all speakers are required to do. With customary West Indian courtesy, she says, "To my pointing father, to the one who opened the service, to all mothers, to the household of faith, and especially to Number One and Number Two sitting on the bench, I must say peace and a pleasant good night." She speaks for a few minutes about the love of Christ. Then she talks about the difficulties of mourning and the importance of keeping faith and "holding on to Jesus." While she talks, the rest of the congregation is engaged in loud *chanting* (humming). They are expected to do so. The humming bears up the speaker and is pleasing to God. Mother Carol catches Spirit and talks in tongues (glossolalia). Leader Timothy catches Spirit, and then starts doption in his seat. He stands, the doption bouncing through his body. Mother Carol beats doption with Leader Timothy. The doption lasts five minutes. The pilgrims continue to sit with eyes closed, feet marching. Mother Carol gathers herself after the doption, readjusting her headtie, straightening the apron on her uniform. She raises her hands to the congregation, saying, "This is the desire of my heart. Peace and a pleasant good night." She sits down and I note the time at 9:55.

Nurse Ford comes forward to give a word of encouragement to the pilgrims. As she speaks, a very heavy rain falls. The pounding of the rain on the corrugated iron roof is too loud for her to be heard. Some nonbelievers who have been standing outside and watching rush in out of the rain. They will go back outside when the rain stops. Nurse Ford stops speaking, but stays at the front. Chanting continues. Pointer Jeffries is sitting on a chair on the altar dais. He calls out, "Something moving down the line." At the time, I do not understand why the pointer calls out phrases like this from time to time. Those who have a spiritual connection do, though. Several catch Spirit when he says this. Nurse Ford quickly finishes what she has to say.

Another mother gives a word. Then the (carnal) child of one of the pilgrims.

At 10:15, the pointer rushes into the congregation with his belt in his hand. He strikes a woman in the face. She awakens with a start and begins crying. Others laugh. He tells her, "You didn't come to church to sleep." The pointer exhorts the congregation to sing louder. He says, "If you want a blessing, you have to sing."

At 10:25, there are 43 people in church and several more standing outside, looking in the windows.

Several more people give words or hymns to the pilgrims; some of the speakers dance with the pilgrims. From time to time, someone goes to the front while another person is speaking and raises up one of the pilgrims to dance with him or her. Some of the dances are very graceful. All are joyful. The pilgrims are passive. They cannot initiate any action during the banning. They must wait for others to dance with them. They cannot speak. They cannot sing. They must wait for the nurse to wipe the sweat from their faces.

In all of the dances, in all of the prayers, in the marching of the pilgrims, wax falls from the candles to the floor. The floors of most Converted churches are covered with a thin layer of wax from the dripping candles. In churches with dirt floors the wax is allowed to accumulate and can be several inches thick. It feels soft and comforting under one's bare feet. The church I am in tonight, like most churches in St. Vincent, has a concrete floor. The wax is periodically removed. Teacher Charlotte, the leading mother, scrapes the wax from the floor with a short, broad knife. She is clearing a space for the pointer to draw a wheel.

At 10:40, the chorus, "In the Valley, Me Alone" is sung. Several people speak in Valley language. Valley doption is performed by five or six people at the front, near the pilgrims. One of the pilgrims begins shaking and is lifted to join in the doption. The other is lifted by her nurse, but does not join in the doption. She continues marching. A woman sitting in front of me starts shaking. She moves quickly to the center pole, picks up the brass bell there and rings it three times in four directions. She bows to the pole and slowly goes back to her seat, interrupted twice by brief shaking.

At 10:45, the others engaged in doption and singing, the pointer draws a chalk circle on the floor. This is the *wheel*. Like the wheel that most pointers draw for banning, it is about two feet across and consists of three concentric circles and eight spokes. Within each segment of the wheel additional seals are drawn. The markings refer to the saints, to Jesus, to Biblical passages, and to spiritual locations. Four white candles are set around the outer edge of the wheel. One white candle is placed in the center.

While a mother lights the candles, the pointer addresses the congregation. It is 10:54. He greets the gathering in the name of Jesus and says, "I must say a pleasant good night." The congregation is still chanting, as they have been whenever someone speaks. The pointer sings a hailing: "Ai, Ai, Ai, O, O." The congregation joins in when he sings it a second time. It is only a few seconds long, but several shake with the Spirit on hearing the hailing. The pointer then says, "Somebody receive a warrior [the spiritual gift]." To those in their nine days, the two who came out of the mourning room on Monday, he says, "You chat too much, . . . when you chat some of the keys are lost; pick them up." He tells one of the nurses, "When there is pointing, wear your uniform." She gestures to her sister on the other side of the church, who is not wearing her uniform either. The pointer says, "You are not the only one." Then the pointer speaks to the pilgrims. He says, "I am now about to point you on to Teacher Divine. But you have to pay attention. You are not too young to die, you know."

He encourages the workers to hurry up and assemble at the front so that the pilgrims can be banned by midnight. He says, "Time is already gone" (pointing to the clock). At 11:15, he says, "I will go to work now so we can close."

Several choruses are sung while the pointer calls out people by name to come up and help in the work.

Proofs

The pointer says to one of the mothers, "Get the Bible for Number One and Number Two to prove." The *proofs* (sometimes called *Bible proofs*, or *taking a proof*) are a type of scriptural guidance. They "help the pointer to know where the pilgrim is at spiritually." Hymns are sung while the proofs are taken. The candles are taken out of the pilgrim's hands at this point and are set by the center pole.

The pilgrims are made to kneel. Their eyes remain closed. Leader Timothy stands in front of the male pilgrim, Teacher Charlotte in front of the female pilgrim (each pilgrim has a separate person to take the proof). Each has her or his own Bible. The Bible is placed on the top of the head of the pilgrim. Then the pilgrim is made to hold the Bible with the mother's (or leader's) hands on the outside of the pilgrim's. Held in this fashion, the Bible is moved in the shape of a cross in front of the pilgrim. The pilgrim is next instructed to split the pages of the Bible with her thumbs. The place where her thumbs are placed are the proofs. The mother (or leader) places her thumbs on top of the pilgrim's thumbs and takes the Bible away.

The leader says, "The proofs for Number One are I Chronicles 19:15 on the left, and on the right, I Chronicles 20:4." He then procedes to read for three verses from each proof. The mother says, "For Number Two, the question: Jeremiah 35:15 [she then reads for three verses] and the answer: chapter 36, verse 33 [and she reads for three verses]."

Pointer Jeffries interjects (as he often does when he gets some bit of spiritual knowledge), "Three of them in church are lock up." (The Spirit has put spiritual handcuffs on some people. They received a call to mourn but they have not answered it and the Spirit is punishing them.)

Washing

Pointer Jeffries calls out, "Whose turn tonight?" He repeats this several times trying to get women to come up and assist in the washing of the candidates. Four women are required. Two hold the basins (one basin for the upper body of both candidates, one for the feet), and two dry the candidates with towels (one the upper body of both candidates and one the feet of both candidates). He calls on one woman who was sitting in the back to come up and work. He says, "The back is for people who turn back." Many people laugh. Having assembled the workers, the pointer says, "Look at the time! Come on now, pick up your implements."

The pointer calls for the "washing lesson" and everyone stands. John 13:1–17 is read:

Now before the feast of the passover, when Jesus knew that his hour was come that he should depart out of this world unto the Father, having loved his own which were in the world, he loved them unto the end. And supper being ended; the devil having now put into the heart of Judas Iscariot, Simon's son, to betray him; Jesus knowing that the Father had given all things into his hands, and that he was come from God and went to God; He riseth from supper and laid aside his garments; and took a towel, and girded himself. After that he poureth water into a bason, and began to wash the disciples' feet, and to wipe them with the towel wherewith he was girded.

Then cometh he to Simon Peter: and Peter saith unto him, Lord, dost thou wash my feet? Jesus answered and said unto him, What I do thou knowest not now; but thou shalt know hereafter. Peter saith unto him, Thou shalt never wash my feet. Jesus answered him, If I wash thee not, thou hast no part with me. Simon Peter saith unto him, Lord, not my feet, but also my hands and my head. Jesus saith unto him, He that is washed needeth not save to wash his feet, but is clean every whit: and ye are clean but not all. For he knew who should betray him; therefore said he, Ye are not all clean.

So after he had washed their feet, and had taken his garments, and was set down again, he said unto them, Know ye what I have done to you? Ye call me Master and Lord: and ye say well; for so I am. If I then, your Lord and Master, have washed your feet; ye also ought to wash one another's feet. For I have given you an example, that ye should do as I have done to you. Verily, verily, I say unto you, The servant is not greater than his lord; neither he that is sent greater than he that sent him. If ye know these things, happy are ye if ye do them.

As with every Bible reading, when the washing lesson is finished, the Gloria Patri (in English) is sung by the congregation.

The pointer takes off his belt at verse 4 ("and laid aside his garments") and wraps a towel about his waist. The reader repeats the verse, the congregation joining in, for as long as it takes the pointer to do this. When the basin is mentioned, the pointer takes a glass containing water and a white flower and pours some of the water into each basin (but the washers have already put water in them, along with leaves from a croton). He drips wax from a lighted candle into each basin in the shape of a cross and rings the bell three times over each basin. Again the verse is repeated for as long as the procedure takes.

The face of each pilgrim is washed with the leaf, then dried with a towel. The washing is careful and very thorough. As the pointer washes each part of the body, he gives an exhortation to the pilgrim. For the eyes, he may say, "I am washing your eyes that you may see Jesus." For the nose, he may say, "I am washing your nose so that you may smell the sweet Savior." The ears and mouth are done in like fashion. The hands are next. The "hand," in Vincentian lexicon, includes the whole arm to the shoulder. The entire arm is washed. The hands are dried and then clapped together. The pointer gets on his knees and washes the pilgrims' feet (the leg up to the knee). As he washes one foot he may say, "I am washing your feet that you may be able to stand." For the other, he may say, "I am washing your feet so you can walk straight." When each foot is dried, it is stamped on the ground by the pointer. The pilgrims are made to drink water from the glass three times. The first two times they spit it out into the basin, the third time they swallow.

The pointer begins the washing while the lesson is being read. When the lesson is finished, the pointer is usually still washing the pilgrim or pilgrims. The congregation sings a hymn that is sung during any of the rites that require washing. The words are by Charles Wesley:

> For ever here my rest shall be,
> Close to Thy bleeding side;
> This all my hope, and all my plea,
> For me the Saviour died.
>
> My dying Savior, and my God,
> Fountain for guilt and sin.
> Sprinkle me ever with Thy blood,
> And cleanse, and keep me clean.
>
> Wash me, and make me thus Thine own,
> Wash me, and mine Thou art,
> Wash me, but not my feet alone,
> My hands, my head, my heart.

The pilgrim may be danced with at this time to the tune of the above hymn. But tonight, the pointer goes right into the anointing. The time is 11:26.

Anointing

The pointer pours olive oil from a small bottle into a cow's horn. Leader Timothy rings the bell over the horn. A second leader reads the anointing lesson. Some churches use I Samuel 16. In St. Stephen's church the twenty-third Psalm is used:

> The Lord is my shepherd; I shall not want. He maketh me to lie down in green pastures; he leadeth me beside the still waters. He restoreth my soul: he leadeth me in the paths of righteousness for his name's sake. Yea, though I walk through the valley of the shadow of death, I will fear no evil: for thou art with me; thy rod and thy staff they comfort me. Thou preparest a table before me in the presence of mine enemies: thou anointest my head with oil; my cup runneth over. Surely goodness and mercy shall follow me all the days of my life: and I will dwell in the house of the Lord for ever.

The pointer waits until the phrase, "Thou anointest my head with oil, my cup runneth over" is reached. He then procedes to anoint the pilgrims. The entire congregation repeats the phrase until the anointing is finished. Sometimes the anointing is as thorough as the washing. Tonight, the pointer makes a cross with the oil on the temples of the pilgrims, on their foreheads, the palms of their hands, and on the soles of their feet. He then pours a generous amount of oil from the horn on the top of the head of each pilgrim (the headtie of the woman having been temporarily removed by a helper), rubbing thoroughly in a circle. The pointer and those helping him drink the remaining oil from the horn. The leader and the rest of the congregation finish reciting the psalm. The Gloria is sung.

Sealing

The pilgrims are made to stand. Pointer Jeffries says to Number Two, "I am going to send you on this journey for the first time. I am sending you in the East. I am sending you in the West. I am sending you in the North. I am sending you in the South." At each direction, the pointer faces the pilgrim in that direction. Then the pointer spins her three times. He says, "In the name of God the Father [he spins her], in the name of God the Son [he spins her], in the name of God the Holy Ghost [he spins her]." He then seats the pilgrim and [referencing *The Pilgrim's Progress*] says, "Pointer the Evangelist when he was sending Christian to the Wicket Gate said, Do you see that light over yonder? And Christian said, I think I do. Pointer the Evangelist said keep that light in your eye. I am telling you this evening to follow the light. The light is Jesus."

To Number One, the pointer says, "I'm sending you on this journey you have been on many times," and he repeats the words about the Evangelist and gives a few more words of encouragement.

He asks a third leader to read Revelation 7:

> And after these things I saw four angels standing on the four corners of the earth, holding the four winds of the earth, that the wind should not blow on the earth, nor on the sea, nor on any tree. And I saw another angel ascending from the east, having the seal of the living God: and he cried with a loud voice to the four angels, to whom it was given to hurt the earth and the sea. Saying, Hurt not the earth, neither the sea, nor the trees, till we have sealed the servants of our God in their foreheads.
>
> And I heard the number of them which were sealed: and there were sealed an hundred and forty four thousand of all the tribes of the children of Israel. Of the tribe of Juda were sealed twelve thousand. Of the tribe of Reuben were sealed twelve thousand . . .

The rest of the tribes are named and numbered. I have omitted them, but the entire chapter is read during the banning. When the reader gets to the phrase "till we have sealed the servants of God in their foreheads," the congregation repeats the phrase until the pointer has finished sealing the foreheads and temples of the pilgrims. When the pointer begins to seal (that is, draw the chalk symbols on) other parts of the pilgrims' bodies, the reader continues. When the reader gets to the numbers of the tribes, the congregation calls out "twelve thousand" with each "twelve thousand" the reader reads. The pointer continues by putting seals on the palms of the hands, on the soles of the feet, on the chest, shoulders and back. If the pilgrim is wearing dark clothing, the seals can be seen on the clothing. They are the same as the seals that are put in the wheel and on the bands and in various places around the church. Two tall crosses are brought and the pilgrims kneel before them. The crosses are put on the right shoulder of each candidate while the congregation sings the chorus "Beneath the Cross." The crosses are returned to the corner. It is 11:35.

The Bands

The pointer says, "I'm going to blindfold you, now." But first he has each pilgrim stand. He has them open their eyes and look at the congregation. He asks each of them, "Do you have anything against anyone here?" They both say no. He asks the congregation, "Does anyone here have anything against Number One or Number Two?" The congregation says no. He says that things must be right with one's brother, that "If you don't get this right, that cloth won't carry you nowhere."

The chorus, "Humble Me My Lord" is sung.

The pilgrims are seated with a mother behind each one. Up to this point, 14 different people have helped in the work of the banning.

The pointer removes the red cloth covering the bands and separates the bands into two piles. Each of the bands are 3–4 feet long and 6–10 inches wide. The bands are of many different colors, each band with a purpose. The colors have meaning, but the seals written on the bands give the bands power. The bands have been ritually *signed* by the dripping of candle wax on each one. The bands have nubbled surfaces from the dripped wax. The pointer takes the pile for each pilgrim and removes each band from it, laying the bands over the shoulders of the pilgrim for whom they were prepared. Number One has mourned many times and has over 20 bands. Number Two has not mourned before and has only eight bands.

The pointer takes the bands from the shoulder of Number One and, one at a time, before tying them around the eyes of the pilgrim, holds them over the candles burning on the wheel he drew earlier. Every few bands, the pointer switches between the pilgrims. Because time is running out, two assistant mothers (mothers who have the spiritual gift of being able to assist at a banning) do the actual tying of the bands around the pilgrims' heads, with the pointer taking over from time to time. The bands are tied so tight they hurt.

The bands for Number Two are tied in this fashion: band one laid on the head transverse, band two laid on top of the head front to back, band three tied around the forehead binding the first two on top, band three and four tied around the forehead, band five under the chin to the top of the head, band six and seven tied around the forehead holding the fifth one on. These are then covered with the white cloth that served as the pilgrim's headtie. Band eight is tied around the forehead over the white cloth and all the other bands. Her head has doubled in size with the addition of the bands. Her vision is obscured almost entirely. She can see a little by tilting her head and looking down her nose through a very small space.

During the entire placing of the bands, the congregation is singing in a lively manner. As each band is held over the candles, the pointer may change the song the congregation is singing. While he is tying on bands for Africa, he may lead an African tune. A Valley band will take a song about the Valley. A series of bands may have a single song on a general Christian theme.

The placing of the bands complete, the pointer rings the bell over each pilgrim's head by holding the bell still and moving the clapper once. Then the bell is rung forcefully in several directions. The time is 11:57. The banning is finished.

There is often a sense of urgency about completing by midnight. Should the banning be completed after midnight, the *rising* ritual will take place one day later. The most important journeys usually take place after the rising, and the congregation is concerned that the pilgrims not be delayed in their journeys. The service may continue for a short while after the bands are placed, but the pilgrims are usually led to the room at this time.

Each pilgrim is given two lighted candles. They are danced with by the leading mothers. The pointer gives the pilgrims advice to pray. To Number Two (the first time mourner) he says, "If you do not pray, you will not be able to receive the Holy Spirit. You have to pray that you will be able to see something that you will be able to tell them when they come" (that is, at the shouting). The candidates are then marched to the mourning room by their nurses and the door to the mourning room is closed.

The pointer leads a series of doxologies that everyone recites together. The service is closed.

Putting the Pilgrim Down

Although the service is over, the pointer and the nurses still have work to do. The *laying down* or the *putting down* of the pilgrim is different for each church. Some churches perform the entire banning service in the mourning room. Some, like this church, do the banning in the church and then march the pilgrims to the mourning room.

The elements of the banning themselves are found in almost any order. In one church, the proofs are taken in the mourning room after the banning. The pointer writes the proof on the wall of the mourning room by the pilgrim's head. In that church, the pilgrim is put down in an interesting way. Six people lift the pilgrim, three on each side—a pair for her shoulders, a pair for her waist, and a pair for her legs. They hold her face down and swing her several times while the music continues. She is then laid on her bed face down and all but the pointer and the nurse leave the room.

In most churches, the pilgrim is put down in the following way. The beds (most often a piece of burlap with a sheet on top) are consecrated by a mother or the pointer by ringing a bell over them. One or two stones are placed under a pillow. The stones represent the stone over Lazarus' tomb (John 11). The pilgrims sit quietly or stand and march while the beds are prepared.

Back in St. Stephen's church, the mourning room is a small room about 14 feet by 14 feet with two shuttered windows (no glass), attached to the main portion of the church. A nurse prepares the beds. Pieces of thin carpet are laid down on the floor and sack cloth is placed on top of that. The nurse asks, "Who walk with a sheet?" Only Number One has a sheet. The nurse says to Number Two, "She didn't give you no sheet?" Number One ends up with nice sheets, Number Two has to use some worn ones that were already in the room. Pillows are put at the heads of the pilgrims' beds.

Number One has to go outside to use the washroom. He is led out by a nurse. As she leads him outside, she says, "Did you cross yourself?" He crosses himself and she spins him and then leads him outside. When he comes back in, he spins himself once and crosses himself. For the remaining period of the mourning both pilgrims will have to spin and cross themselves every time they cross the threshold. They will have to cross the glass (or calabash) for every drink of water they have and will have to cross the plate or bowl of everything they have to eat.

Number One and Number Two have been sitting quietly on a bench. A nurse says, "Arise, travelers." They stand up and candles are lit and placed in their hands. Number Two is led to her place and the nurse spins her once. She says, "Spin yourself," and the pilgrim spins herself the last two times. She lays down on her back, holding her three candles. The nurse says, "Number Two, kneel and take a praise." Number Two kneels and prays silently. Number One is led to his place by the same nurse and is told to spin himself. He spins himself three times and kneels in prayer. Then Number One and Number Two lay on their backs, heads on pillows, holding their lighted candles upright. The pointer whispers the password of the church into the ear of each pilgrim. Number Two asks him to repeat it and he does.

The nurse then pulls a curtain to separate the mourners' sleeping area from the rest of the mourning room. The mourners are hidden from view, and I say good night.

Spiritual

Experience

Pilgrim Travelers

T HE CONVERTED ARE ALWAYS GOING SOMEWHERE. They travel in the mourning room. They travel in church. They travel at home, in bed, while sleeping. I do not know every place they go, but I do know the places they most often go. These are the spiritual lands.

In this chapter, I consider the journeys to the spiritual lands. I describe the spiritual world itself and the means for entering and experiencing it, as reported by the Converted.[1] The beings who inhabit the spirit world, the symbols of the various spiritual cities, and the behavior expected of the Converted in the Spirit are detailed. The spiritual world is bigger than one chapter or even a whole book and this must be seen as only an introduction.

The Pilgrim Journey

Seeking knowledge, wisdom, and understanding is the primary reason for the Converted travels in the spiritual world. At a banning, one is very likely to hear the pilgrim reminded that she is going to seek "knowledge, wisdom, and understanding" even as Solomon did (e.g., II Chronicles 1; I Kings 4:29). One gains knowledge by travel.

While some Converted are able to go where they wish in the spiritual world, it is the Holy Spirit who takes them most of the time. Converted who are able to direct their own travels do so by the power of the Holy Spirit, and with his will. Converted primarily travel to the Spirit by mourning (the period of ritual seclusion) and by doption (short collective journeys during the church service). One is said to belong to the places where she has traveled during mourning and is able to travel to those places later during doption. Besides mourning and doption, there are about ten other ways one may enter the spiritual realm.

The first way and the most profound way that people travel in the Spirit is by mourning. We saw in the last chapter the elaborate preparations for the journey during banning. The intention of the *pointing* is to send the pilgrim to the Spirit. In the Spirit, God introduces the pilgrim to events, items, and places for her own edification and for the edification of the community.

The spiritual world is large and consists of a number of spiritual cities (to be detailed) as well as St. Vincent itself and other local islands. More experienced mourners are the ones who tend to go "farthest" or "deepest" in the Spirit. For Converted on their baptismal journey and for inexperienced mourners, most of the activities in the Spirit take place close to home, reflecting their day-to-day experiences in St. Vincent. One may find oneself on a journey in the mourning room itself. Also one may find oneself in one's own house or that of a neighbor, seeing there normally hidden (spiritual) things. The Converted I interviewed reported traveling spiritually to locations in every part of the island, including mountains, quarries, harbors, rivers, caves, the volcano, towns, roads, the fish market, and the market square in Kingstown. It is customary for pilgrims to find themselves in a boat or ship on the water around St. Vincent. In Brooklyn, it was normal for Converted to travel to places they were familiar with (in New York or in St. Vincent, and if they had lived in Trinidad, in Trinidad also). In St. Vincent, mourners would occasionally travel to America, but, in every case that I was aware of, only if they had already traveled there (physically) to work or to visit.

Every place that is seen in the Spirit is the spiritual aspect of that place. The spiritual aspect of St. Vincent is as much the Spirit as are the spiritual cities. Spiritual knowledge may be gained in any place in the Spirit. In a private conversation, one man reported seeing the pointer of another church stuck in mud in a local river. The vision was at the same time symbolic and a spiritual reality. The pointer was spiritually stuck in mud because he was "not right with God."

Many places in the Spirit are unnamed and the pilgrim often does not know where she is. If clues are not available and if the pilgrim does not ask, she will not know. It is not a problem if the name of a spiritual location is unknown; knowledge from unidentified places is as valid as that from identifiable locations. However, knowledge of the identity of a location enhances the usefulness of techniques or other information learned there.

Traveling in the spiritual world is "going to school" for the Converted. Going to school in itself is part of the work of the Converted. The sort of knowledge gained in the spiritual world determines one's ritual role in the physical setting of the church. Pilgrims are reminded to pay attention on the spiritual journey so that they may learn all they can.

The Spiritual Cities

The spiritual cities are one of the most exciting parts of Vincentian cosmology.[2] *Spiritual cities* are discrete locations in the spiritual world. They are not always urban areas. Each *spiritual school* (that is, each church) has a different tradition regarding the number and nature of the cities. However, there are some patterns. In every city, there are a school, a hospital, and a port. Every city has a watchman and a soldiery. Each city has its own recognizable language and flag and dress and song. The spiritual cities have a strong presence in the church. Flags representing the various cities hang from the rafters (along with flags of other significance). Converted individuals who belong to certain cities wear the uniform of those cities when they come to church.

Studies of Trinidadian churches mention cities or spiritual locations, but not much is made of them (e.g., Simpson 1966:545–596; Parks 1981:82; Glazier 1983: 55–58). It is unclear if this is because the churches in Trinidad place less emphasis on spiritual travel or if the research was focused on other aspects. In either case, the Converted of St. Vincent repeatedly told me that their tradition is "more grounded," "deeper in the Spirit," and of a more spiritual nature than the Trinidadian churches.

Every Converted individual has only a partial knowledge of the spiritual world. Although they listen attentively to others' reports of spiritual travels, the Converted base their knowledge on their own experience in the spiritual world. A common response to a query about specific spiritual locations was, "I don't know, I never went there." One day I interviewed a husband and a wife together. They disagreed about whether one could touch the center pole in (the physical) church. The woman said yes. The man said, "No, because in Zion, there is a boundary around the pole so you can't touch it"—and (because the physical ritual goods stand for a spiritual reality) one is not supposed to touch the one in church either. The woman said, Oh you're right. I asked if everyone sees the center pole in Zion (the spiritual city). They both said, Yes.

One man, when I asked him about the spiritual cities and how they are differentiated said, "Each port does have a flag, like Grenada and St. Lucia and Barbados and St. Vincent each have their own flag, and when you see the flag you know where you are." This put me on to an intriguing line of questioning and I realized that for him and for many of the Converted, the spiritual world is perceived as a series of islands. The pilgrim frequently arrives in a spiritual location by boat. Songs that may take one to a spiritual city are sometimes called *ships*. While not the case for each Converted, many, and maybe most, view the spiritual cities as islands like St. Vincent (for most Vincentians, the only topography they know). The spiritual world is like the physical world as perceived from St. Vincent. Spiritual cities are not thought of as some heavenly or otherworldly place. They are conceived as a spiritual part of the physical world.

The classification of the spiritual lands presents some difficulty. In some churches, every spiritual land is called a city, but that is not the case in each church. One pointer told me, "There are five cities, don't let anyone fool you." Another Converted person said, "There is seven cities." Others said they did not know how many there were but "there are lots of cities." Below I discuss the basic information I have about each place. However, I do not include the tunes of the cities. The tunes (also called songs, although they are usually without words) are what carries one to specific spiritual lands. Each land has one or more tunes.

While trying to get at the nature of the spiritual lands, I asked time and again if one could draw a map. Although it seemed like a possibility to many of my respondents, none of them had ever thought of it that way. The question usually brought on a pondering silence. One person said, "Zion is the boundary . . . It is the last city." Another said, "Zion is always the first city you go to." Another person said, "I think China is the farthest, because I heard one man say he went to China and it took a long time to get there." One man whom I asked several times told me I should stop trying to think of the spiritual world as separate from the physical world, that it is the same thing. I asked one woman if, when she went to Africa, it was a spiritual Africa or the actual physical Africa that one hears about on the news. She said it is a spiritual Africa, "but it could be the physical one, too, because God can work miracles." There is not a catechism regarding the spiritual lands.

Finally, I asked a group of people one night if one could make a map of the spiritual world. One man said, "No, it is the sounds. The sounds are the route." All in the group agreed. I think that is the correct way to understand the spiritual world and the travels of the Converted in it (especially at doption). I present here the nonmusical aspects of each spiritual city, but understand that the music is more important. Also understand that the information for each city is partial and in most cases is not the same in every church.

Here is a list of all of the spiritual cities to which more than one Converted told me they traveled: Zion, Africa, India, China, Valley of Dry Bones, Canaan, Jericho, Israel, Beulahland, Jerusalem, Bethlehem, Syria, Arabia, Egypt, the Sahara, Sea of Glass, Sea of Tingeling, Nations of the Sea, Indian Sea, Red Sea, The Nations, Valley of Peace, Valley of St. Philomene, Jacob's City, South Pole, North Pole, Prosperity, Victory, Babylon, Hell, Sodom. No one was able to name more than ten at a single sitting (but that does not mean that they had not been to more than ten—just that they were unaccustomed to dealing with the cities in that way). I am certain there are more cities. These are the ones I heard referenced more than once.

One's knowledge of a spiritual city is expected to come from one's experiences there. As people have different things to learn, the Spirit shows them different things. If a pilgrim is not well prepared with prayer and intention of her purpose in the Spirit, she will not go as far and will not see as many things as when she is prepared to go. Likewise, those with more experience "know the way" and are able to go further.

Some cities are mentioned more often than others. The most frequently mentioned city is *Zion*. Zion itself is understood differently according to one's experience. Some equate it with heaven, some with the Mount Zion in (the physical) Jerusalem. Zion is not described in the church setting, although people regularly journey there by doption while the rest sing a song about Zion. Mount Zion is equated with Zion by some individuals, but according to others it is the heavenly mountain and not a city at all. Zion, like the other cities, is populated with spiritual beings and spiritual institutions. Several people said that the flag of Zion is white and blue, but others said the flag is white only.

Zion and Mount Zion are described both in *The Pilgrim's Progress* and in the Bible (I Kings 8:1; Hebrews 12:22). In *The Pilgrim's Progress*, "Mount Zion" and the "city of Zion" seem to refer to the same thing. Both are mentioned in hymns and choruses sung by the Converted. A very significant one is "Old Ship of Zion Going to Sail," a chorus used also by African American churches as a promise of escape from oppression (cf. Pitts 1993). Mount Zion, the location where the physical city of Jerusalem is built, is usually synonymous with Jerusalem in the Bible. It becomes two entities for most Converted and for most Christians—the city and the mountain. Mount Zion in the Converted spiritual world, although generally free of spiritual dangers, is steep and hard to climb. "Most people," one pointer told me, "have to climb a mountain" (on their spiritual journey). The mountain is usually Mount Zion. Again, due to Vincentian notions of propriety, if one does not hear a song about Mount Zion or meet a spirit on the way who identifies the mountain as such, Mount Zion will not be named in the shouting. An unnamed mountain, however, is often assumed to be Mount Zion.

While the mountain is difficult to climb, and one may be in danger of falling off, visitors to the *city* of Zion never mention feelings of anxiety there. Like other cities, Zion has a school, a doctor's shop, and a watchman at the gate. A common activity in Zion is pumping. There is a "waterwheel in Zion spinning round." There is a pool in Zion and one has to fill it: "you got to pump, man." One of the doptions that may take one to Zion involves movements that look as if the individual is pumping water from a hand pump. Zion is a highly-valued spiritual location. It is a pleasurable and pleasant place to go. Most people are able to go there. No one ever described to me any trouble in Zion.

The Valley, however, is a dangerous place, as may be Africa, India, and China. These four are mentioned in church with about the same frequency. The Valley is the Valley of Dry Bones. In most churches the Valley is synonymous with *Ezekiel Cave, Valley of Jehosaphat* (Joel 3:12), *Emmanuel Graveyard, Babylon Graveyard, Ezekiel Cemetery, Ezekiel Ground*, or *Emmanuel Ground*. Some of these terms refer to separate places in some churches. Many Converted told me that when one mourns one always must go through a cemetery of some kind, whether it be Ezekiel's Ground or another place. The experience of the Converted in the Valley is usually similar to that of the Old Testament prophet Ezekiel in that place:

> The hand of the Lord was upon me, and carried me out in the spirit of the Lord and set me down in the midst of the valley which was full of bones, And caused me to pass by them round about: and behold, there were very many in the open valley; and lo, they were very dry. (Ezekiel 37:1–2)

In Ezekiel's account, the bones are raised up by the Spirit of God. In the Converted experience, the bones rise up and dance. Many Converted, but not all, said that one learns the basic doption from the skeletons (or from a single skeleton), although the

Valley has a doption of its own. One Converted told me with a smile, "A skeleton can teach you to dance." If it seems that two locations, the cemetery and the Valley, are being conflated, that reflects the reports of my respondents. It reflects, as well, differences in perceptions according to differences in Converted churches and experiences of individual Converted. The Valley is also associated with judgment (Joel 3:12), and those who wear black, the color of the Valley, are sometimes said to represent Judgment.

The main symbol of the Valley is bones. The language of the Valley is the sound of bones knocking together: "*kip kop skip kop kip. . . .*" The flag of the Valley, usually solid black, may have a skull and crossbones on it—that is, it is sometimes identical with the pirates' Jolly Roger or "The Banner of King Death" (Black 1989:19–21). The song most commonly sung while people are traveling to the Valley by doption has the words: "Go Down in the Valley, Count Them Bones." The motif is one of overcoming fear, and many reported to me great fear at being surrounded by animated bones and skeletons. However, once one's fear is overcome, one has power—not only from the courage generated by surviving a dangerous challenge but also by possession of the skeleton's doption to travel to further places. Although churches differ, the preponderance of accounts suggests that once into the spiritual lands, the Valley (or a cemetery) and/or a mountain are the first things encountered.

In the Valley, one frequently meets dogs who guard the way. If one is not prepared, spiritually, to enter the Valley, the dogs will keep her out. In the church service, Converted people themselves may become the dogs, barking at each other. This is usually a fun time, the congregants laughing and enjoying the performance, but it has serious implications. It refers to the spiritual vigilance of the church members and may indicate that one not spiritually prepared is trying to enter the spiritual lands. "Watch out them Valley dogs don't get you" is a warning one may hear in a church service. The appearance of the Valley dogs in the church is rare, but I presume this varies by the specialty of the church.[3] Some pointers are known as "cemetery men" and I expect that their children (that is, their congregation) would have more experience in the Valley. Converted who belong to the Valley are called "Valley people."

Africa, India, and China represent spiritual lands of a different type. *Africa* is by far the most important of these. When I first met him, a widely regarded bishop told me of the Converted, "It's a real African religion." Most Converted say that the "work" came from Africa and was incorporated with Christianity in the island. In St. Vincent, the band (the blindfold) representing Africa, which is intended to point one on to Africa, is one of the last placed, often the very last. It is usually bright red. The African dance is one of the most elaborated of the spiritual dances (see chapter 4). The African flag is either solid red, red and black, or a tricolor of red, yellow, and green stripes placed vertically or horizontally.

Africa is one of the largest places in the spiritual world. It has many parts to it, most significant of which is *the Jungle*. One who belongs to Africa may be called a "Jungle man" or a "Jungle woman," but usually just an "African." As with most of the spiritual lands, different groups inhabit Africa, called *tribes*. From the tribes, one may learn various spiritual techniques. Most mourners only meet one kind of African, those who look like themselves (but with a different dress). Only those who go deep into Africa will meet other tribes, such as the tiny *Chiptees* (the pygmies). When their language was imitated by a Converted who had met them, the high-pitched musical sound seemed to me rather like the songs of the pygmies of the Ituri forest. The *Ethiopians* are another tribe of very small, very dark people in Africa. One has to be deep in the Spirit to meet them. The African language spoken in church is: "*Ga ga gee ga ga gong. . . .*" Like all the spiritual languages, a series of syllables (seldom more than 12) is called out by one person who has entered Africa. Others who belong to Africa then call out a similar response. The song of Africa has no words, but is a tune that inspires immediate excitement on the part of the Converted. Africa, especially in its deeper parts, is characterized by voluptuousness, as suggested by the rolling of the hips in the African dance. Africa also represents spiritual skill, demonstrated by balancing a calabash on one's head while performing the African dance.

India is another large place. India is often described as the most dangerous place. When one is taken hostage, it is usually in India. When one gets lost or stuck in a cave or hole, it is often in India. India has many parts to it, many tribes, and many flags. However, the color of India is always yellow, usually a deep saffron. A Converted person who belongs to India wears a yellow uniform and is called an "Indian" or a "Wild Indian." Indians of the sort from South Asia, whose descendants one may see on St. Vincent, are sometimes found in (the spiritual) India. Most people, though, only see Amerindians of the type found in the American West, as portrayed in Hollywood Westerns (cf. Pollack-Eltz 1970:828). Most of India is described as a desert. The Indians of the desert can be very hostile. One must know the song of the Indians to pass through the land and learn what there is to learn there. If one does not know the song, he may be taken hostage until the pointer, equipped with the proper song, can convince the Indians that he is "on their side" and that they should release the pilgrim. The most common vocalization by a person who belongs to India is a whooping while patting one's mouth with the fingers of one hand (the kind of war cry proffered by Hollywood). "Apaches" are one of the tribes one may meet in India. Converted say that some cities have a number of tribes, but most people said of India, "There is a lot of tribes there."

China is another place, like the others, referred to as a city. In some churches it is described as quite large. The language of China is: "*Chong ching chong chong. . . .*" Some parts of China use a different language: "*See saw see see saw saw. . . .*" In some churches, the doption of China involves hopping on one foot. The flag of China is usually blue and white (but may be red and white). People who belong to China usually wear a blue (or red) and white headtie and a blue (or red) and white uniform.

Israel, Canaan, and *Jericho* are spiritual cities mentioned nearly as often as those above. The Converted enter into them in the church service as often. People from Israel are normally known as Israelites, but on one occasion they were referred to as Israelis. I do not think the person misspoke; the notion that the spiritual Israel has a connection to the modern state of Israel reflects the connection the Converted make between the spiritual lands and the physical lands of which they are a part. The uniform of Israel in many churches is red and white checked. The flag may be the same, but is sometimes solid white. Many Converted wear the uniform of Israel, but although the uniform of Canaan was described to me, I never saw it worn. Canaan's flag is also solid white, but is a different spiritual city from Israel. The doption for Canaan represents the joyous entry of the people into that land. Canaan is often described as a valley. However, any valley not the Valley of Dry Bones must be lexically marked (e.g., Canaan Valley). Jericho is a city that must be entered on horseback. In the Jericho doption, one looks like he is riding a horse. A pointer may call out, "Look at the ponies!" during the Jericho doption. People may also call out, "Ride, Jerichonians!" [4] I could not find a uniform for Jericho, and some say that Jericho does not have one, although at the services I attended, people did the Jericho doption more than that of any other spiritual city except for Africa and the Valley. Many people belong to Jericho.

The Nations is the next most frequently mentioned location in Converted churches. The Nations is not one location, but all of the nations in the spiritual world. One may belong to The Nations. The Nations has no particular song or doption or language apart from those of each of the individual locations. However, it does have its own flag. Sometimes called the flag of All Nations, it is always a multicolored flag. In some churches it is a quilt-like combination of colors and patterns. In some churches, any red, white and blue flag is called a Nation Flag or the flag of all nations. In several churches, the "Flag of All Nations" is the Union Jack of Great Britain. The uniform of The Nations is a multicolored, multipatterned gown or dress (with apron and headtie), made of strips of different fabric. Sometimes it is called a "coat of many colors" (in reference to Genesis 37).

All other spiritual locations are mentioned far less than those described above. Each church uses them differently. Some I only found at one of the churches I visited, and it is probable that a number of other locations exist peculiar to certain churches or schools who know how to go there (spiritually). Locations mentioned by people across a broad spectrum include the other Biblical locations. The rest of the locations are places to which people may go during doption, but to which they are more likely to travel during mourning.

Beulahland, Jerusalem, and *Bethlehem* are places many Converted visit in the Spirit. Beulahland is a word found in hymns but not in other sacred scriptures. In the Bible (Isaiah 64:4) and in *The Pilgrim's Progress* (Bunyan 1979:166), it is referred to as "Beulah." In Converted churches, it is always called Beulahland. I was unable to elicit a specific doption for Beulahland, Jerusalem, or Bethlehem. According to some Converted, the three cities are all in the same area. One person put Beulahland on a mountain or cliff overlooking the Valley of Canaan. She was very specific, describing the topography of the mountain in detail, as well as the dress and manners of the inhabitants of both places. This type of vivid recollection is common, because the spiritual locations are places in which Converted spend time and where they are expected to notice as many things as they can. In the experience of this individual, Israel was part of India.

Syria, Assyria, Arabia, Egypt, and *the Sahara* are cities that I elicited in interviews, but that I did not hear mentioned in church. With the exception of the Sahara, these are all places named in the Bible. I never observed a doption, language, or flag associated with any of these, but I was informed that Saharan and Egyptian doptions do exist. One respondent placed Syria, Arabia, and India all in a similar location, because people from there "all look the same."

While nearly all Converted at one time or another find themselves on top of the ocean in the spiritual world, the places that most excited my imagination were the places that the Converted would go *under* the sea. Often these are cities as well. I asked a Converted teacher in St. Vincent if the locations under the sea had schools and hospitals like the other cities. He said, "Yes. Everything that is on the earth is in the sea." One man who had been under the sea told me with evident pleasure at the memory, "Some parts are dry and you can walk, and some parts are wet and you have to swim." Not everyone can go, and if one does it signifies a special preparedness in the Spirit. Most of these places are described as "under the sea" or at "the bottom of the sea." However, some of them do have names. The two that several of my respondents had visited were the *Sea of Glass* and the *Sea of Tingeling.* Both are submarine locations. The Sea of Glass is characterized by being able to see all the way across to the other side or for very long distances (and may be a reference to the "sea of glass" of Revelation 4). "What is important about the Sea of Tingeling is the song," one respondent told me. It is the sound that gives the name to the sea (tinkling)—the sound of "steel and thing" hitting each other. The song is very pretty. When one returns, one must be able to sing the song to prove that one has been there. (As a general rule, once one has been to and thereby belongs to a city, one must know the song and be able to sing it when required.) Other locations my respondents reported knowing of people going to in the Spirit, but that they had not visited, were "the Nations of the Sea," "the real Indian Sea," and "the real Red Sea." All of these would be the bottom of the respective seas. Every time one was on the top of a sea, the sea was not named.

Other locations vary by church and there is not a consensus as to what they represent. The Jungle and the *Desert* are both spiritual locations to which many people go. They are usually described as part of Africa, and of India, respectively. The *Valley of Peace* and the *Valley of St. Philomene* appear to be similar green Valleys. *Prosperity* and *Victory* are cities in some churches and are characteristics of other cities in some other churches—prosperity and victory being things one can attain in the Spirit. Jacob's City, Babylon, Hell, and Sodom are places for which I have scanty information. The latter three are bad places, for there is bad in the Spirit as well as good. Converted people can learn from everything they encounter in the Spirit, good and bad. I received other names, mostly from bannings where pilgrims were told some of the places they might go. I was unable, however, to verify if anyone did go to those places. Since the names were given as advice on the departure for the pilgrim journey, I assume that at least some people had been in those locations. Two examples are Judgment Hall and the Pool of Shiloh.

The North Pole and the South Pole were only mentioned in one church I visited (people I asked at other churches had not heard of these as spiritual locations). The North Pole and the South Pole were places that one pointer sent his spiritual children. The exact words are these:

> You about to go to the North. East, West, North. You going to meet soldiers. I want you to stand like a brave. You going to meet the chief commander. When the soldiers say, Bam!, you say, Beem! Beem! [that is, when they shoot you, you shoot them back].
>
> You about to go to the South Pole, where you will meet the King and the Queen of the Ocean. They going to take you to dive. To the depths of the depths. To the bottom of the water. Tell them Pointer [Jelico] sent you and you come seeking understanding, knowledge, and wisdom.

This quote provides a good example of the range of sources from which the words of spiritual instruction are taken. "Stand like a brave" is from a Charles Wesley hymn. "To the depths" is from Psalm 107. Firearm-bearing soldiers in the Spirit as well as a king and queen (or father and mother) of the ocean are common in Converted parlance. Their association with the North and the South may be related to Daniel 11 (but was not mentioned as such), which discusses a lengthy battle between the seafaring kings of the North and South. Converted use words such as these to help them organize and understand the experiences they have in the Spirit.

One pointer, just before placing the bands on four pilgrims who were sitting on the bench, addressed them as several other speakers had done that evening. The pointer told the pilgrims about some of the things they might see on their journey. He said:

> You are about to enter into a snake valley. You are about to go into a snake valley! You are going to go into a valley full of dry bones! You are about to meet a mermaid. Hear, now. When you go, there is a city and some people just small like that [indicating about a foot high] so that you're afraid that if you walk you are going to mash them because they are so short . . . —it's a nation of people, we call them the Gypsies, and when you see those people start to dance, you are going to want to dance with them. Further in, there is a city where the people don't walk in flat shoes; they wear spike heels. You might enter there; they might teach you to dance. But today, you see—to you, Number One to Four, there is some good people over there. But, you see, if you go to an area where there are Indians, they aren't just good—because when the Indians tell you to do this and you ain't do it, oh, they will put you down . . .

This chapter and anything else I may report can describe only a portion of the richness of the spiritual world.

Spiritual Beings

The most important spiritual being is God. He is perceived as a trinity composed of the Father, the Son, and the Holy Spirit. Converted often meet Jesus, God the

Father, or the Spirit in the spiritual world. The Father and the Spirit are often stern; Jesus is usually gentle. The actions of each of the three are variable.[5]

Satan is next in importance after God the Father, Jesus, and the Holy Spirit. He strives constantly to lead Converted travelers off their path. He deceives them by appearing as a trusty saint or as one's pointer, changing into his true form only after succeeding in getting the pilgrim lost, after being defeated by the pilgrim or the pilgrim's pointer in combat or in a test of wits, or when the pilgrim repeats her password. Like God, Satan appears in daily life in a way that the other spiritual beings do not. He intervenes in one's affairs in an effort to make the Converted lose faith in God. He may speak through one's friends in a way that disparages the Converted; he or his demons may cause physical mishaps; he may speak inside one's head while one is on the *mourning grounds* to discourage the pilgrim from continuing her journey. Exhortations given at the banning often urge the pilgrim to "resist Satan." At a shouting, the returned pilgrim is congratulated that she has made Satan "a very angry man" by completing her pilgrim journey.

Vincentian Converted identity is enhanced by the concept that spirits other than God need not be supplicated for favors in the spiritual world. The Converted can go to the spiritual world and do the work themselves. This contrasts with most Caribbean religions, where the emphasis is on spirits coming to the site, to the person, to the aid of the situation (Murphy 1994). However, the Converted do work "with spirits." Each Converted person has a saint who helps her. The saint acts as a spirit helper, pointing the way or imparting knowledge in the spiritual realm. Saints in Vincentian Converted cosmology are not iconic beings like the Catholic saints with highly specialized niches. They are more like generalized spirit helpers. Some Converted people do not know the name of their saint but can give a vivid description based on encounters with the saint in the spiritual world. The most commonly named saints (e.g., Catherine, Philomene, John the Baptist, Michael) are the same as those recognized in Shango (Herskovits and Herskovits 1947:331). However, rather than a saint possessing someone's body, as in Shango or Orisha, the Converted person meets with the saint in the spiritual world for instruction and guidance. The Converted person "works with" the saint; the saint does not work through the Converted person. It is the Holy Spirit that does that.

Saints are common in religions in the Caribbean. In both Vodou and Shango, members of the religion associate with particular saints who have specific powers to assist. The Converted also associate with individual saints. Unlike the Vodou and Shango powers, each Converted saint is extremely varied in his or her attributes. The colors of a saint and the city the saint is associated with are so inconstant as to appear almost random.

When I asked Converted to describe the saints to me, their powers, and the lands to which they belonged, I was more often referred to "the Catholics who have books" about them than I was told anything about them. Although this may have been to protect knowledge, the forthright nature of the Converted in all other matters leads me to believe that knowledge of saints is rather unimportant to them except to know with whom they work. Saints do not do specific things for the

Vincentian Converted, but instead act as guides in the spiritual realms. (The situation is probably different for the Trinidadian Spiritual Baptists who pray to the saints and have multiple images of them in their churches.) One's saint will often accompany one to all of the spiritual lands, but not always. Additionally, if the Converted person does not ask the name of an individual she meets in the Spirit, she will not know just who it is that is assisting her. Generally speaking, the male saints work with male Converted, and female saints work with female, but this is not always so.

All of the saints that Converted told me they work with are: St. Michael, Ezekiel, St. Anthony, John the Baptist, on the male side; St. Catherine, St. Philomene, the Virgin Mary on the female side. Although churches carry the names of many more saints (e.g., John the Evangelist, Francis, Joseph, Jude, Malachi, Peter, Phillip, Ann, Elizabeth, Theresa), the six listed above were the only ones that Converted told me they work with. Two additional names of churches, St. Sullivan and St. Bethel, are not in the Roman Catholic canon. Although a number of churches are named St. Bethel, I was told by others that St. Bethel does not refer to a saint, but that "they just call the church that."

The only recurring associations I did get for the saints were that Ezekiel works in the Valley and his color is black, that Michael works in Africa and his color is red, and that Catherine and Philomene are associated with the ocean. Two respondents referred to Philomene as the mother of the ocean and Catherine as the grandmother of the ocean. Philomene (sometimes called Philomena) was associated with brown or with green and yellow, but not by the same people. Catherine was sometimes associated with red. Far more often, the people did not know. If they had noticed, they could describe whatever the saint wore when they saw him or her.

One woman told me she did not like to wear her spiritual clothing in church if she could help it, because "the spiritual clothing is heavy—most people don't realize, if you get it in the Spirit—because the spirit sits on it." She said she did not like to wear her solid brown uniform because then people would know that she worked with St. Philomene. Although the saints that Converted work with are actually few, they do not think of it that way. They do not say, for instance, that Philomene and Catherine are the Converted saints. Converted can work with any saint. I think they do not realize that so few saints actually are met with in the Spirit. That does not mean the Converted do not feel affection for and dedication to and identification with their saints. They do. However, they do not usually pray to them.

Four beings sometimes referred to as saints seem to have a special quality. These are *Nurse Dinah, Brother Cutter, Sister Clearer*, and *Bramble Picker*. Apart from being picturesque and somewhat Bunyanesque, the names seem to belong only to the Converted (unlike the other saints).[6] None of my respondents worked with any of these four specifically. They appear to be saints who work with all Converted all the time. Unlike other saints, these four are often invoked in Converted prayers.

Common phrases in prayers are, "send Brother Cutter, Lord, to cut the way straight," "tell Sister Clearer to clear the path," "send Bramble Picker to pick out her stony heart," "send Nurse Dinah with her clean towel of salvation." Brother Cutter cuts the road (through Vincentian-style tropical growth) on which the pilgrim walks. Sister Clearer clears the way of debris and danger. Nurse Dinah is a nurse in the Spirit. Bramble Picker "picks the stones" out of a hardened heart.

Spiritual beings not described as saints also inhabit the spiritual world. These may be members of the tribes of various cities including soldiers and warriors of those tribes, various unnamed people described as "gentlemen" or "ladies," as well as short men or short women. More than once, the short man told the pilgrim that he was "the Lord thy God." One pointer said that the "short, fat, woman" was the "Queen of Africa." These are all good spirits, or potentially good spirits. Bad spirits also live in the spiritual world. One was described as a "jumbie" (a ghost), but usually bad spirits are identified as "Satan" or simply as "bad spirits."

Even though people from one's daily life are mainly found in (the spiritual) locations around St. Vincent and not necessarily in the spiritual cities, still they may be found there. One's pointer is met with on the way at many times. This is because the pointer is *tracking* one and will be seen from time to time on one's travels because he actually is there in the Spirit keeping an eye on his spiritual child. He is watching progress, checking to make sure she is not getting into trouble. Besides one's pointer, the most common people from the "natural" world one sees in the Spirit are one's fellow travelers (should there be more than one pilgrim in the room at a time), members of one's family and household, deceased pointers, and other deceased people.

Other figures with whom one may interact in the Spirit are trees, bushes, rocks, and animals. No one I asked had talked with rocks or vegetation. This was always characterized as a lapse of attention on their part: If they had been paying attention they would have known to ask the rock or tree for knowledge. Converted say, "So et-e come, so et-e go" ('as he comes, so he goes') and, "So carnal, so spiritual." That is, if one is attentive and inquisitive in one's physical existence, one will be also in the Spirit, and ask the right questions. In addition, experience helps. The more one mourns or enters the spiritual world in other ways, the more experienced one becomes, learning to ask the right questions for the most effective experience.

Many of my respondents had talked with animals. The animals most often mentioned were dogs and snakes. Frogs, rats, ants, roaches, and donkeys also were described as imparting knowledge to Converted pilgrims in the spiritual lands. A man told me, "In the Spirit, the rat is a wise animal, and the ant is the cleverest animal." One pointer allows no one to kill a roach or an ant in the mourning room (although it is natural daily behavior for Vincentians). He said that he killed a roach in the mourning room one time, and then he went on a journey where roaches were playing a very difficult song that he had to learn. He said, "The tune those roaches were playing, Oh!"

Actions in the Spirit

The purpose of traveling in the Spirit is learning. Mourning is "going to school." Although the pointer is the spiritual teacher, the Holy Spirit is "Teacher Divine," who takes over in the spiritual realm. For most Converted, travel to specific cities is passive. The Spirit takes them and shows them what they are to see. However, by application, the pilgrim can direct her travels and enhance her experience. The pilgrim is admonished during the banning to ask whomever and whatever she meets for useful information, to ask about her whereabouts, and to ask for the identities of the individuals she meets. She is also given a *password* (or *pass*) for use in dangerous situations, to find her way when lost or to gain admittance to places from which she may be barred. The password is not a single word, but a sentence, sometimes a Bible verse. It is one secret that is always secret. No one told me their password, nor did I ask anyone to do so. Divulging one's pass can lead to death or madness. Everyone agreed on this. However, a pointer or pointing mother usually only has one password to give, and all of his (or her) spiritual children share the knowledge of the pass. "The same word you have is the same word I have," Converted may say to those who have had the same pointer, reflecting a feeling of a common bond.

There is danger in the Spirit. In almost every case, it is a sort of benign danger that can be converted into useful knowledge on the part of the pilgrim. Danger may take the form of animals who may oppose one—most likely snakes and dogs. If one overcomes one's fear, as the pilgrim who is prepared is able to do, the animal will teach one what it has to teach. The snake teaches a dance that sometimes is seen in the churches. The dog teaches vigilance in the Spirit, as we have seen in the case of the Valley dogs. Other potential violence comes from soldiers with swords or firearms to whom the pilgrim must respond, as well as from hostile Indian tribes. One must approach all creatures in the Spirit, human or otherwise, with respect. That is why the pointer tells the pilgrim to tell the people she meets in the Spirit who she is and who sent her as well as what her purpose is. Prayer helps with all of these, as does the password. If one uses the password when taken hostage by Indians, they may then teach one their song and their ways. The password may also bring one out of the spiritual world and back to oneself in the mourning room.

One may also get *locked up* in the Spirit. It may happen while one is on her spiritual journey, where she may be placed in spiritual handcuffs or in a spiritual jail. Or she may be taken hostage or kidnapped (usually by Indians). This sometimes happens if the pilgrim goes somewhere she is not prepared to go or if she becomes afraid and forgets to use her pass. The pointer may redeem the pilgrim by paying bail to a jailer or ransom to kidnappers. The pointer may also accomplish the effect of releasing the individual by singing the appropriate song.

Being locked up, *lock up*, or *in lock up*, however, usually happens when one is not on one's spiritual journey. The effects of this are identical to what is generally known in anthropology as "soul loss." One Converted individual who was suffering from being locked up in the Spirit told me, "It feels like a weight on your life" and "like you can't go nowhere." Asked to elaborate, she said, "You can't get anything done. Nothing goes right." Others described the feeling as similar to depression. The solution to being locked up in the Spirit is to go mourn. In other words, in Converted religion, the cure for soul loss is to go get it yourself. This reflects that all Converted people act as shamans by doing work in the Spirit as well as practice the Converted Christian (Wesleyan-Arminian) tenet that one's salvation is dependent on one's own actions.

Fighting in the Spirit is a task most Converted are called on to do, sometimes on the pilgrim journey, but also in church. In the *spiritual fighting* in church, the observer sees a dancing kind of fighting, with the hands held as if they are swords, hands open, palms flat, striking with the narrow outer edge of the hand. Two people (but sometimes more) usually engage in this activity, called *sword fighting*. Sometimes it is an outward view of what is occurring in the Spirit (the two fighting in the Spirit). Sometimes it is an exercise performed by the pointer to prepare his children or to check the preparedness of his children. The Bible is described as a sword (Ephesians 6:17). One pastor told me that if the members of his church had been studying the word of God, they would respond well to his sword fighting. In most cases, the sword fighting turns into firearms. The hands are held as pistols, the forefinger being the barrel of the handgun. The pistol fighting escalates (and accelerates) into the use of (invisible) rifles, and finally rapid-fire automatic weapons. There is no victor in these contests. They are didactic. I am referring to the normative behavior. Some variation does occur. Here is an excerpt from one of my field reports:

> [I] was watching a group of ten or so Baptists "work doption" in a church smaller than a [city] bus. They were all doing one doption which indicated they were in Zion; two men switched to an African doption. Then they began to fight spiritually. The hands were used as swords and they chopped and parried for a moment. The pointer who had his eyes closed—"tracking" the people in the Spirit—called out, "No Fighting." The fighting escalated to the use of spiritual firearms—the fingers held as pistols and rifles. An assistant pointer went over to intervene. Later one of the fighters told me, "We were in Africa and I saw him coming at me, so I had to defend myself."[7]

Another form of violence in the Spirit is *getting lash* or *getting licks* from the Holy Spirit. For sin or disobedience to a specific spiritual directive, the Holy Spirit may whip one with a spiritual whip. The results of the whipping are visible to those in the church as a bodily reaction on the part of the one getting lash. The body is wrenched in reaction to the blows of the whip. One or more people get lashed at most services. After church services, I was sometimes shown bruises by Converted who said it was the result of a spiritual lash. Sometimes, my walk home was accompanied by a Converted who was limping from a spiritual lash. This sort of violence is well within Vincentian norms of authority and subordination. The pointer beats his spiritual children (see chapter 3), the (carnal) teacher in government or parochial schools beats his students, parents beat their children (cf. Abrahams quoted in Beck 1979:304, fn. 37). The violence is also upheld by scripture. Some Converted quoted

Hebrews 12 to explain the whipping: "For whom the Lord loveth he chasteneth, and scourgeth every son whom he receiveth." The chapter goes on to explain that if a father loves his children he will chasten (and presumably whip) them. This is why some Converted complain if their pointer (their spiritual father) does not use his belt often enough. The whipping theme occurs throughout the Bible, and it is graphically depicted as being performed by an angel in *The Pilgrim's Progress* (Bunyan 1979:145–146).

Physical actions the Converted perform during the church service are one way the spiritual world becomes partially visible to those, like myself, who do not enter it. The sword fighting mentioned above is one example. Another way is the playing of musical instruments. As described in chapter 4, the Holy Spirit gives each Converted a musical instrument. Some pointers require mourners to play their (spiritual) musical instrument in the mourning room before the shouting, to be sure "they are really a musician."

Glossolalia (speaking in tongues) is another window into the Spirit. It is not only spoken in relation to the cities, although that is the predominant form of glossolalia. An antiphonic echolalia is spoken (one person leading, all others repeating), but usually in connection with the cities. Even those who do not belong to a certain city may participate in this sort of glossolalia. The languages spoken in this way let the congregation know in which city the others are traveling.[8]

Almost all other actions in the Spirit take place away from the view of those not actually in the Spirit (or looking into the Spirit). One action that may take place both in the church setting and on one's pilgrim journey is the collecting of tools or treasures. On several occasions, Converted told me of seeing (spiritual) golden keys during church services that had been dropped by others (i.e., the one who dropped the tool was not using it properly or had neglected its use, and it had fallen away). On one occasion, the person seeing the tool did not pick it up, but at other times the person did retrieve the tool, adding it to the tools they already had. The acquisition of tools, though, is one of the main activities in the Spirit. Crowns, keys, and crosses are the usual tools found by Converted on their journey, but others, like the pointing tools described in chapter 3, are common.

Three of the most common actions in the Spirit are going to school, working on a ship, and entering a hospital. Each involves gaining spiritual knowledge for work. If a woman finds herself in a hospital, taking care of patients, it usually indicates that her spiritual gift is that of nurse. On the other hand, one may enter a hospital to be cured of a sickness. A common prayer said for a pilgrim at a banning is for God to take the pilgrim to "the doctor's shop in Zion." [9] If one finds oneself working on a ship, one may be a spiritual captain. On the other hand, a ship may be just a means of conveyance from one spiritual city to another. Many of the lessons in the Spirit take place in school. Pointers' knowledge is most often acquired in school. Several pointers, pointing mothers, and assistant pointers reported sitting in a classroom while a man (or the Holy Spirit) wrote on a chalkboard pointers' seals and explained pointers' work. The seals of each pointer are expected to be different.

Although they may have the same form as those of other pointers, they often have different meanings.

Perhaps the most startling Converted phenomenon is the acquisition of practical skills during mourning. Skills commonly learned are reading, sewing, and cooking. One man told me he learned how to be a baker completely in the Spirit and then went to work as a baker. Before that he had no specific job skills. Although he has since gone to work in the health care industry, he still uses his baking ability to raise money for the church. Others told me with amazement that they learned how to sew or to cook. The skills are often learned in a classroom in the Spirit. I never met anyone who did not know how to read and was taught in the Spirit, but many Converted told me they had firsthand knowledge of cases where that had happened. References to the acquisition of skills in this way are made regularly in church to remind Converted of the power of God.

The remarkable circumstance of individuals learning practical and trade skills in a spiritual world is also found elsewhere in the Caribbean. Tessonneau (1983) reports a wide range of skills learned while sleeping—in dreams—in Haiti:

> In the case of the carpenter and of the seamstress, the evidence is consistent. They are able to make the object without a model. These (illiterate) people say, "I was not able to let the money go. So I accepted the work. When I went to bed, I asked myself how I was going to pull it off. That night, in sleep, someone appeared to me and showed me how to do it. The next day, I was able to make the requested piece very easily. Since then, I work in the same way and am able to do a job regardless of whether or not I have a pattern." (Tessonneau 1983:70, translation mine)[10]

Sacred skills are learned by Haitians and by Converted in the same way. But it is the process of learning practical skills in a nonphysical environment that should attract the interest of secular scholars (cf. Murphy 1992:323–324).

Preparation for Spiritual Travel

How one enters the Spirit depends on one's preparation. Pointers and other experienced Converted are able to enter the spiritual world at will by meditating on that intention. While less-experienced Converted may enter the spiritual world by doption, most are only able to enter the spiritual world during mourning or in one's baptismal journey. Preparation for the pilgrim journey begins for the individual in the weeks of baptismal candidacy—sitting humbly, palms up, eyes closed, being danced with, prayed for, preached to, absorbing all that occurs in the church. In preparation for mourning, the pilgrim is expected to pray harder than normal, to abstain from sinful acts, and to establish a spiritual mien so that she may go further in the Spirit.

The candidate is also supposed to read the Bible to help prepare himself. In St. Vincent, most Converted households I visited had a copy of *The Pilgrim's Progress* by John Bunyan, which is a kind of guidebook to the spiritual lands. When Converted told me that their journeys are like those of Christian, the character in *The Pilgrim's Progress*, they were not merely using a convenient metaphor. For the Vincentian Converted, *The Pilgrim's Progress* is a major source of inspiration, a holy scripture secondary to the Bible. In some churches, members are instructed to study the book so that they "will know where to go" in the spiritual world. It is a "true and good story" and if the Converted "walk right" they will go on the road that Christian walked and they will arrive where he did (the Celestial City).

The Pilgrim's Progress has a strong literary presence in Vincentian society. It is taught in the schools and it may be viewed as a true story by more than the Converted. Perhaps it was only a coincidence, but when I checked the Kingstown (St. Vincent) Public Library, *The Pilgrim's Progress* was listed in the card catalog under "Adult Non-Fiction." Like a true literary classic, Bunyan's tale is property of the world. That it should speak to descendants of Africans in the Caribbean is not a surprise when we consider that it has recently been read as a Hindu morality tale (Gupta 1993). The British West Indies, perhaps even more so than India, has been affected by English literary hegemony, and as such may have more to learn from *The Pilgrim's Progress*.

Signing of the Bands

Preparation for the pilgrim journey is also undertaken by the traveler's pointer. The most important act on the part of the pointer before the banning (the sending of the pilgrim to the spiritual lands) is the signing of the bands themselves.

Most Converted do not see the spiritual lands set out before them as on a map. In Converted doctrine, one's physical nature prevents one from seeing things in the Spirit. It is only as Converted people become more spiritual that vistas in the Spirit become clear. We have already seen in the banning the various symbols used to orient pilgrims as they begin their journey. Most important of these, from the Converted point of view, are the bands tied around the eyes. The bands are sacred implements that have been inscribed with holy power. Each band does something for the pilgrim. The manner of preparing the bands is given to the pointer in the Spirit. Each pointer's method is slightly different. Indeed, if a pointer were to sign his bands in the same way as another pointer, his authenticity would be suspect.

The seals are images drawn in chalk as a sign to the pilgrim and to the Holy Spirit. They set apart a space, a room, or a person as dedicated to a spiritual task. The seals are chalked on the walls of a room at a house blessing; they are placed on the floor and in various places of the church during the regular services. They are placed on the table at a thanksgiving. During a banning, they are placed on the bench, on the floor, on the bands, and on the pilgrim himself. The seals themselves are often small (two to five inches) images and letters representing saints, Christian principles, spiritual tools, and places. A group of them are often set in a *wheel*— that is, a larger chalk circle or a set of concentric circles. Thompson (1984:111) calls the seals of the Vincentian Spiritual Baptists a "remarkable Afro-Caribbean calligraphic art" in which "largely alphabetically derived ideographic signs float like sidereal dust." He refers to them as a "visual glossolalia" (113). That may be so. However, like the glossolalia of the spiritual cities, the seals have directed meaning.

When placed on one's bands at mourning, the seals help carry one to particular places in the Spirit as well as protect one and help one to unlock certain areas of knowledge in the Spirit. It is unlikely the pilgrim would know which seals are placed on her bands. It is usually unnecessary for her to know. Although some pointers explain some of the seals to their mourners, I do not think any explain them all. Likewise, the bands themselves are seldom explained. If the pilgrim is astute, she will know what the bands mean by the content of her travels.

It may be instructive of how the spiritual world is perceived and explained to quote extensively from my fieldnotes. I have edited the following quote for spelling and in the omission of irrelevant passages. The event below took place in St. Vincent after I had been in the island for three months. A pointer invited me to watch the usually secret signing of the bands:

> Although I was invited, getting information from this pointer was very difficult (but similar to all the others). It would go like so: Me: Does this have a meaning? He: Yes. Me: Am I allowed to know the meaning? He: Yes. Me: What is the meaning? He: It is a symbol. Me: A symbol of what? He: It is a sign. Me: What is it a sign of? He: Well, of the city. Me: Of what city? He: Victory. Me: The city of Victory? He: Yes. Me: I want to get this right, it is a symbol of the city of Victory, that is the name of the city? He: Yes. This went on for all of the 20 bands he signed—each with 5 or 6 symbols each. He was patient to do the same kind of asking and answering for each band.
>
> I confirmed with him that the ritual of putting on the "bands" is spelled "banning." I made him spell it for me because the banns are what one puts forth in preparation for marriage in the Anglican churches.
>
> He had an unpainted plywood board about 3 feet long and 10 inches wide. On this board were some fresh chalk seals. "That's an African seal," he said, "I belong to the African tribe." He said, "You can work all the cities, but you have one that you are living." On the table were the board, a candlestick, a metal (pewter or aluminum) plate (like an offering plate), and an open Bible with a piece of chalk resting in the center. The Bible was open to the 51st Psalm—which he repeated to himself throughout the ceremony. He said he used a different psalm for each person as he was led by the Spirit. I think he repeated a different verse for each band, but he did not do these aloud. At one point he turned to me and said, "Now I'm doing the second verse."
>
> He lit a candle and placed it horizontally in the plate to get it started for dripping (the pointy wax tip was removed first so that the wick was about twice as long as normal). Each band was a triangle of cloth of different sizes and colors. "Red and black is always longest," the pointer said. Each cloth was folded so that it had three folds and formed a trapezium about six inches wide and three feet or so long. Each cloth was then placed on the board points up. None extended over the ends of the board. Each cloth was stuck together with one drop of wax. (He said he buys a yard or two of each color—each cloth was about a yard or less.) He then drew on each with

chalk—the "sealing," and then dripped wax drops in patterns on top of the seals—the "signing." (Not the other way around as one might think.)

The first cloth was royal blue and was the "School Signature." In the center was a palm, and on the left side was a stylized "S" for 'saint' and on the right was a stylized [initial omitted for privacy] for the name of the saint (which was also the name of the church).

The second cloth was the "Pilgrim Traveler." This was on a white cloth. The pointer did not have any colored chalk and so just signed instead of sealing. In the center were nine arches. I asked what they were and he said, "nine arches." On the two sides were spirals.

The third cloth was maroon in color. He said, "Now I'm going to do a ladder." I asked what the ladder means. He said, "Climbing." This was sealed with four ladders and 3 letters. The letters were K, T, and R. I asked him what they were and he said letters. I asked what they meant. He said the K meant "Keep on traveling," the T means "Determine to go to a city," and the R means "Religious." (Mispellings and apparent misappropriations of initials do not represent orthographic naiveté but mysteries in the instructive [e.g., Elysian, Masonic] sense.)

The fourth cloth was purple. He said, "This is the Wheel." . . . The wheel was described as a compass—to put one on a wheel to spin. The wheel keeps the pilgrim spinning to different directions.

The fifth cloth was black. This was "The Valley of Ezekiel." . . . It featured "bits and pieces of bones," a "skeleton" (actually a skull), two bones crossed, a rib, another skull, and the words: THE VALLEY OF EZEKIEL.

The Pointer was sweating heavily and concentrating very hard. It seemed obvious he was putting tremendous effort into his task. He decided to take a break. We went outside and stood in the breeze. . . . After about 20 minutes, we went back inside.

The sixth cloth was royal blue and was just signed and not sealed. (The pattern was hard to see because there were no chalk markings. . . .)

I did not write down the colors of the seventh, eighth, and ninth cloths. They were only signed. I asked what the signings meant and he said, "The words from the chapter." He said he recites the words to himself as he works.

The tenth cloth was chalkboard green. He said, "Now I'm going to do the Alphabet." He put the alphabet in chalk on the band—A through P on one line and Q through Z underneath. I asked what the alphabet does. He said, "It carries you straight to school."

The eleventh cloth was white. It was sealed in "Chinee letters." . . . The letters were exotic looking, but did not look Chinese to me. There were five letters. The first was the signature of the city (the city of China). The second letter stood for "upliftment." The third letter was "prosperity." The fourth letter was "protection." The fifth was "watch over me." Because the bands are different for each individual "according to their degree," I asked if he would always do one for China. He said, "You always do one for China."

The twelfth cloth was brown and was the "Signal." There were several images. Each representing a signal (flag) of a city. One was a key. The key "is to open the cities that you're going." The signals were Africa, India, and China. . . .

The thirteenth cloth was yellow (India) and was only signed.

The fourteenth cloth was grey (the sky) and only signed.

The fifteenth cloth was light blue (the city of Victory) and only signed.

The sixteenth cloth was also light blue (the Virgin Mary) and only signed.

The seventeenth cloth was cream (India) and only signed.

The eighteenth cloth was also cream and was both sealed and signed. He said, "This is my number." There were four sets of images. The first was a [number omitted], the next was [number omitted], then a circular seal, then [number omitted]. The circular seal was the school—St. [name omitted]. . . .

The nineteenth cloth was red and was "the African band." There were six images. . . . The first was the "shepherd rod." The second was the ladder. The third was a signal: a three-pointed flag with five circles inside. The fourth was "a pan to play" (the musical instrument known as a "steel pan"). The fifth was a ship—with an anchor (at stern), a signal (flag at stern), and three masts. The sixth was the word "AFRICA." Underneath that was to go the pilgrim's name. He left the space blank until the pilgrim arrived.

He then quickly sealed some smaller "hand bands"—one for the right hand (wrist), one for the right foot (ankle)—and the "revealing band" (that goes under the chin). I asked why it was called the revealing band. He said because you remove it (on the third day at the ritual called "rising" or "rising morning" . . .). He said, "Some don't remove it, but according to the scripture you have to remove it." . . .

Those were the bands he signed for just one of the pilgrims he was to point that night. The procedure took over two hours.

This account of the signing of bands demonstrates the deliberate character of journeys into the spiritual world. Preparation for the pilgrim journey is extensive on the part of the pointer, who is the one sending the pilgrim on the journey. He must know where she is to go so that he can track her progress. Even though the meaning of the bands is seldom explained to the pilgrim, it is believed that solemn preparation of the bands on the part of the pointer has spiritual efficacy. The large number of 20 bands signifies a pilgrim who has mourned before. The pilgrim in this case was quite experienced and had a lot of places to go in the Spirit. At a baptismal banning, it is common to see as few as three bands placed on the candidate. Pointers sign their bands in different ways. Some use plaid or striped cloth. Some use very long *swaddling bands*, which are up to eight feet long and are wrapped around the head several times. Some pointers sign their bands in the mourning room itself. Some sign theirs in the presence of the pilgrim. All, however, use chalk and dripped candle wax.

Ritual States of Consciousness in Converted Religion

In an effort to address problems related to the comparability of anthropological terms for spiritual behavior (e.g., trance, possession, dissociation), I use the term *ritual states of consciousness* for altered states that have a sacred place in the culture in which they occur (Zane 1995). The questions of whether or not possession or dissociation or any specific state is really occurring that occupy so much of the discussion of other researchers (e.g., Henney 1974; Ward and Beaubrun 1979) can be avoided by leaving the determination up to those in the culture under study. The ritual states can then be analyzed for cultural relevancy—that is, for the nature of the ritual experience—as well as compared cross-culturally with other culturally significant states. Although not as clean as definitively placing a particular behavior in a category such as trance or possession and thus making it directly comparable to types of behavior identified as trances and possessions in other cultures, this approach does have the benefit of relating directly to the experience of the people under study.

The ritual states model has enabled me to identify numerous culturally relevant altered states that have never before been recorded; it has also allowed me to find out how the Converted differentiate between those states. Most of the Converted ritual states relate to the spiritual world. Most of them are ways of entering the Spirit. Ritual states of consciousness identified by the Converted are: shaking, doption, traveling, gazing, seeing, meditation, dying away (or dying off), pilgrim journey, vision/dream/journey, tracking, reading.

Shaking (or *catching Spirit*) is characterized by uncontrolled jerking and spasms under the influence of the Holy Spirit. This is usually described in the anthropological literature as "Holy Spirit possession." The Converted view it in a variety of ways, describing it as "the Spirit in you," "on you," or "taking" or "seizing" one. The activity may be quiet and stationary or loud and accompanied by sudden movements.[11]

Trying to get at the experience, I asked Converted over and over to help me understand the process of the shaking. Many said that the Holy Spirit is always inside a Christian and he just takes over at those times when the shaking is apparent. Quite a few Converted told me that the shaking begins with "head raise" or "skin raise" (that is goosebumps or gooseflesh) and a coldness in one's foot or leg that extends rapidly to the rest of the body. Bodily awareness recedes as the shaking takes over. Some are oblivious during the shaking, having no memory when they return. Others said that they are taken away by the Spirit: "You feel like you are flying" and "You go far away."

Allen (1991:164) describes Holy Spirit possession in African American churches in New York City as feeling light, good, and hot (but not cold, as with the Converted). Holy Spirit possession in African American Pentecostal and charismatic churches is described as always pleasurable (cf. Sherrill 1964:128). Most Converted have a different experience. While it felt good to some, most who expressed a preference told me that they did not like the shaking. It made them hot and sweaty, messed up their clothing, and frequently led to physical injury (but the experiences of spiritual travel were usually described as pleasurable).

Doption (or *rejoicing*) is different from shaking.[12] Prolonged shaking is frowned on in most churches. Converted people are spiritual workers, and they must "work the Spirit." They must "beat doption." In most of the churches I frequented, the shaking person was supposed to gain control of the shaking and transfer the spiritual power into doption. Those shaking are told to "Work it out." "Working the Spirit," "working penitent," or "jump Spirit" is an ordered sort of Holy Spirit possession. Doption is a spiritual journey taking place during the church service. Some novice Converted did not describe doption as a journey. They described it in other terms, such as "people whispering things in your ear," and "something you just have to do, you have no control." Usually it is a collective spiritual journey, with the Converted who are doing doption traveling together from one spiritual city to the next. Doption is sometimes described as "walking the road." However, the church is a *ship* and the *captain* leads the doption, shifting to different doptions as the people go to different cities. In either case, the people doing doption are usually grouped together, often facing each other or touching each other. They are traveling together.

Doptions are different beats taking one to different places. A description of the most common doption (*Number One doption*) is identical to descriptions of "labouring," "trumping" or "groaning" in Jamaican Revival (Simpson 1980:169; Chevannes 1978:8; Seaga 1982:7), although the Converted meanings are different. The individual stamps on one foot while bending from the waist, then breathing sharply while straightening up (the precise order varies). Ward and Beaubrun (1979:483) describe Trinidadian Spiritual Baptist doption as "rhythmic sighs." Bourguignon (1970:92) calls it hyperventilation or overbreathing. As these terms suggest, the sounds are an integral part of doption. They set a compelling rhythm. When I asked Converted what was the important part of the doption, I was told that the movement was more important, the sounds secondary. I must emphasize that there are numerous doptions (at least ten that I recorded). Doption indicates travel to the spiritual lands. The Number One doption (the one like the Jamaican forms) is almost always the first doption engaged in by a group of Converted. Other doptions emerge from it.

I saw the Number One doption in every church I regularly attended. It is sometimes called "one foot," "the one foot doption," or "working the pump." In some churches, the Number One doption takes one directly to the city of Zion. In others, it is a general doption used to transport one to different cities: The people who are jumping Spirit then switch to the specific doption of the city when they enter (but this varies as well). In some churches, Zion is the city that must be visited first during doption (as an entry into the Spirit). In other churches, it may only be visited last (as the last city possible—that is, heaven). Doption always occurs during the church service, and it occurs in most church services.

Other doptions occur less often than the Number One doption. The Jericho doption entails a motion as if one is riding a pony, as does the Jerusalem doption. In the Valley doption, the people are bent over with their arms hanging toward the ground. The African doption may seem licentious, bent from the waist with back straight, legs kicking out, and the women pulling up their skirts, the men pulling up their gowns. It is not scandalous that women sometimes pull up their skirts during doption. Throughout the world, possession or other ritual states temporarily exempt one from the normal rules of society (Edgerton 1985:58–61).

Those doing doption gather together. If one who is shaking transforms her shaking into doption, she moves, engaged in doption, to the huddle so that she may travel with the others. In some churches, the captain takes over, calling out the rhythm of the doption and indicating the stops and cities along the way. Stops are indicated by a loud *"beem!,"* at which the people doing doption stop with eyes still closed. The captain starts the same doption after a few seconds and the others join in for a few more seconds. The pause is so that the captain may talk to the watchman of the gate of the city to which the group is traveling. When the group is admitted to the city, they enter by the same doption that took them there. Usually the captain leads those doing doption to a series of cities, switching doptions for each city. There is some delay between the actions of the captain and those of the rest of the group during doption, because the captain is in front of the other people (that is, he is in front in the Spirit; in the physical world, he is in the huddle) and it takes longer for them to reach the spot where he has stopped. In some churches, *shuttling*, a vocalization without a specific rhythmic movement, is used to switch from the doption of one city to that of another. The sound is *"Supsupsup-sup . . ."* In some churches, the Number One doption is used for most cities, without a visible shift, and only those with spiritual eyes can tell in which city the group is traveling.

The *Number Two doption*, also called the "two foot doption" or "two foot," is seen in a few churches. This is a double-time doption. Some told me that it is used "to stand" (to rest between different cities). Others told me that the Number Two doption is a way of getting to cities quicker. However, in some churches I was told that the only doption identified with a number was the Number One doption. *The Alphabet* (or *the Letters*) doption looks like a sort of marching, and it takes one "to school." While one or more persons are engaged in the Alphabet doption, each letter of the alphabet is chanted from A to Zed (the British "Z"). When Zed is reached, that letter is repeated for as long as the doption lasts. The congregation usually joins in the chanting. One pointer told me that the letters A, B, C, D, and Z each have their own doption, but I was unable to elicit this in other churches. Those not doing doption help pilgrims on their travels by their actions—by singing the tunes of the cities, by marching, clapping the correct rhythm, or imitating doption.[13]

In a religious "shout" in America (Lincoln and Mamiya 1990:352), the participants are "bumped" by the bodily percussion of those on the sidelines. A similar procedure takes place in Converted doption. The doption carries the person to the spiritual lands. In both the language used and in the detailed explanation of the process of doption, it seems that many Converted spirit journeys involve some level of culturally trained synesthesia. For instance, the songs as well as the doptions are called ships or roads. They take one to a certain spiritual city. They help one to "go through" into the Spirit. The sound of the music not only implies motion but is the experience of it. The sound is felt as motion. This appears similar to Cytowic's (1989; 1993) synesthesia patients as well as Irwin's (1985) synesthetic model of out-of-body experiences.

Mourning is the pilgrim journey. It is the period of ritual seclusion in the mourning room (see chapter 7). The baptismal journey is usually not considered mourning, but it does take place in the mourning room after banning (for two to four days only) and the events in the Spirit are usually identical to those in mourning. Mourning is traveling spiritually.[14]

The Converted may also journey in the spiritual realm in a vision or a dream in normal sleep. In a *dream*, one may travel to any of the places in the Spirit that one may go in the pilgrim journey. Dreaming differs from mourning in the lack of a purpose. The person dreaming has not been "sent" by her pointer. A dream, whether or not it has a spiritual quality, is sometimes described by Converted people as a *journey*. A *vision* is a dream with a message. It is usual for visions to be reported in the church service. Anyone may get up and "give a vision," and many churches set aside time in the service for those who have something to say to get up and say it.

All of the above-mentioned ritual states are entered into by all Converted. The others (seeing, meditation, traveling, gazing, dying away, tracking, and reading) are not experienced by all. They require a deeper level of experience and commitment. Usually it is only the most experienced Converted who enter the states that require more skill.

Meditation and traveling are connected. According to some respondents, they are the same thing. They both take place most often while one is sitting in the church during a service. *Meditation* is closing one's eyes and by quiet intent entering the spiritual world, during which travel may occur. *Traveling*, however, may happen without meditation and without intent. In both cases, the places to which one may go are the same (that is, anywhere in the Spirit). Either traveling or meditation may lead to physical action. In the church service, most of the actions in the Spirit are accompanied by physical action on the part of the person in the Spirit. The physical body may perform the actions done in the Spirit, so that those in the church may only see the person bending over or raising a hand or spinning around in response to spiritual stimuli. Otherwise, some physical person sitting in church may be seen in the Spirit (by the person who is in the Spirit) with, for instance, a flower or a leaf in her hand or tucked into her headtie, and the person in the Spirit gets the item from the altar or the center pole (plucking off a piece if necessary) and placing it on the person. If he (or she) sees a lesson written with seals on the ground in chalk, he will write that as well, or tell a pointer to write it if he has not been given the power to do so himself.

Reading is the knowledge of past events in a person's life as well as of one's current state, spiritual and/or physical. The spiritual gift of prover is characterized by the ability. It is sometimes done by divers and may be done by most pointers. Reading seldom involves an outward sign of change in consciousness.

Seeing is seeing things in the Spirit of any sort while fully engaged in the physical world, but it also may refer specifically to seeing the future. The terms "seerman" and "lookman," sometimes applied by outsiders to those who have the gift, have implications of obeah (sorcery) and are avoided. Seeing may happen to Converted people unexpectedly. Many told me they were shocked the first time they "saw" in the Spirit.

Gazing is watching a specific scene in the Spirit without being there oneself. This often occurs in the context of a pointer watching those traveling together in doption to ensure they walk the right road and do not encounter danger.

Tracking is the action by a pointer of watching a specific individual. The pointer may watch an individual's physical actions. (One man told me in awe and fear how a pointer described the exact layout of his bedroom.) Tracking is most usual in the context of mourning, the pointer keeping an eye on his spiritual children on their travels. I was told, "If a father loves his children, he's going to know where they are." Tracking is almost always carried on during the pointer's daily actions at work or at home. It often involves no overt change in consciousness but may be accompanied by meditation. The idea that a pointer can be engaged in the church service or in his daily routine and still tracking a pilgrim is special, but not unique. Eliade (1958:207) describes a Tantric technique of entering different spiritual worlds but at the same time maintaining "lucidity and self-control" (cf. Hultkrantz 1973:28).

Although I observed all of the above ritual states dozens of times, *dying away* or *dying off* is a rare action that I only saw twice. Dying away, according to my respondents, can last for hours or even days. Both of the ones I saw lasted less than an hour. The person experiencing the dying away loses locomotive power and falls to the ground or is supported by others. It appeared to be a bodily arrest of the sort characterized by respiratory alkalosis brought on by hyperventilation (Singer 1995:128–131). Dying away is the source of profound travels. In the dying away, the person travels in the spiritual world and reports what he or she sees while others gather around to hear. What is remarkable about the dying away is that it is an occasion when a saint may take over the body of the Converted person and speak through him or her. I did not observe this, but I did talk to two people to whom it happened. They said they could feel the voice coming through them. The Converted, besides practicing Holy Spirit possession also have more traditional spirit possession, though it is rare, and without the loss of knowledge on the part of the person being possessed.[15]

Several consciousness-altering techniques accompany the ritual states: auditory driving, kinetic driving, meditation, hypnosis, sensory deprivation, sensory bombardment, culturally learned synesthetic imaging, and socialized lucid dreaming. Converted do not describe the alterations in those ways, however. To the Converted, all of the actions in the Spirit and ways of getting there are accomplished by the Spirit of God. Ward and Beaubrun (1979:483) identify the experiences of the Spiritual Baptists during mourning as a result of destabilization between the sympathetic and parasympathetic systems by overexcitement. I think the fact that spiritually skilled Converted are able to experience the sensations of travel and the other world without movement (that is, by gazing, meditation, seeing, etc.) shows that not only does destabilization not have to be the case; but because overstimulation (and/or deprivation) is unnecessary, it is not central to the nature of the experience. The social context of the ritual states is far more important than physiological influences.

The Converted, though, do accompany changes in consciousness by physical and physiological action. Singer (1995:139), in another context, identifies techniques of "physiological persuasion:" "hyperventilation, repetitive motions, changes in diet and in sleep and in stress levels, body manipulations, and relaxation-induced anxiety." These are techniques used in mourning to persuade the body that it is traveling to the desired locations. But they are not the only techniques. Reichel-Dolmatoff notes a similar multiplicity of choices for inducing altered states among South American shamans. He reports (1975:201) that, in addition to drugs, "prolonged fasting, dietary restrictions, sexual abstinence, physical exertion, intentional deprivation of sleep, breath control, and concentrated thought are practiced by many people, apparently quite consciously, in order to produce certain desirable states of mind."[16]

As an example of how these aspects might work, let me quote from a letter I wrote from the field. The event is a *fasting*:

> In spite of my Epicurean vow and complaints about 11-hour services, I attended a 12-hour one on the 29th–30th of July. I was sort of shanghaied on this spirit journey, but at least I got to go on a journey. I intended to stay only a few hours, but there were only eight of us and no one was supposed to leave the room and everyone was praising God so much for my presence and had already made my bed (three sheets and a blanket on the hard floor); I couldn't bring myself to disappoint them. And they sacramented me just like the Baptists, so I got first-rate data. All my exposed parts were washed and dried vigorously by four people, with ritual exhortations given at my eyes, ears, nose, mouth, hands, and feet. That felt great! Then with equal enthusiasm, all those exposed parts were rubbed with lots of olive oil, precipitously reducing my pleasure. I was made to kneel for 32 minutes in prayer—no fake kneeling here, body vertical from the knee up, and no bench to lean on. Try that for 60 seconds! While holding a candle dripping happily on my hand. At another time I had asked the Baptists if that hurt them. "Yes, burn plenty," I was told, "but you just pray harder." I was getting twitchy, not from hot dripping candle wax, but covered with oil, I was afraid of combustion! At least I was glowing a pretty yellow. Then we lay down in prayer and waited for visions (sometimes identical with dreams). The hard floor, the sound of the ladies peeing into the enameled metal chamber pot just on the other side of the curtain from my bed (a sheet separated the men from the women), and the boy on my side of the curtain rolling hither and thither, kept my sleeping periods short and the dreams fresh. I had six dreams of water and urination, which I did not recount in the period allocated for this at the morning service—at 4:30 A.M. One I told was of me somewhere in America (the journey) talking to a man and a woman at a fireplace who said, "It is a good book" (publishers?). Numerous "Praise God"s at this.
>
> We were in the building which serves as the mourning room and although what we did was called a "fast" (but slow, slow), it was in effect a mini-mourning. In my public prayer (my private meditations were not churchable), I asked God to help me to write the book on the Spiritual Baptists in a way that people will want to read it because it says something important for their own lives and not just about the Spiritual Baptists. This said while staring at the candle in my hand for half an hour and hearing the others pray for me to write well the "notes of the Lord" must have influenced my

dreams (two total about writing, all the rest connected with the chamber pot). I imagine the same thing going on for the Baptists—but the preparation for real mourning is far more intense.

The above excerpt suggests that belief is more important than technique for altering consciousness. All of the Spiritual Baptists who were in the room with me traveled to culturally appropriate places during the fasting. The social setting may be the most important part of what happens to the Converted.[17]

SEVEN

Mourning

BANDS SO TIGHT THEY CUT YOUR EARS. Skin hot in a small hot room. Skin arms legs hands itching. Days-old sweat. Floor so hard it bruises your knee. Three days and nights on your right side lying. Seven days praying on your knees on the concrete floor. Seven days sleeping on concrete and the same dirty sheet that was clean when you came in. Ten days begging God. Eleven. Twelve. Twelve days unwashed bodily stench. Twelve days of inaction. Twelve days confined. Twelve days blindfolded. Every bodily need tended by others, accompanied by others. Twelve days speaking in a whisper. Twelve days of discomfort. Twelve days of sacrality.

It could be more of course. I had heard of pointers going as long as 40 days. In Brooklyn, seven days is a norm. Some people in St. Vincent go only nine. For the baptismal journey, the norm is three days. Most of the mourners I knew went 12, 13, or 14 days. It is up to God and the pointer when the pilgrim will come out. Sometimes a shouting will be expected one day, and the pointer will say the pilgrim needs to stay in for a few more days.

I have visited mourners in the room. The discomfort is thick and wincing, even for the observer. But they endure it. One man had mourned 22 times in 15 years. Why? In previous chapters I have given an indication: The spiritual world is vast and beautiful and full of means to acquire knowledge, wisdom, and understanding.

The mourning cycle comprises three community rites: banning, rising, and shouting. Each has distinct parts. We have already seen some of what happens at the banning (chapter 5) and the shouting (chapter 2). I will now discuss what happens in the *inner room*.

The mourning room is sometimes called the *secret room*. In many churches, what occurs in the mourning room is secret, and non-Baptists are not allowed inside. Some churches even do the banning in the mourning room. One Converted shepherd told me, "Don't let anyone tell you that God doesn't have secrets. God does have some secrets" and he quoted the Bible: "The secret of the Lord is with them that diligently seek him" (Psalm 25). He added, "The Bible doesn't lie." However, secrecy of knowledge is variable in Converted religion. Some information that was kept from me in one place was openly disclosed in another. Some told me I must go to mourn myself to know what happens, but others who said that I should write "everything" told me all I wanted to know. I do not present anything here that was told me as a secret. But because secrecy is assumed by many, the following information is suitably disguised by taking some portions and descriptions from sections of my fieldnotes regarding other churches or individuals.

We accompany a young Baptist on her first mourning. She has, however, already experienced a trip to the inner room before—at her baptism. There she received the gift of nurse. The following account is taken from the public ceremonies I attended for this pilgrim's mourning and a series of interviews after the event. I did make one visit to the mourning room by myself to read a chapter from the Bible to the pilgrim (as do many Converted), where I was able to ask a few questions. Although many of the journeys during mourning may be idiosyncratic, I leave those out and only mention the ones that are consistent with the reports of several people. The pilgrim is a 19-year-old who lives with her mother and several sisters close to the church. She has no children. She works from time to time as a housekeeper, even though she has a secondary education.

❊   ❊   ❊

The church is an hour's walk from Kingstown, in a village of about 600 people. The mourning room is adjacent to the church, in a room accessible by a door beside the altar dais. The pilgrim is banned on Friday night.

At her banning, six people "stand up to give the pilgrim a word." More people want to speak, but there is not enough time. One man says, "You are going to see Jesus. You are going to kneel meekly at his feet. Tonight, you will be led to the number one Lord of Zion and he will take you to Africa. Nurse Dinah will be there to nurse you on your pilgrim journey. Hold on to Jesus. Ask Brother Cutter to cut the rugged road. Ask Sister Clearer to clear the way." A woman says, "As you climb the hill to the Wicket Gate, you will see a light." She shakes with the Spirit and cries, "Glory," "Jesus," and "Yes, man." She continues by saying, "You are sitting there with tears in your eyes [the pilgrim was crying], let the tears flow from your heart. Any time you are in trouble, use your pass." All of the speakers make numerous references to Jesus as well as to the importance of having faith in the difficult days of mourning to come. There are more songs than words of advice. Some of the songs will reappear in the spirit journeys.

The pointing mother proceeds with the banning. She says to the pilgrim, "I have seen the belt passed on your back tonight. Inside there, you licked. People come here and think they can fool me." Twice this evening, the pilgrim had suddenly wrenched her body in response to a (spiritual) whip or belt strap. I had interviewed the pilgrim the evening before her banning. She said that she was trying to purify herself before she went to mourn. She said, "We have sin you see and sin you can't see."

The pointing mother says to the pilgrim, "To you, toil on. As you about to go to the other world, I about to lead you on." The bands are put on the pilgrim and she is led to the mourning room, a mother and the leader of the church spinning her along the way. The bands are placed on her head and she is put down before midnight.

❉   ❉   ❉

The (spiritual) mother who acts as the nurse sleeps in the room with the pilgrim, but during the days goes home and cooks for her family. The pointing mother comes in periodically during the day to tend to the pilgrim. Her house is adjacent to the church and the pilgrim can ring the bell should she need anything (for instance, to be escorted to the toilet).

The pilgrim is told that she may lie on her right side or on her back, but that she should not lie on her left side. The pointing mother says, "Some people say that if you lay on your left side you will get bad *tracks* [journeys], but that is not true. If you lay on your left, you won't remember your tracks." It is very important to remember one's tracks. They form the basis for one's spiritual life. The pilgrim also may not put her hands under her head while lying on her side. If she does so, she will forget her tracks as well. In this spiritual school, the pilgrim sleeps with a pillow, but in others, the pilgrim places her head on a Bible or a stone. The pilgrim is not supposed to cross her arms or legs while in the mourning room or she will block her journey and she will not go anywhere.

The pilgrim is told to pray like she has never prayed in her life. She recites the Lord's Prayer (called the "Our Father prayer" by the Converted) and the Apostle's Creed almost like a mantra. At six in the morning, at noon, at six in the evening, and at midnight, the pilgrim is told to get up by the nurse. A candle is lit and placed in the pilgrim's right hand. The nurse holds one as well. Both kneel, arms rocking as mourners are supposed to do (to keep the journey going). The nurse prays out loud. The pilgrim prays silently. The pilgrim will have only one bowl of porridge between the banning and the rising. She drinks water from a calabash. No cold water is allowed in the mourning room at all. "Cold water does chill the Spirit," the pointing mother says. After the rising, the food gets better. However, it is supposed to be "no pleasant food" (Daniel 10:1). The meals mainly consist of breadfruit and salt fish. Sometimes the pilgrim gets fresh vegetables and rice.

✵   ✵   ✵

The *rising* begins at 6 A.M. on Sunday morning. It has been only 30 hours since the banning, but it is the third day. In some churches, rising takes place at night and is called *rising night*. This church has a *rising morning*. Eight people are gathered in the mourning room. The pointing mother has laid the pilgrim on her back, her arms laid straight out to the sides in the shape of a cross. Four unlit candles have been placed around the pilgrim, one each at the head and foot, one each at the sides. In some churches, a sheet is placed over the pilgrim, but here the pilgrim lies without a sheet. Her clothes appear wrinkled, but still relatively clean.

As with every ceremony, most of the ritual is accomplished with and by songs. After singing and prayers, the congregation recites Psalm 91 from memory:

> He that dwelleth in the secret place of the most High shall abide under the shadow of the Almighty. I will say of the Lord, He is my refuge and my fortress: my God; in him will I trust. Surely he shall deliver thee from the snare of the fowler, and from the noisome pestilence. He shall cover thee with his feathers, and under his wings shalt thou trust: his truth shall be thy shield and buckler.
>
> Thou shalt not be afraid for the terror by night; nor for the arrow that flieth by day; Nor for the pestilence that walketh in darkness; nor for the destruction that wasteth at noonday. A thousand shall fall at thy side, and ten thousand at thy right hand; but it shall not come nigh thee. Only with thine eyes shalt thou behold and see the reward of the wicked. Because thou hast made the Lord, which is my refuge, even the most High, thy habitation; There shall no evil befall thee, neither shall any plague come nigh thy dwelling. For he shall give his angels charge over thee, to keep thee in all thy ways. They shall bear thee up in their hands, lest thou dash thy foot against a stone.
>
> Thou shalt tread upon the lion and adder: the young lion and the dragon shalt thou trample under feet. Because he hath set his love upon me, therefore will I deliver him: I will set him on high, because he hath known my name. He shall call upon me, and I will answer him: I will be with him in trouble; I will deliver him, and honour him. With long life will I satisfy him, and shew him my salvation.

While the people say the psalm, the pointing mother and the leader of the church scatter petals from flowers of different colors around the pilgrim and on the pilgrim. The pointing mother places a white rose in the mouth of the pilgrim.

The pointing mother calls for John 11 to be read. She pulls the back of her dress forward between her legs and tucks it into the front of her belt, girding herself. The leader does the same with his gown, tucking it into the cords at his waist. A mother reads the 11th chapter of the gospel of John. This is the story of Jesus raising Lazarus from the grave. The chapter is read from verses 1 through 45. I reproduce it here from verse 25. Mary has just expressed doubt that Jesus can bring her dead brother back to life:

> Jesus said unto her, I am the resurrection, and the life: he that believeth in me, though he were dead, yet shall he live: And whosoever liveth and believeth in me shall never

die. Believest thou this? She saith unto him, Yea, Lord: I believe that thou art the Christ, the Son of God, which should come into the world. And when she had so said, she went her way, and called Mary her sister secretly, saying, The Master is come, and calleth for thee. As soon as she heard that, she arose quickly, and came unto him. Now Jesus was not yet come into the town, but was in that place where Martha met him. The Jews then which were with her in the house, and comforted her, when they saw Mary, that she rose up hastily and went out, followed her, saying, She goeth unto the grave to weep there. Then when Mary was come where Jesus was, and saw him, she fell down at his feet saying unto him, Lord, if thou hadst been here, my brother had not died.

When Jesus therefore saw her weeping, and the Jews also weeping which came with her, he groaned in the spirit, and was troubled. And said, Where have ye laid him? They said unto him, Lord, come and see. Jesus wept. Then said the Jews, Behold how he loved him! And some of them said, Could not this man, which opened the eyes of the blind, have caused that even this man should not have died? Jesus therefore again groaning in himself cometh to the grave. It was a cave, and a stone lay upon it.

Jesus said, Take ye away the stone. Martha, the sister of him that was dead, saith unto him, Lord, by this time he stinketh: for he hath been dead four days. Jesus saith unto her, Said I not unto thee, that, if thou wouldest believe, thou shouldest see the glory of God? Then they took away the stone from the place where the dead was laid. And Jesus lifted up his eyes, and said, Father, I thank thee that thou hast heard me. And I knew that thou hearest me always: but because of the people which stand by I said it, that they may believe that thou hast sent me. And when he thus had spoken, he cried with a loud voice, Lazarus come forth. And he that was dead came forth, bound hand and foot with graveclothes: and his face was bound about with a napkin. Jesus saith unto them, Loose him, and let him go. Then many of the Jews which came to Mary, and had seen the things which Jesus did, believed on him.

While the first part of the chapter is being read, the pointing mother picks up a good-sized stone, a flattish river stone about two pounds in weight, and draws seals in chalk on both sides.

At verse 33, "he groaned in the spirit," the reader pauses and the group sings a melodic groan three times. The stone is placed on the belly of the pilgrim.

At verse 38, "groaning again in himself," the leader and a mother shake the pilgrim at her legs, arms, and shoulders while the rest of the group again sings the melodic groan.

At verse 41, "and they took away the stone," the stone is removed.

At verse 43, "Lazarus come forth," the group repeats "Lazarus come forth" three times. The pilgrim is lifted up. The congregation sings the chorus, "Up from the Grave He Arose." The pointing mother spins the pilgrim. The leader spins the pilgrim. The pointing mother spins the pilgrim again.

At verse 44, "Loose him," the band under the chin (the *revealing band*) is removed. This band under the chin represents the cloth that is tied under the chin of a deceased person in St. Vincent to prevent the mouth from opening. In some churches, it is called a "dead band," but in most it is called a revealing band because it is removed. The band around the wrist is removed and the band around the ankle is removed (but they are not taken off in every church). The chorus continues and several church members take turns dancing with the pilgrim.

Everything in the room is removed, all of the candles, the bedding, the bench that the nurse sits on, glasses of water, spiritual flags. The wax from the candle drippings is scraped from the floor. The floor is swept. The walls and floor of the room are washed with water from a basin that has green leaves in it.

The various elements are put back in the room in different positions from where they were before. Fresh candles go in each of the corners. A group of candles goes at the head of the pilgrim's bed. The pilgrim's and the nurse's beds are consecrated again by ringing the bell over them.

The dancing has continued throughout. Vigorous doption breaks out.

The pilgrim is seated on the bench. The cloth covering the bands is removed. Then all of the bands are removed and tightly retied. The cloth that covers the bands is replaced.

The pilgrim is lifted so that she is standing again and dancing resumes to the chorus, "We Are Climbing Up Mt. Zion Hill."

The pointing mother dances with the pilgrim. She hunches down in her dancing, dangling her arms as she faces the pilgrim. The pilgrim is tilting her head so she can see under the bands. The pointing mother lunges at the pilgrim in spiritual fighting. The pilgrim is ready and counters the thrust with a forearm parry. The pilgrim does not do any thrusting herself, only wards off the thrusts of the mother, then the leader. The pointing mother fights with several of the church members in turn.

Dancing and singing continue for a few minutes more, and the pointing mother says, "We going to let the pilgrim get some rest now." There is no closing to the service because the pilgrim is continuing on her journey. The group repairs to the main part of the church where coffee and fried salt fish (a common Vincentian breakfast) is served. The nurse and the pilgrim remain in the room, where the pilgrim again lies down on her bed.

※　※　※

Up to the rising, the pilgrim had not had any tracks that seemed significant to her. They seemed like dreams. She said at the shouting, "After three days, I was laying there, and I saw a bright light, brighter than any light I've ever seen." After the appearance of the light, she began to travel in a sharply cogent way. She went to Africa and to China, learning the languages, songs, and dances of those places. She traveled in many places in St. Vincent. She learned secrets about members of the congregation. She traveled on a ship. In a certain place a snake bit her. In a house she met people making crowns of gold. She traveled to a desert and met John the Baptist. She traveled to Jerusalem. She met soldiers who trained her to march. She was given a sash that she is henceforth to wear in church. She found herself in a hospital taking care of children (reaffirming her previous gift of nurse). She went to school in two different cities. In one, in an unidentified city, she was standing in front of a blackboard and a teacher was standing there showing her numbers and names that she was forbidden to reveal. She found herself by a waterfall and was led to a cave behind the waterfall. In the cave was a Bible and many treasures— golden crosses and swords and crowns. A man told her, "These are the treasures of Solomon." Those are just the events she reported at her shouting. She told me more later.

�֎   ✖   ✖

After the rising, well-wishers visit the pilgrim daily. Sometimes one or two, sometimes a small group. They sing, give words of encouragement, read from the Bible. They dance with the pilgrim, pray with her. Reinforcement of the value of mourning, description of the spiritual world, and encouragement to continue the journey are given by everyone. Whether or not the pilgrim is sleeping or traveling, she must get up and listen to those who have come. In some churches, however, the pointer lets the pilgrim continue on a journey if she is on one.

Similar encouragement was given at the usual Wednesday evening service and the usual Sunday evening service (which had been replaced by the 6 A.M. rising the previous Sunday). For the services, the pilgrim is taken out after the service is opened and returned to the room before the service is closed. Her journey must not be interrupted by a closure and an opening is unnecessary because she is consecrated the entire time.

I visited the pilgrim on one morning on her tenth day in the room. As I approached the church, I saw the pointing mother in the yard hanging up the wash. She saw me and knocked on the shuttered window of the mourning room, calling to the pilgrim. She then knocked on the door to the room (it had a door to the outside as well as into the church). The pilgrim had been asleep and took a few moments to answer.

The pointing mother led me into the room, asking why I had not come to visit the pilgrim sooner. The nurse was away. The pilgrim's headtie (the cloth over the bands) had come off and the mother went over and retied it so that the pilgrim's eyes were completely covered. I was left alone with the pilgrim. She sat up in her bed. She moved slowly. The room was dark, but light came through chinks in the shutters. The first thing I noticed was the strong smell of body odor. It kept pushing itself on me while I was there. The pilgrim had on the same clothes as at the banning. Empty candle boxes and stumps of candles were piled under the bench on which I sat. Two dirty bowls that had contained food were on the bench next to me. The sheet on the nurse's bed was crumpled.

I asked the pilgrim if she was allowed to talk. She said she could, but "not too much." She spoke in a very low, very quiet voice because she had been speaking very little for the previous ten days, only to ask her nurse for something or to tell her tracks to the nurse or the pointing mother. I asked how many people had come so far. She said, "A fair number." She said that she was able to keep pretty good track of the time while she was in the room, but that she seldom knew the time of day. She was unsure if it was morning or evening when I was there. Because Converted always say that the harder one prays the looser the bands become, I asked if her bands had come off at all while she was in the room. She said, Yes, but she usually retied them herself. I asked if she had any stones under her pillow. She said no, but pulled her revealing band out of her pillowcase to show me. She commented several times that her bands itched. In order not to disturb the bands, she could not reach her finger under them to scratch. Instead, she hit her head with the heel of her palm. This behavior is also commonly seen in church among women who do not want to loosen their tightly-tied headties.

I said a brief prayer. She quickly lit a candle and knelt in prayer next to me. Then I sat on a bench and read to her from the Bible—the book of Jude. I asked a few more questions, but left shortly so I would not distract her too much from her journey. She did tell me that she was not supposed to know when her shouting was, but that she knew it was in two days because she heard the pointing mother calling it out to someone on the road.

�֍   ✖   ✖

In the morning on the day of the shouting (Wednesday), the pilgrim is released. The *releasing* is usually a private ritual. It is described to me later. The pilgrim lies on her bed and the pointing mother *takes her tracks* (listens to the journeys that the pilgrim remembers). Sometimes the pointer is dissatisfied and delays the shouting for several more days (I knew of only one time that a delay occurred during my fieldwork). On this day, the pointing mother would tell me that the pilgrim "performed well." The mother stands up and says to the pilgrim, "Roll up your bed and drop it by the door. You are no longer mourning." She does so. The nurse brings a glass of water and sprinkles some of it on the bed. The pilgrim is told to remove the bands and put them on the bed. This also is done. She tells me later that the light is too strong for her and she must keep her eyes closed. The bands are sprinkled with water. The nurse gives her three sips of the water.

The pilgrim is led back into the room and is washed thoroughly by the nurse and the pointing mother. Then a freshly prepared set of bands are tied on the pilgrim's head. (But in many churches, the old bands are not removed and the same bands are left on for an additional nine days.) The pilgrim is allowed to put on different clothes (but in some churches the same clothes are worn for the shouting).

The pilgrim is not free to go. She must sit quietly in the mourning room, meditating, and perhaps still journeying, until the shouting this evening. She must still say her prayers at noon and at 6:00. The shouting will be at 7:30.

❌ ❌ ❌

The shouting is attended by visitors from several Converted churches. Members of one church have come by a chartered van. The church building has been cleaned and looks bright and pretty. The service is opened by the leader. Several people pray for the pilgrim. The greeting hymn is sung. The female members of the church put on their veils and enter the mourning room. The pilgrim is then marched from the outside door of the mourning room to the front door of the church. She is wearing a newly made uniform. It is one that she received in the Spirit during mourning. The pointing mother had it made by a seamstress in the last few days. The uniform is a red and white dress with a white apron and a red and white headtie. She is still blindfolded and the headtie is tied on the outside of the bands.

The pointing mother greets her. With the pilgrim standing outside the door, the leader reads the Ten Commandments (Deuteronomy 20). After each commandment, the congregation sings, "Lord have mercy on us and incline our hearts to keep this law." The Beatitudes (Matthew 5) are read. After each beatitude, the congregation sings, "Grant us this grace, we beseech Thee, O Lord."

The leader reads Psalm 122. The pilgrim is brought into the church as the psalm begins:

I was glad when they said unto me, Let us go into the house of the Lord. Our feet shall stand within thy gates, O Jerusalem. Jerusalem is builded as a city that is compact together: Whither the tribes go up, the tribes of the Lord, unto the testimony of Israel, to give thanks unto the name of the Lord. For there are set thrones of judgment, the thrones of the house of David. Pray for the peace of Jerusalem: they shall prosper that love thee. Peace be within thy walls, and prosperity within thy palaces. For my brethren and companions' sakes, I will now say, Peace be within thee. Because of the house of the Lord our God I will seek thy good.

The pointing mother says to the pilgrim, "Number One, I am welcoming you into St. Luke's church." The benches having been pushed into the center of the church, most of the congregation joins in the procession around the inside of the church. Three times counterclockwise, three times clockwise (but most churches do only three in either direction). The leader is in front ringing the bell; the flag wavers all have their flags waving; the cross-bearer carries the cross. The congregation sings the chorus, "We Shall See the King."

The pilgrim is seated on the mourner's bench, which has been sealed by the pointing mother. Several people get up to give words to the pilgrim, encouraging her to stay on the right path. The pilgrim is told, "Satan is a very busy man. Tonight, Satan is very angry with you. Satan is bruising your heels and mashing your toes." She is told to "hold on to Jesus," and to "toil on." She is also warned that life will not necessarily be easier since she has mourned. A visiting pointer tells her, "The road ahead is rough and stony." But there was some encouragement,

"The bud may have a bitter taste, but sweet shall be the flower." Others give praise to God because "We see that she is not bruised, no bone have been broken, we see tonight that no ambulance backed up, no policeman came." All of these are standard Converted sayings.

The pilgrim is washed and anointed in the same fashion as at the banning.

The pointing mother says, "Whoever have gifts to give can come now." The pilgrim stands facing the congregation and her nurse stands next to her. The pilgrim holds five lighted candles—two in the left hand, three in the right. Members of the congregation line up with packages of candles in their hands. The congregation sings a hymn ("We Plough the Fields and Scatter") with the refrain:

> All good gifts around us
> Are sent from heaven above:
> Then thank the Lord, O thank the Lord,
> For all his love.

One of the candles in each package is lit. The person giving the candle holds it in front of the pilgrim and says something similar to what one woman says this evening: "I am giving you this light. Tonight, I want you to know the light of the world is Jesus. Hold on to Jesus. In the name of the Father, Son, and Holy Ghost. Amen." The candle is extinguished with the fingers and the package is handed to the nurse who lays it in a pile with the others on the floor. After the gifts are gathered (the gifts are always candles), they are blessed by the leader. Then the hymn "See Israel's Gentle Shepherd Stand" is sung. The hymn is sung three times. The last verse is:

> We bring them, Lord, in thankful hands,
> And lift them up to Thee;
> Joyful that we ourselves are Thine,
> Thine let our children be.

One of the church mothers stands behind the pilgrim while the song is sung, taking the pilgrim's hands and holding them out, dancing the pilgrim to the cheerful tune. At the phrase "lift them up," the pilgrim's arms are lifted, then for the remainder of the verse the pilgrim is made to bow to the right, then the left, and to lift her hands again. At each bow, her hands touch the ground. The flashing about of the lighted candles is very attractive.

The pilgrim must now give thanks. On her knees, she prays a singing prayer. But the congregation can hardly hear her because her voice is so weak. Her voice does gather strength as she speaks. After the prayer, the pointing mother lifts the pilgrim's bands a little bit so that she can see the people (but her vision is still mostly obscured). The pointing mother, with an admonition to "talk hard" (loudly), tells the pilgrim to stand up and give her tracks. The pilgrim stands up and speaks. After telling 13 journeys, the pilgrim says, "The rest I will keep to myself." The pointing mother addresses the congregation, "Believers is satisfied?" The congregation answers yes. It had been a very good shouting—lots of singing and doption and the pilgrim had many tracks. The pointing mother explains why. She says,

"[There is] a road to Glory. You have to put the pilgrim's name on the bands. A lot of people don't get nothing because they don't have their name on the bands." She tells the pilgrim, "Then you is going out. You go with a book [the bands]."

The service ends with the usual doxologies and the pilgrim is free to go.

The pilgrim was in the room for 13 days.

※   ※   ※

The process is not over though. Now the pilgrim does her *nine days*. She will still receive visions for the nine days and still has an aura of sacredness about her. The bands assist this feeling. During the nine days, she is expected to wear her bands without taking them off. If she must take off her bands to go to work, then she places them carefully in a Bible and ties one or two of the bands around her waist. When she returns home, she puts her bands back on. She wears a different set of bands for the shouting and the nine days (but one band from the first set was included with the second set). The first set of bands must be kept in a safe place until she is ready to mourn again. Then she takes them to her pointing mother (or to another pointer if she is directed by the Spirit), who may use some of them for the next mourning. Both sets of bands must not be washed for a long time, some say not before a year has passed. If the bands are washed too soon, the pilgrim will forget her tracks. She may, at any time, put one of the bands on her head if she wants to travel in her dreams. She may wear one under her headtie when she goes to church. Some have told me they wear one or two of their bands for protection when going to a new church or when traveling to and from church. Some wear one or more of their bands to church "to be more in the Spirit." It is common to see women in church with bands under their headties. Sometimes one cannot tell, but sometimes a flash of color shows at the edge of the headtie. If men wear one or more of their bands to church, they put a *headwrap* over the bands.

The pilgrim must keep up her four-times-a-day praying regimen for the nine days. She must light a candle, kneel facing east, and rock her arms during the prayers. The pilgrim cannot handle money or a knife or soap for the nine days. She cannot be around fire or cook for herself. She must abstain from sex.

※   ※   ※

The pilgrim visited me several times during her nine days. I think she was tempted by her boyfriend and saw a visit with me as a way she could keep a sacred purpose in mind. Another man may have tempted her, but all I wanted to do was to talk about her spiritual experiences. On two of these visits I was able to conduct lengthy interviews.

I noticed a marked sense of maturity about her after her mourning. She became confident in her answers to my questions, whereas before she was usually tentative in what she had to say on spiritual matters. In the interviews, she told me at least twice as many tracks as she said in her shouting. She gave me more detailed accounts of those that she did tell in her shouting.

She told me the names of people that she did not disclose at the shouting. She told me about sin in other people that was revealed to her in the Spirit. She sang to me many songs and related to me many things people told her in the Spirit. Some things were secret and she kept those secret. She told me things I heard from no one else and many things I heard from everyone else. She told me her gifts: nurse, flag waver, surveyor, preacher (she wasn't sure how to call this, but she said, "I'm supposed to preach.")

But there is one thing more. I have come to a matter that I am unsure how to treat. My intent is not to report all that the Converted told me. That is not possible, and even what they told me is a small portion of what they experience. My purpose is to put forth patterns of Converted experience that tell us something about the religion and its place in the world. The matter is this: some Converted engage in sexual acts in the spiritual world. This is not something that Converted discuss with each other. It is not something, usually, that is told to one's pointer. Knowing that people in other cultures may have sexual experiences in a spiritual realm (and that the condition may be common in the world), I asked as many people as I could if it happened to the Converted as well. Some people told me that it did happen to them, but that I should not write it in my book. Others said I should write everything. This pilgrim did not say either way. Like nearly every one of the Converted I talked to, this pilgrim answered my questions matter-of-factly. What might be embarrassing to reveal to a fellow Converted or a fellow Vincentian may be unburdened easily on a dispassionate researcher. Far more people said they had not had sex in the Spirit and had never heard of anyone having sex in the Spirit than those who told me they had.

The pilgrim had sex with a man in the spirit world. I asked who it was and she said she was unsure. She said that if one does not pray hard, they can get on the wrong path. She said that if one is not pure going into the mourning room, one can have a bad track. I got the impression that she did not feel it was very bad. In another track, she got married to a woman in the spirit world. She said she kissed the woman, but did not elaborate further. She said that she had not told these tracks to her pointing mother. Much later, an older Converted told me that if one goes too deep in Africa, that will happen, because they practice lesbianism in those places. She said, "If you do it in the Spirit, you going to do it when you come out, too."

Sexual matters are less bothersome in the Caribbean than they would be in an American setting. The pilgrim soon became a fiery preacher who could sing beautiful prayers and who could be seen waving her flag at shoutings in many neighboring churches.

PART III

Vincentian

Context

EIGHT

Work and Travel

HAVING DESCRIBED THE BASIC elements of Converted religion, I want now to turn to the contextualization of the religion, showing how it is an essential part of Vincentian culture and how it is built from Vincentian life experiences as well as from general human life experience. I consider the work of the Converted and their spiritual travel, and I compare the practices of the Converted to shamanic practice around the world. I begin with a brief discussion of shamanism, then present a typically shamanistic Converted event, and later give explanations for common shamanic experiences.

The comparative examples I use may strike the reader as distant from the assumed sources of Converted religion—that is, from other African and European religions. This is intentional. Although it is interesting to trace the historical lines, African and European connections are to be expected and do not elucidate the importance of the Converted very much. When religions around the world are surveyed, and one sees the same practices as the Converted in cultures with a different material base from St. Vincent, a different social structure, and with no direct historical ties, then we may surmise that we are looking at similarly human actions rather than culture-specific traits. The Converted are in a special place in relation to exemplifying these, because their practices are at the intersections of many of the usual categories (e.g., Christian, shaman, African, European). The position of the Converted in the history of religions is not just as an interesting study of Caribbean religion but as a system that reveals normally hidden structures of basic religious tendencies. One of the most basic of these is the shamanic impulse.

Shamanisms

The classic work on shamanism and still the standard point of departure is Eliade's *Shamanism: Archaic Techniques of Ecstasy* (1964).[1] He looks at numerous shamanisms around the world and finds three things in common: interaction with spirits, soul flight (spiritual travel), and spiritual work on behalf of the community. Integration with the local community is an important part of the idea of shamanism. We usually think of shamans as existing in small-scale societies, in a horticultural village perhaps, or in a community of hunter-gatherers. Shamanism in these societies is not a separate religion; it is a type of work or service at the disposal of the members of the community. Generally speaking, one does not believe or disbelieve in shamanism; it is an expression of the worldview of the culture where it is found. Not everyone in these societies is a shaman, but everyone uses the services of the shaman. This is what sets the Converted apart from other religions that incorporate ecstatic techniques but are not usually thought of as shamanism (e.g., Pentecostalism, Spiritualism). The Converted are the psychological workers of St. Vincent. If a Vincentian has a problem (a disturbing dream, a persistent illness, a death in the family), normatively he or she seeks out the Converted. It is just the thing to do.

I am not trying to prove that the Converted are shamans. They are the Converted. They do fit most of the definitions of shamanism (to be discussed), but the argument is not whether the Converted are one or another type of religion, but rather: What can the Converted tell us about human nature? Shamanism, found in society after society, exemplifies a general human tendency. A new kind of shamanism should be explored for what it may reveal about that basic trait. What the religion of the Converted does show is the historical sources of a shamanic cosmology. This is important because it demonstrates the power of the imagination within the constraints of environment. Study of the Converted also clearly shows the manner in which ecstatic techniques are taught and why they are successful. Because the Converted are an indigenous Western shamanism (or, at the least, an ecstatically mystical tradition incorporating all of the traits of shamanism), the nature of shamanism in Converted religion is easily accessible to the student of religions.

The Converted are not obviously shamans. Their otherworldly experiences are veiled to the noninitiated and couched in seemingly metaphorical language. Many structural elements in Converted religion are not normally associated with shamanism (like the large numbers of spirit-traveling participants and reliance on a scriptural authority). Also, the confusing array of people required to conduct the service, all with different roles to play, the reference to many spirits and saints, and the exorbitant paraphernalia all make the Spiritual Baptists stand out as unlike other Christians. Glazier maintains they are polytheistic (1983, 1988), whereas Houk (1995) and Simpson (1966) describe them as a Protestant denomination, and Herskovits and Herskovits (1947) term Spiritual Baptist religion an "African-Protestant synthesis." Malm (1983) describes the Spiritual Baptists as a "monastic order" and claims that anyone can lead the service. Young (1993:165) describes the church as having an unformalized hierarchy, whereas Henney (1974) and Glazier (1983) note a strict internal hierarchy. Although the Converted could be analyzed along any of these lines, their outstanding combination of spiritual methods is the most striking and may have the most to impart about the nature of religion.

Atkinson (1992) has described the difficulties in defining shamanism and selects the term "shamanisms" to allow both for different techniques of direct contact with the spiritual world and different manners of approaching the same data by scholars. With Taussig (Atkinson 1992:307), she is uncertain of the utility of the concept of shamanism, "eschewing the term entirely except in reference to a body of scholarly literature" (ibid., 309). Nevertheless, shamanism is recognizable enough for it to be an elemental part of introductory anthropology texts (e.g., Harris 1991; Havilland 1996; Ember and Ember 1996). I use the term specifically because it does refer to a body of scholarly literature from which the Converted (and other Spiritual Baptists) have been excluded and to which they can be suitably compared. Because the Converted operate a shamanism that developed in a Western setting, their practices are able to illumine much of the nature of shamanism that is potentially obscured by the otherness and lack of historical record in the development of non-Western shamanisms.

Walsh (1990:10–11) identifies five characteristics of shamans that are useful in thinking about the Converted: "shamans can voluntarily enter altered states of consciousness;" "they experience themselves 'journeying' to other realms;" "they use these journeys as a means for acquiring knowledge or power and helping people in their community;" "interaction with spirits;" and "contact with an ordinarily hidden reality." Primary among these is the use to which these experiences are put— helping people. The main way the Converted help themselves and others is by saving them from eternal damnation. Secondary for them is the treatment of physical problems such as illness or conditions described in anthropology as "soul loss" (e.g., Hultkranz 1978:35) and by the Converted as being "locked up in the Spirit."

Shamanism is a type of work. Hultkrantz (1985:453) reports that "[t]he main quality of the shaman is his ability through ecstasy to create contact with the supernatural world; whether he makes a soul flight or calls on the spirits is a question of professional choice and cultural ways." He also establishes (1978:30) four constituents of shamanism: an ideological premise, the shaman as actor on behalf of a human group, inspiration granted him by helping spirits, the extraordinary ecstatic experiences of the shaman. The notion of work in a spiritual realm is perhaps the most important (Krippner 1985; Siikala 1985). Shamanism is work in a spiritual world. It not only entails work in the spiritual world, it is the manner of work in the spiritual world, a "special form of performance of religious rites" (Basilov 1976: 156). The audience is central to the shape and outcome of that work (cf. Laderman 1991). In the case of the Converted, in that all in the congregation are at the same time workers, the audience are the performers themselves. From the Converted perspective, the audience is larger—the performance, public or private, is done always under the watchful and critical eye of God.

Like other shamans, the Converted use their powers to heal, guide, and prophesy, but unlike other shamanisms, the performance is not centered "on an ecstatic individual" (Winthrop 1991:255). The behavior is centered on a performing congregation instead of on a single individual (cf. Harner 1972:154; Lee 1993:117). Winthrop also states (1991:256) that "the powers that the shaman exercises are attributed to his mastery over various spirits . . . , both those who act as familiars, and those malignant spirits whose powers the shaman must overcome." For the Converted, the spirits they work with are partners; they "work with" the spirit (their saint). According to the Converted, for one to "have a spirit" is always bad. They are, however, always subject to the will of the Spirit (the Holy Spirit). They can never have mastery over the Holy Spirit, but they can become masterful practitioners of the spiritual arts by anticipating the will of the Holy Spirit.

Langdon (1992:16) writes: "In all its expressions, the one role that is constant in these shamanic systems is that of healer." The healing function appears among the Converted, but it is always subordinate to the larger Christian effort of eternal salvation. A common understanding in anthropology is that shamanism is "first and foremost oriented to curing and recovery" (Hill 1992:177). But that is a narrow view. Shamans do many different things (Winkelman 1992). They are not just healers or even primarily healers as many writers emphasize. The healing is just what is readily observable. For some shamans (e.g., the Baruya [Godelier 1986:113–116]), guidance and protection of souls, including the shaman's own, is the bigger job. This is accomplished by positive conscious activity by the shamans in the realm of spirits.

The work of shamanism requires the acquisition of spiritual knowledge. Pollock (1992:42) states, "In an important way, shamanism is a quest for knowledge, and knowledge of the sort they seek is power." Manning (1976) portrays shamanism as a profession operating at the edge of knowledge that is subject to change as knowledge changes. This lines up with the Converted openness to change and enhancement of knowledge and experience. One Converted pastor whose church I frequently attended explained differences between his practices and those of other Converted by saying, "Knowledge increases." The sort of knowledge, though, is important. It is knowledge learned directly from spirits. That is, it must be learned in the spirit realm. The Converted stress this continually. With me they were willing to discuss their knowledge of the spiritual world because they understood the nature of my enterprise, but with someone truly seeking after spiritual knowledge, not spiritually disinterested as was I, the response is "come and taste." Their answer is: Converted knowledge cannot be described; it must be experienced.

When shamanism exists with priestly (state-sanctioned) religions, it is subjugated by the other (Winkelman 1992), borrows symbols of power from the other (Miller 1975; Basilov 1984; but cf. Mumford 1989), but maintains its own practical goals (e.g., curing and recovery). In areas of the world where shamans exist in a Christian context (e.g. Mexico, Knab 1995), the shamanic elements are considered to be something separate from Christianity, something auxiliary, or inferior, or dealing with a different realm (see Basilov 1992, for the same relation between shamanism and Islam). A major difference with the Converted is that the shamanic technique is united with the Christian goal (world salvation through individual effort). The Converted spiritual realm is a Christian spiritual realm. The Converted may be seen to practice a Christian shamanism.[2]

Eliade prefigures this identification of Converted religion with shamanism (as a Western embodiment of ecstasy): "We shall find shamanism within a considerable number of religions, for shamanism always remains an ecstatic technique at the disposal of a particular elite and represents, as it were, the mysticism of the particular religion" (Eliade 1964:8).

Vincentian Wakes

When I arrived in St. Vincent, I was not thinking about shamanism. The high importance to the Converted of spiritual work, work with spirits, and spiritual travel seemed to me just another ecstatic form of Christianity. When I started learning about Vincentian wakes, the shamanistic nature of the religion began to stand out boldly. A wake also reveals the close association of Converted religion with the rest of Vincentian culture.

I never did attend a wake in St. Vincent. I would have if I was invited, but I was not. Abrahams (1983) described a wake, Gullick (1971) described a wake, Young (1993) got to see at least one. I watched one from afar in my village, listening to the songs, watching the activity on the outside of the house of the deceased. I asked many people about wakes. No one was hesitant to tell me about them. I said I would like to see one. But no one invited me.

It is properly called a *memorial*. Some people do call it a wake. But most people call it a memorial. Most households have three memorials for the dead—on the ninth night after death, on the fortieth night, and on the first year anniversary of the death. These are called *nine night, forty days*, and *one year's memorial*. They are common to all of the West Indies.

What is special about the memorial in St. Vincent is that the Converted almost always conduct the service, even when the deceased and the family of the deceased are not Converted. The Converted are the spiritual workers of the island. They are the ones to call when it comes to spirits. "Most people use them . . . because they are good with spirits," I was told by a non-Converted Vincentian. They can "put the spirit [of the loved one] to rest," she said, "No one wants a spirit roaming the earth." And that is why the Converted are called. One woman told me that Apostolic and Pentecostal preachers may lead prayers and singing at the wakes in some households, but that "most people want the Baptists."

Some people have a memorial on the third night, too—the "rising night." One woman said that they do it on the third night because that is when "they [the spirits of the deceased] get up, like Jesus." One Converted man said he used to be confused about the rising night. He said sometimes when he is there in someone's house, they will say, "Move aside, he want to pass" or other things that indicate the dead person is wandering around the house, but he never saw anyone. He said, "I don't think the person is really there [physically] because the Bible say that the dead can't return to his house." But he said, the "spirit [of the deceased] usually does visit."

I knew the pointer who conducted the wake that I saw from a distance in my village. I asked him about it the next day. I asked what was different about the wake from a regular service. He said, "Nothing really." I was to find out he was mostly right. It is the sacrality of the Converted that accomplishes the work, not any specific ritual they do.

A Wake in Brooklyn

Below I describe a Vincentian wake to illustrate both the shaman-like character of the Converted in relation to other Vincentians and the congruence of Vincentian society with the services provided by the Converted. It may seem strange to use an event in Brooklyn to discuss the Vincentian context of Converted religion. However, Vincentians in Brooklyn are no less Vincentians for living in New York. When someone dies in Brooklyn, Vincentian customs are followed as much as they can be even though St. Vincent is very far away. I want to use the wake to emphasize that, although the Converted are possibly only 10 percent of the Vincentian population, all Vincentians are affected by the Converted; nearly all have some kind of ritual contact with them and nearly all use their services. Without Converted participation at wakes, Vincentian culture would lose some of its distinctive quality.

The forty days was in a basement apartment in a Brooklyn brownstone. It began on Friday night at 8:30 P.M. It ended after 2:30 A.M., over six hours later. It was my first memorial service. (I would later attend one other.)

Mother Jarreau and I arrived shortly after 8 o'clock, and we were the first people there of the Baptist party. We were led into the kitchen (the largest room), where the service was to be held. The kitchen table had been cleared and several chairs arranged around it. A vase with flowers was placed in the middle of the table. Other chairs were set apart from the group at the table.

We met the bereaved family and were seated next to the table. Not one of those present (or the deceased) was a Spiritual Baptist. Eventually all the Baptists and me were seated around the table and the non-Baptists sat well away from the table.

Pointer Parker came in about 8:30 and began to draw a *wheel* on the table (arranged around the vase) with a mixture of (unpopped) popcorn, farine (casava flour), and rice that he had mixed up on a plate. It ran out and he called for the hostess to bring over some more. As he prepared more of the mixture, the bag of popcorn fell over, spilling the corn in a pile on the table. He sucked his teeth at the bother, and he and the hostess picked up the kernels and put them back in the bag. It promptly fell over again, the spilled kernels effacing much of pointer's previously made design. For a moment, Pointer Parker looked upset. But then he laughed and said, "Somebody like corn, eh?" The hostess, who was the deceased woman's daughter, smiled and said, "Yes, even though she didn't have no teeth." Pointer Parker said, "When people die, they aren't dead. Their spirit is still around." Only those seated at the table and a few others heard this as he was talking rather softly. However, he later said to the gathering, "I am not here to do anything for the dead because the dead is already dead."

Pointer Parker took out his leather strap and hung it around his neck while he worked. He took eight thick white candles that he had the hostess wash in water and placed them around the edge of the wheel. The hostess then gave him several other candles and he put them inside the wheel: 2 white, 1 yellow, 1 blue, 1 red. We had not entered a solemn part of the proceedings, and I asked the hostess why the candles were those colors. She said that she called up Pointer Parker and he told her what to buy. The pointer had the hostess light the candles and while she did that, he unwrapped his bell and placed it at the head of the table where he was to sit. He set his strap next to the bell and put his Bible on the table directly in front of his chair. Candles were placed in the corners of the room and lit.

While he was doing all of this, people were asking questions. Only two people present were not from St. Vincent. One woman from Tortola said that on her island the wake is held the night of the death and goes all night. She said, "This is all very interesting to me." The hostess asked Mother Jarreau, who was sitting next to me, what the symbol drawn on the table meant. Mother Jarreau said, "It is a wheel." She then added, "I shouldn't be telling you what it means." Two of the Baptists next to me were discussing mourning. One said, "I have to make a trip to the room." The other said, "I have to go, too." She said, "My time past due but I'm waiting for a vacation."

Pointer Parker commented on the flame of the candles, "The lights burn steady. When the light burn steady you know the house [is good]."

At nine o'clock, Pointer Parker said, "We will open the service now. We will begin by singing the [consecration] hymn 'Peace Be on this House Bestowed, Peace on All that Here Reside, Let the Unknown Peace of God, With the Man of Peace Abide.'" Then he motioned for me to start it. I was mortified and almost did try to start it (which I'm sure would have been a disaster—but I think it was important because he treated me as if I was there to do the work rather than to just observe). Fortunately, a genuine leader was there and he did start it (after an awkward momentary silence), and I was very relieved. Two of the Converted women consecrated the room. Then Pointer Parker recited from memory the long version of the Morning Prayer and I read along in the *Methodist Hymn Book*. The eight Converted people there were from four different churches. The long version is done in only a few churches. All the other Baptists recited the liturgy where it coincided with the short version.

Some in the audience began to cry for grief as the service started. One adult son was crying and kept repeating, "Mommy's gone, Mommy's gone." Others held him and patted his back and stroked his neck.

The pointer introduced a hymn. Then another. And several more. The pointer called out the words to the hymns as we sang. No one was singing except the Converted people and myself. The others in the room were watching the performance, not participating. The pointer switched to choruses, which are easier to get the words to, and encouraged everyone to join in. He cited a proverb from St. Vincent, "[If] you can't sing, you can *la la* and *do re*, just don't go away."

Shortly after we began a lively chorus, several of the Baptist women started shaking with the Spirit. The hostess and her sister-in-law began shaking, too. In St. Vincent, I had sometimes seen non-Baptists at the edge of the service, only watching, be overcome with the Spirit and start shaking.

At one point shortly after the service started, the husband of the deceased, who was sitting near the door said, "She here." Then putting his hand out, he said, "Rest in Peace."

As in the normal service, three scriptures were read. They were scriptures of comfort: Psalm 91, I Corinthians 15, and John 14.

The pointer, then the leader, prayed. The pointer asked the hostess and the other lady who caught Spirit to pray. When the hostess (daughter of the deceased) prayed she did not know what to do. She kneeled in silence for a moment. But then she sang her mother's favorite song, "On the Other Side of Jordan." Pointer Parker smiled. The song was sung for a while and the hostess again shook with the Spirit. Some of the Converted shook as well. One called out, "Push the key in!" (the key is the song). Pointer Parker called out, "She singing!" (referring to the deceased). After the prayers, the pointer said to the hostess, "Your mother is very happy that you sang that song."

More songs. Some dancing. There was quite a bit of catching Spirit and several different periods of doption. The leader was going pretty heavy at one time, singing "*tink a tink-a-tink.*" His hands were moving at waist level in front of him. Mother Jarreau saw me watching him and called out to me, "He playing a pan, man!" (a steel pan).

Before the close of the service, both the pointer and the leader and two of the mothers stood up and said a few words to the gathering. The leader said, "I don't know what you expect to see when you invite us here tonight, [but we came here to] serve God." One of the things the pointer said is that when the hostess called him to ask for a forty days, she asked how much he charged. He said, "I told her I don't charge anything."

The service was closed by the reciting of the usual doxologies.

As we prepared to eat, Mother Jarreau whispered to the hostess, "Your mother [is] very happy."

A wake is indeed without monetary charge. However, there is a ritual payment. Here is how I described it in a letter from the field:

> I knew I had to go to a wake (I should say, a nine night, forty days, or one year's night) but was hesitant to impose the complications of my skin color on someone else's grief. The wake is the one most visible act that establishes the Baptists as shamanic practitioners. They come in to perform a service (setting the spirit to rest), while all others watch, and are given a meal and at the end a ritual payment—of sweet buns and cocoa tea!! "We always give hot cocoa and buns to the Baptists [back home]," the non-Baptist says, and I ask a pointer if the non-Baptists always give buns and he says

(actually it is the usual wearying fieldwork stalking where you ask 20 questions [6 this time] without trying to lead too much and then, gratifyingly, he answers this:) "I wouldn't say that, but you always looking for your buns and cocoa tea."

The forty days I attended was clouded by some initial confusion over my whiteness, but I happened to know some of their relatives in St. Vincent, and as soon as I started singing they considered me as just another Converted, and at the end gave me to take home the same they gave to all those who came "to do the work"—a package of hot-cross buns and a 46-ounce can of Hawaiian Punch (!) in lieu of the traditional hot chocolate. There were nine of us Converted and ethnologists (eight Converted, one ethnologist), and we did an entire service of five hours length while everyone looked on. And we deserved those buns because we had to work so hard because we were so small in number and everyone was watching so strongly.

Comparative Shamanic Experience

Work and travel are the two driving metaphors in Converted discourse. The work the Converted do is determined by their spiritual experiences. The Converted can put the spirit of the deceased to rest at a wake because they are able to communicate with spirits. Spiritual travel, spiritual work, and interaction with spirits—all things that distinguish the Converted in St. Vincent—make them comparable to other shamans. Having considered the work the Converted do as a type of shamanism, I want now to discuss the experiences of the Converted in the spiritual world.

Other researchers have described the spiritual experiences of the Spiritual Baptists as deriving from the African forebears of the people who become converted as Spiritual Baptists (Herskovits and Herskovits 1947:305) or from the Methodist origins of the religion (Bourguignon 1970). Although those are reasonable conclusions, and although Converted religion is certainly an African religion as well a Christian religion, a comparative view leads to a third source. Most of the similarities to African practices in Converted religion are also found in shamanic cultures elsewhere. I want to show that the experiences of the Converted are similar to shamans in places far from Africa geographically and historically. The content of spiritual events in Converted and other cultures derives from lived daily experience.

Most of the traits described as African or from the African American south (Glazier 1985a; cf. Hackshaw 1992:78–79)—blindfolding, seclusion in "mourning," traveling to other realms, speaking in other languages, separation of soul or spirit from body—are, I contend, bodily and social metaphors informed by the local context. First I will establish these as common in the shamanic tradition and not necessarily connected with Africa. Then I will show how they are natural symbols, not inevitably derived from diffusion. All of this is to show the larger context. I am not saying that Converted religion is not African or not Christian, only that it is not *only* African and not *only* Christian.

Kalweit (1992:18) notes that many societies have what amounts to "shamanic schools." He reports of the Yamana of Tierra del Fuego that on the last evening of the school, the new initiates perform for a gathering of invited spectators. All present join in the songs and chant to provide background for the "tumultuous boat journey" performed by the initiates (30). By witnessing the spectacle, all become part of the journey. Like the shaman, the Converted person recounting his experiences at the shouting is making his appearance "not as an individual but rather as the embodiment of his community which together participates in the trip beyond. . . ." (Kortt 1984:289–306). Similarly, the Converted church service is a communal event. Unlike those in most shamanic cultures, nearly every Converted event is a communal experience.

In all general descriptions of shamanism, patterns emerge: ascending travels, descending travels, travels to different countries, quests for visions, bones and skeletons, animal spirit helpers, human-like spirit helpers, small people in the spiritual world, deceitful spirits, androgynous behavior, spiritual battles, different grades of shamans, blindfolds, seclusion for initiation, and other categories into which all of Converted behavior may be placed (e.g., Eliade 1964; Noll 1985; Walsh 1990). Shamanism is not a culture apart from the cultures in which it exists. It persists because shamanic cosmology is believed in by the people who use the services of the shaman; it is not only believed in by the shamans themselves.

I detail here some similarities between shamanism among the Wana of Sulawesi and Converted religion. I select the Wana not only because of similarities to the Converted (almost any shamanic tradition would do) but because Atkinson (1979; 1989; 1992), who studied the Wana, is especially aware of a wide range of possible "shamanisms." The Converted may be a new type of shamanism in the anthropological record, one where the techniques are the same as shamans elsewhere, but where the goals are those of Christianity.

Much is different between Wana and Vincentian life. The Wana are swidden horticulturalists in a relatively egalitarian society, whereas the Vincentians are small farmers and laborers in a highly stratified society derived from the colonial plantation system.

The song of the Wana shaman is called a *jaya*. A Wana *jaya* is at the same time a road and a means of conveyance. The Spiritual Baptist tunes are also called ships or roads that carry one to the spiritual lands. "The shaman has his spirits construct a *jaya* resembling a boat and provide the locomotion by rocking it. The journey is a long one, requiring an all night chant detailing the travels of the *walia* [spirit helpers] as they move along, stopping at every place along the way" (Atkinson 1979: 267). Some *jayas* are slow, lasting all night; some are quick. The Wana shaman's seance is a journey that may take a long time (like Converted fasting or mourning) or may take a short time (like doption). Some of the physical actions of the shaman seem to be similar to doption. "Bending" and "bouncing" and flexing of knees characterize both doption and the Wana shaman's dance (Atkinson 1979:263; 1992: 121,164). The bouncing is the manner in which Wana spirit familiars propel their vehicle on a journey. Wana shamans may travel together, as do the Converted. Atkinson (1992:271) writes, "On one occasion I witnessed, three shamans and two novices all went together on a journey to Pue."

Events in the shaman's journey might be visible to other shamans but not to his "non-shaman" audience (Atkinson 1992:271). Spiritual events may produce physical actions on the part of the shamans by which those not traveling with the shaman may know where he is and what he is doing, as with the Converted. Wana shamans also perform ritual dueling without weapons. Like the Converted, they "feint, but do not fight" (Atkinson 1989:154–155; cf. Laderman 1991).

Shamanic experiences are human capabilities, available to people in every culture. The similarities between the experiences of individuals in very different cultures point not to distant historical events (Eliade 1964) or to archetypes embedded in the human psyche (Ripinsky-Naxon 1993) but to similar ways of being in the world. The sources of the metaphors of shamanic experience are not hidden in remote sections of the brain, but derive from daily experience in the world—sometimes biological, sometimes environmental.

Many of the shamanic metaphors are bodily metaphors. As such, they are natural symbols. "The human body is common to us all," Douglas wrote in *Natural Symbols* (1970:vii). She discusses cultural norms that are expressed in attitudes toward and of the body. Her premise can be equally reversed. To Douglas, the body is a medium of expression of cultural norms. Shamanic worlds, in part, amount to cultural expression as a medium of bodily norms.[3] Shamanic experience is a "conditional universal" (D. Brown 1991): When people have shamanic experience, they experience it in similar ways.

The ascent of the shaman to an overworld and the descent to an underworld are what Lakoff and Johnson (1980:14) call "orientational metaphors," tied to the physical orientation of our bodies. As they point out, "up" is good because we feel good when we are up, while death and sickness are associated with "down" because we are usually lying down when sick or dead. Although on the face that may seem simplistic, the most important bodily orientation is the vertical axis. Disturbance of one's sense of balance leads to debilitating sickness (vertigo). The *axis mundi* (Campbell 1968) is none other than the *axis hominis*. The common Converted spiritual events of climbing a mountain and climbing a ladder are both natural symbols (that is, bodily symbols), because they take elements from the environment to match the bodily metaphor. The cave and the bottom of the ocean are similarly orientational metaphors (our bodies have a hidden inside, some parts dry, some parts wet, opposed to an exposed outside). The bodily metaphors are externalized and put into a place that reflects the person's (the shaman's) experience. Similarly, dogs are found throughout the anthropological record in the underworld land of the dead because of the universal association of dogs and bones and death and bones (cf. Mumford 1989:171). Shamanic commonalities in diverse places are less the result of diffusion than of a universal human capability influenced by local context. However, shamanic techniques are taught, and shamanic cosmologies are passed on. They are retained over generations because they speak to the lived experience of practicing shamans.

Dreams, Lucid Dreams, and Senoi Dream Theory

Converted sometimes describe their journeys as dreams and sometimes as "like dreams, but not exactly." Many of the spiritual journeys experienced by the Converted may be likened to "pattern dreams"—dreams that are significant in a particular culture and expected to take a particular form by members of the culture. These are described by Lincoln (1970:326) as being induced in three ways: conscious autosuggestion, formal suggestion or instruction, or formal parental suggestion "with instruction to the child vision seeker to keep dreaming until he dreams right." All of these methods are found in Converted religion, though the latter is directed by one's *pointing parents*. In most of the Converted spiritual schools I had contact with, the pointer sometimes sends pilgrims back to a specific spiritual city if they did not receive the appropriate knowledge or missed an important spiritual gift to be had there.

Lincoln's research that led to the concept of pattern dreams was conducted among American Indians. One Converted man told me of an American film he saw depicting a Lakota vision quest. To him, it looked like mourning. The similarity may be more than superficial; the Lakota referred to their vision quest by a term glossed "crying" or "lamenting": "everyone was expected to seek at least one vision, both for the personal upbuilding that it provided, and for the benefit it gave to the tribe by adding to the cumulative store of power which was gained through the totality of all the visions of all its members" (Dugan 1985:134). Converted mourning may be seen in the same way.

Sambia dream phenomenology in New Guinea is the same as that of the Converted in the West Indies: "What I call a dream was an event my soul experienced in another, parallel world, which my thought recalls and I—my self—share" (Herdt 1978:56). This is a common concept regarding dreaming found in the cultures of the world (e.g., Merrill 1978; Roseman 1984). Converted people in St. Vincent often recount dreams about others with the expectation that it was an actual encounter that the other person might recall. The phrasing is usually similar to what a Converted said to me one evening: "You visited me last night. Do you remember?" Converted people sometimes report dreams in church. If the dream involved another person, they may say, "I don't know if she remembers." From the point of view of many cultures, dreams can be seen as "a real cosmological environment," in which contact with spirits and other dreamers is possible (Wright 1992:158; cf. Knab 1995: 59).

Empson (1993:101–106) notes a "continuity between waking skills in integrating visual material and in the coherence of dream reports." The Converted dictum, "So carnal, so spiritual" applies here. It is by intent and preparation that the pilgrim is able to travel. When the sensual material of the journey is correlated and reinforced by the words and songs of others, as in the Converted case, then we can see how similar experiences may be reported by many different people (cf. Watkins 1976).

Clinical researchers have found that dreams are not limited either to a particular kind of sleep or to sleep at all, and that dreaming has a "multi-state basis" (Foulkes

1993:11–12). Because many of the ways Converted enter the spiritual world are like dreaming, the various ritual states of consciousness practiced by the Converted may be interpreted as multistate dreaming and vice versa.

Lucid dreams bear a lot of similarity to Converted journeys to the spiritual lands. A lucid dream is one in which the dreamer is aware of the dream and is able to direct the action of the dream. LaBerge (1985:19) lists the dream of a fifth-century Carthaginian, Gennadius, as the first recorded lucid dream. Gennadius had two lucid dreams on two successive nights, interacting with the same character. Like the Converted journeys (or lucid dream-like events), Gennadius' dreams took place in a heavenly land in which a guide appeared to answer questions. In the second lucid dream, Gennadius remembered all that had happened in the first (displaying a unitary consciousness).

LaBerge (1985:72–90) demonstrates that events of lucid dreaming have the cognitive character of events in external reality. One Converted told me about her first experience in the mourning room on her baptismal journey. She said she found herself in front of a steep hill and it stretched very far upward. Having heard many such accounts by that time, I asked her if she went up. She said, "No, everything was so confusing. I just turned away and I came back to myself." Her pointer told her that she had to go back and climb the hill. The use of the password is another example of the lucidity of Converted spiritual journeys. Converted use the password when they are in a dangerous situation in the Spirit and are unable to extricate themselves. In a shouting, it is common to hear, "I used my pass to come back to myself."

Another way that Converted journeys are like lucid dreams is in a sort of reality testing. Converted often report in their shoutings, "How I got there I don't know" or "I said to myself, how did I get here?" (see chapter 2). This kind of questioning often leads to a switch from ordinary dreaming to lucidity in lucid dreamers. On almost every journey, the pilgrim is aware of the journey and her purpose on the journey—interacting with the beings in the spiritual world, introducing herself, saying where she came from and who sent her, and asking questions to gather knowledge.[4]

Culture, of course, makes the difference as to how what happens is perceived to have happened. As the Converted know, one can be fully aware in dreaming or waking, or in any of their ritual states, and the awareness can later have immense influence on their normal waking life (cf. Trigger 1969:114–120; McManus, Laughlin, and Shearer 1993:39; Purcell, Moffitt, and Hoffmann 1993:242–243).

Senoi Dream Theory attempts to make the influence intentional as well. Senoi Dream Theory is a Western psychotherapy developed in the 1950s by anthropologist Kilton Stewart (1990) that he claimed was derived from the daily practice of the Temiar Senoi in Malaysia. Briefly, he claimed that the Senoi trained their children to dream lucidly, that they strove for positive action in their dreams, and that this led to the peacefulness in person and in society for which the Senoi are noted (cf. Dentan 1968). There is quite a bit of evidence that Stewart made it all up (Domhoff 1985; Dentan 1988).

In his critique of Senoi Dream Theory, Domhoff (1985:90) reports that there is "evidence that dreams cannot be controlled even to a small extent within dream groups or experimental situations." The findings of Barrett (1993) that dream content can be controlled counteract this assertion only a little. Although statistically significant, her results were not strong. Certainly Domhoff's large body of negative evidence would seem to disconfirm Barrett's one case of interested dreamers. Domhoff writes (1985:95) "As with many other dream ideas, Stewart's principles about dream sharing and dream control remain hopeful possibilities that rest largely upon the intuitions of a unique dream theorist and the reports of success by a few individuals." Pending the discovery of convincing new ethnographic data, the case appeared to be closed.

I think the Converted data encourage a reconsideration of Stewart's ideas. What is at issue is not whether lucidity is possible—that is uncontested (e.g., Grackenbach and LaBerge 1988)—but whether an indigenous culture exists where it is taught and used for positive purposes. Dentan (1988:58–59) reports that an "examination of all Senoi ASCs [altered states of consciousness] known to me or recorded in the literature uncovers no phenomenon unequivocally like the lucidity postulated in Stewart's account." Others looking for lucidity among the Temiar also failed to find it (59). Dentan does offer that a "close examination of shamanic activity elsewhere may turn up some clear cases of lucid dreaming/trancing" (59).

Converted religion does not lead to the same kind of peaceful psychological existence that Stewart claims for the Senoi (but Dentan [1995] discounts that as well). However, Converted practices do produce positive psychological benefit. Griffith, Mahy, and Young (1986) and Griffith and Mahy (1984) found that Spiritual Baptist mourning, the period when the most significant and most lucid spiritual traveling takes place, is a significant source of improvement in both life satisfaction and physical health.

I read Stewart's description of Senoi action in the dream world to several Converted:

> According to the Senoi, pleasurable dreams, such as flying or sexual love, should be continued until they arrive at a resolution which, on awakening, leaves one with something of beauty or use to the group. For example, one should arrive somewhere when he flies, meet the beings there, hear their music, see their designs, their dances, learn their useful knowledge. (Stewart 1990:196)

With the exception of sexual love, every Converted responded in the manner of one man who said, "That sounds like us." Like Stewart's Senoi (but not the ones described in more responsible anthropological literature [Roseman 1984; Domhoff 1985; Dentan 1995]), the Converted in the spiritual realm must convert potential enemies into friends (e.g., the Indians who may take them hostage). They must learn the dances (e.g., the doption from the skeletons) and the music, and in the case of the pointers, the very important designs (the pointers' seals).

Stewart claimed that, with experience, Senoi dream life becomes "more and more like reflective thinking, problem solving, exploration of unknown things or people, emotionally satisfying social intercourse, and the acquiring of knowledge from a dream teacher or spirit guide" (Stewart 1990:201). While that may not be true of the Senoi, that pattern does hold for Converted mourning and other spiritual travel.

Some Converted, when telling me about the spiritual world, became very excited. One said, "It was so real, just like looking with your natural eyes." They understand that it is theoretically (or doctrinally) possible to go there, but when they are finally carried to the spiritual lands, it was always described to me with wonder and, it seemed, a bit of surprise. Like lucid dreamers, the pilgrim is aware of her status as a pilgrim on the journey, asking the proper questions, prepared to say who she is, where she comes from, and who sent her, if asked, prepared if challenged by spiritual beings to give the secret password of her church that the pointer whispered in her ear just as she began her journey. She is aware that her purpose is to learn useful information and skills. Unlike most lucid dreams, a single consciousness continues throughout separate journeys. The pointer frequently sends a pilgrim back to a specific spiritual land to get some spiritual item or bit of knowledge that he knows is there and the pilgrim did not get. Many pilgrims are able to do so. Many, also, are able to travel together to spiritual lands, together experience unique events, and separately describe to me the same event when they return.

Spontaneous Shamanism

Further support that Converted phenomena arise locally rather than from diffusion can be found in the spontaneous creation of shaman-like religions.[5] Monroe (1971; 1985; 1994) provides us, in a clear way, the development of a religion based on nonphysical travel and direct experience of other worlds. In 1958, Monroe began having out-of-body experiences. Eventually these enlarged into travels in an elaborate otherworld landscape. He established the Monroe Institute to study the phenomenon. He trained others to leave their bodies as he did, and they traveled to the same places he described. The Institute eventually began providing workshops and extensive training. By his 1994 book, *Ultimate Journey*, he had to provide an extensive glossary to include the large spiritual landscape he had developed. The places he goes and the experiences he has are similar to shamanic experiences around the world (although he does not acknowledge that). His spiritual landscape and cosmology are taken directly from his experience in a technologically oriented America (although he does not acknowledge that, either). Some of the names of locations in his universe are "H Band," "KT-95," and "(M) Field." He experiences these places as real and makes no allowance that they may not be real. Monroe's is a very Western, very American example of spontaneous mystical experience, influenced solely by his own experiences as a television producer and executive who was middle-aged by the time of his first experience. However, by training others in his experience, by establishing an institute that produces proof and genuine believers, his is a spontaneous shamanism, a shamanic culture passed on to others.[6] His example shows that not only can the experience arise unexpectedly, as it did with him, but that others can be socialized into the experience and that a culture may develop around that experience. In the space of a very short time (30 years), the plan can develop into a complete religion, embracing a whole ontology and cosmology.

Monroe is not the only one. Similar patterns are followed by Silva (1977), whose weekend workshop empire, Silva Mind Control, trains people to engage in a type of (shamanic) behavior based on a spontaneous series of events that happened to him; and by Argüelles (1987; 1988) whose mystical (pseudo)translation of a Mayan Codex led to the 1987 Harmonic Convergence and whose nonphysical travels throughout the universe have enabled him to establish a large following. However, Argüelles does not train others in otherworldly travel. He retains control of the experience and of the power for determining the future.

Anthropologists are not immune to spontaneous shamanism. Harner (1980) and Castaneda (1968; Epstein 1996) come to mind when one thinks of anthropologists creating shamanic cultures. However, they do not represent spontaneous inventions. They both appropriated existing shamanic traditions. Goodman (1990) is a good example of an anthropologist who has developed her own techniques of shamanic travel and has taught them to others. Her experiences are based on her own interaction with spirits and experiments with spiritual travel. Like Monroe, she has established an institute for the study of such matters.

One last author I will consider is anthropologist Hank Wesselman (1995), who periodically inhabits the body of one of his descendants 5000 years in the future. His book is not a novel: Wesselman genuinely experiences what he writes. The book jacket reads, "Without abandoning his scientific objectivity, Dr. Wesselman abandoned himself to the mystical, sometimes frightening, yet always luminous experiences that took him beyond the boundaries of ordinary consciousness." He does the latter, not the former. He accepts what he experiences as the truth and, while using archaeological and some ethnological information to support his experiences, he in no way addresses the fact that the prophecies and worldviews he cites are often incompatible with each other. The prophecies point to a common psychological process, but not to a shared truth. How Wesselman argues that his experiences are true is typical and revealing. He explains to a fellow anthropologist that he knows what he experienced is real and not a figment, because not only did he experience it, but because, since he is perceiving it through his subconscious and the subconscious is noncreative, it cannot lie, and therefore the experience must be the truth (278). Wesselman's proofs are similar to those put forth in the famous exchange between Luther and Zwingli over the nature of the Eucharist. Each man insisted that the Holy Spirit had convinced him that his own interpretation of the scripture was correct. Circular logic does not fail when upheld by sensory and/or social experience (Festinger 1957).

Rather than looking at these people as wacky folks, I think it is important to take seriously the occurrence of highly trained professionals driven by life-changing exotic experience to risk ridicule for the sake of what they perceive as the truth. While Monroe was cautious, as was Silva, the behavior of José Argüelles (a former University of Chicago professor), Felicitas Goodman, and Hank Wesselman show the completely unhinging capability of the mystical experience. Not only will life never be the same again if the sensual reality of the mystical experience is accepted as external reality, but it cannot be. That is especially the case if others verify one's experience with their own (or as their own). In the case of Monroe, others not only left their bodies, but went to the very same places he did. The same with Goodman. In the case of Argüelles, hundreds of thousands of others around the world validated his experience by participation in the Harmonic Convergence (Argüelles 1988).

These people do not have a fault of experience, just of integration. On every basis of every reality that they were ever taught was real in the real world (e.g., "pinch me to see if I'm dreaming"), the other world is experienced as "as real" or "more real" than anything in the physical. "As a matter of psychological fact, mystical states of a well-pronounced and emphatic sort *are* usually authoritative over those who have them. They have been 'there' and 'know.' ... The mystic is, in short *invulnerable*, and must be left, whether we relish it or not, in undisturbed enjoyment of his creed" (James 1982:423–424, emphasis original; cf. Reichel-Dolmatoff 1975:182).

The Converted have had no less of a lifeway affirming (and/or changing) experience. For the professionals noted above, like the Converted, the "real" view of the world that they have requires an urgent message to the world—that it is living on the basis of a lie. Although that may not be a general fear, once it becomes a cognitive possibility, it may be a life-changing one.

Colonial Experience, Vincentian Experience

Even though the capabilities for spiritual travel are shared by people in different parts of the world, the spiritual landscapes, the nature of spiritual beings, and the actions in the spiritual world are shaped by local context.

The Converted go to Africa and India and China, the sources of British colonial labor. They go to the Biblical cities of Jerusalem and Jericho. They also visit more usual shamanic locales such as the bottom of the sea or The Valley of Dry Bones, where skeletons teach them to dance. Each city has one or more flags to represent it that are hung in the church. The Valley of Dry Bones has the same flag as the elemental pirate war standard, the Jolly Roger. It is hard to get more Caribbean than that. In some churches, as a representation of all of the spiritual nations, and called "the flag of the Nations," one finds hanging from the center pole the flag of the British Empire, the Union Jack.

Converted religion is a spiritual reproduction of the Vincentian secular world (cf. Stoller 1995). Every spiritual city has a school, a hospital, a port, a watchman at the gate, a flag, a particular style of dress, and one or more songs. Leaving the others aside for the moment, the (spiritual) school is a British colonial school. It is a Vincentian school. The students sit at desks while the teacher stands at the chalk-board. The teacher may, like the physical teachers, beat unruly children with a leather belt. In the physical setting of the church, so must the pointer, as the teacher of the church, and others in a teaching position in the church, wear a belt and use it for corporal punishment. Each school in each spiritual city has something special to teach the pilgrim traveler.

Not only the school, but everything in the spiritual world is for instruction, for knowledge, for instituting the Converted pilgrim travelers as responsible spiritual workers. On a ship, one may learn how to be a captain (spiritually). In a hospital, one may learn how to be a nurse. In a field, one may learn how to be a shepherd. By the knowledge gained so, a Converted becomes a teacher, a nurse, a warrior, or a captain, and is addressed as such in the congregation—connoting a respect they would be unlikely to obtain in the secular world. The Spiritual Baptists become by name and title police inspectors, corporally punishing teachers, captains of ships. The oppressive structures are not erased in the spiritual world. In the spiritual world, the Converted take control of the structures that rule their daily lives.

Douglas writes (1970:80) of West Indian charismatic sects in England, "On my thesis, it is expected that the London West Indians should favour symbolic forms of inarticulateness and bodily dissociation more than the Londoners with whom they interact. Their religion is not a compensation, but a fair representation of the social reality they experience." Ecstatic religions are fair representations of social reality, but they are also a compensation. Converted religion, like Pentecostal religion, does compensate by putting the poor and powerless in direct contact with the source of power. Converted spiritual reality is also a compensation by being a representation of their social reality, only inverted. They get to experience the other side of Vincentian social life.

Roseman (1984:432) writes that symbolic inversions "which invert, contradict, or negate categorical distinctions—perform an interpretive function, furnishing a framework within which to comment upon or question the accepted order of things." The nature of the Converted spiritual world may also be seen as a sort of moral judgment, Converted people working to "transform their social baggage into gear that suits urgent situational needs" (Beidelman 1986:203).

The work the Converted do inverts their position in colonial society without abrogating the colonial structure. Like other shamanisms, the landscape, actions, and beings in the Converted spiritual world derive from human biology and the historical/cultural environment. The spiritual world is not separate from the physical world. For the Converted, it is a reproduction of the physical world, but one where the Converted are able to vanquish foes and gain access to secret places by use of an all-powerful *pass*. It is one where they can leave any time things get difficult or confusing. Powers denied the Converted in the physical are exercised by them in the Spirit.

Converted Cosmology

CONVERTED RELIGION, LIKE OTHER social fabrications, is a product of its biological, historical, and social environment. In previous chapters, I have detailed the structure of Converted cosmology. In this chapter, I look at specific elements of Converted practice and show how they are products of Vincentian society, itself set in a process of colonial history.

Eliade had a persuasive way of explaining religious processes. He said, "I always compare the world of the religious imagination with that of the poetic imagination. It makes it easier for someone unfamiliar with the domain of religions to enter it" (Eliade 1982:138). Converted cosmology is imaginative in two senses. First, it must be experienced largely in a nonphysical (imaginative) realm. Secondly, it is a charmingly creative (imaginative) reordering of the world. Vincentian Converted religion is ritually made and remade in the setting of the lived experience of continuing Vincentian history.

Pointers' Seals

In the last chapter, I introduced the concept of "natural symbols," those cultural facts that derive from or are operated on the body. They appear in the Converted (shamanic) world as cultural norms that derive from bodily orientations common to all of us. Here I want to emphasize that bodily metaphors may be incorporated as cosmology. The metaphors are perceived as true because they reflect one's bodily experience. Pointers' *seals*—the chalk drawings they use for spiritual effects—are natural symbols that are, additionally, historically derived.

Pointers' seals are one of the main sources of power for the Converted. The power of the seals derives from the method in which they are obtained. They must be received entirely in the Spirit; they may not be learned or borrowed from another pointer. A pointer's seals may be taught to him in a classroom in a spiritual city, or may be seen in a dream, or may appear in the air or on the ground during the church service. They are often revealed by the Holy Spirit as the pointer signs the bands for pilgrims in preparation for mourning. Here, again, the pointer often sees the different seals appearing on the band or in the air before his eyes. Converted seals look similar to the images of the Desana shamans (Reichel-Dolmatoff 1975). They resemble patterns in cave art in Western North America (Hedges 1993). They are also similar to the symbols in the visions of St. Hildegard (e.g., Sölle 1989).

Like the symbols of the saints and shamans listed above, Converted seals most often look like mandalas. The most important Converted seal is the *wheel*. The wheel is a ship's wheel. When a pointer spins a pilgrim, he is spinning her like a ship's wheel, to send her (spiritually) in a different direction (see Gell 1980 on the use of vertigo to initiate altered states). The wheel that is drawn on the pilgrim's bands, on the floor of the church, or on the ground at a crossroads is to keep the person, the people, the place "spinning to different directions." The wheel the pointer draws represents a ship's wheel and looks like one, too, normally consisting of three concentric circles and eight spokes.

Even though Converted seals are supposed to be different for each pointer because the Spirit reveals to each what he wishes them to have, the seals consistently use the same images. Every pointer has a wheel. Every church has a wheel at its center. Some Trinidadian churches in Brooklyn have an actual (physical) brass ship's wheel at the center of the church that is rotated by the captain of the church throughout the service. The Vincentian Converted usually draw their wheel on the ground in chalk, radiating from the center pole. The Vincentian captain must rely on his voice to steer the ship of the church. If a church has no center pole, the wheel is drawn in chalk at the center of the church and a candle is placed in the center of the wheel.

When a pointer signs the bands, he knows what to put on the bands because the Spirit shows him what to put on each one (each set of bands must be made specifically for each pilgrim). While the bands are *sealed* by drawing the designs in chalk, they are *signed* with candle wax. The wax is dripped over the entire length of each band. Signing each band takes five to ten minutes. The pointer must stare at the light of the candle as he signs his bands to be sure that the drips of wax make the appropriate design. One pointer told me that for several days after signing bands he sees spots before his eyes. Nearly everyone has experienced phosphenes (Bednarik 1990:77), things that are "seen" that are within the eye itself (such as the "stars" many people see if they stand up too fast or the spots before one's eyes after staring at a light). The seals are, or derive from, phosphenic patterns on the retina (cf. Reichel-Dolmatoff 1975; Hedges 1993).

The pointer's wheel is the retinal pattern itself. The "bits and pieces" of dancing bones that the pointer sees when he signs the band for the Valley of Dry Bones are fleeting phosphenic impressions. The "tree of life" placed on the band for the city of Zion is the image of the branching blood vessels within the eye. These sorts of

symbols (wheels, trees) are common throughout mystical religions. What is important is not that they are seen, but that to some people they have cultural importance.
If one thinks of the spiritual items the Converted see as hallucinatory activity (e.g.,
Henney 1974), that obscures the cultural reality of the images. The trees and bones
and other images the Converted see are experienced as real events by them. As with
the cave art and other mystical symbols, pointers' seals are the "images of a distinct
reality" (Hedges 1993:689).

Thompson (1984:179–191) notes a convergence of Fon and Ki-Kongo influences
on Haitian art. Some of these are shared by the Converted, most notably the center
pole and the ground drawings (*veves* in Vodou, *seals* in Converted religion). These
same African influences are also found in St. Vincent.

However, both the center pole and the veves (seals) could just as easily be derived
from human physiology. Converted seals are not formulaic as are the veves; they
may only be drawn when one sees them in the Spirit (which further suggests a
phosphenic—or entoptic or eidetic—connection). This is a good example of cultural
selection. The seals (ground drawings) of the African ancestors were retained as
important cultural symbols because of experiential saliency.[1]

Other features of Converted religion are shared by too many cultures for them
to be other than natural symbols, ones connected to a common biology or a common
lived experience. For example, at the shoutings of first-time mourners, most report
as their first vision a great light or a light "brighter than any light I've ever seen."
A great light is expected to be the first thing one sees, as predicted in *The Pilgrim's
Progress* (Bunyan 1979:27). Referring to the widespread appearance of a great light
in religious experiences, Morse (1994:48) wrote, "As far as I am concerned, a bright
light is the sign of a mystical experience" (cf. Kroll and Bachrach 1982; Henman
1986:229).

Although many symbols are based on physiology, the spiritual world must be
continually reexperienced and refashioned. Systems of meaning of all kinds require
"ceaseless imaginative effort by individuals; otherwise, the metaphorical vivacity of
these images becomes atrophied and ineffective" (Beidelman 1986:203).

Historical Symbols

By "historical symbols," I mean those that have cosmological significance that are
taken from cultures separated from the receiving culture by time or space. The two
I consider here are the Converted institutions of the *African warrior* and the *Indian
tribes*. In the absence of written history or a consensus oral history, the historical
attributions I make to these features must be speculative.

In Converted churches in St. Vincent, one of the spiritual gifts one may receive
is that of African warrior. Of singular interest is the tradition that the office may
only be held by a woman. She is known to be "fiery hot" and "cannot sit still" in
the service; she is "always moving around" under the influence of the Spirit. She

may wear a (Converted-style) soldier's uniform, but it is not necessary. By her constant movement, the African warrior is one of the easiest spiritual roles for the observer to detect.

I noted above the likely presence of a Fon (Dahomean) influence in Vincentian (Converted) culture.[2] While it may not be known for certain if the Converted African warrior derived from the Fon, the Fon did have complete divisions of female warriors in their standing army. The institution of female warriors (known in European literature as "the Amazons") was in existence at the time of the slave trade although not formally made part of the Fon army until 1818. The Amazons were the most militant of the Fon warriors and formed "the core" of the Dahomean army (Diamond 1996:177). It was the Amazons, "not the ordinary male conscripts who were systematically steeled against fear in combat, who were trained to razor sharpness, who were taught to die rather than retreat in the King's name" (173–174). Every Converted is a soldier for the Lord. However, only women may be "warriors." Like an echo of the Converted expectations placed on their African warriors, Diamond (ibid., 174) tells us that the Amazons were engaged in "continuous military maneuvers" at the royal court. Not only are Converted warriors expected to be in constant movement, but the Converted churches are often called "courts" (e.g., "the court of St. Michael's").

There is one interesting parallel between the military organization of the Fon and the organization of Converted religion. For the Dahomeans (the Fon), every male office head in the military or in the royal court had its female counterpart or "mother" (Sanday 1981:86). Among the Converted, the same sort of organization prevails (e.g., pointer/pointing mother, leader/mother leadress, assistant pointer/assistant mother). Among the Converted, a woman may head a church as well as a man. But each church must have a father and a mother. They perform different tasks, but what they do varies according to the tradition in each congregation. If a small church lacks one of either a pointing father or a pointing mother, neighboring churches assist in important rituals. Sometimes this is referred to as "borrowing" the individual(s) from the other church.

One possible reason for the retention of a female African warrior (providing it came from the Fon) is that the preservation and expansion of Fon culture was considered a sacred trust to every Fon individual. According to Ross (1978:146), "The sacred duty of the living was to perform the various rites which ensured the perpetuation of the Fon world and to pass on to their descendants, intact, the kingdom which they themselves had inherited from their ancestors."

On the other hand, a ritual female warriorship (contrasting with the Fon active one) existed in other parts of West Africa. Among the Ibibio, who along with the Igbo made up most of the slaves brought to St. Vincent (Collins 1803), a ritual office of female warrior can be found today. It is a possibility that the Converted African warrior is related to the tradition of *dike nwami* (brave woman) among the Ohafia Ibibio—women who "do what men should have done but failed to do; they are driven by circumstances to defy the limits of the feminine role" (McCall 1996:

127). Could this be connected to the subjugation of the Africans by the Europeans and that the female Converted African warrior now militates spiritually the way enslaved male African warriors were unable to do physically? The Converted institution of African warrior may descend from a female role in Africa, or it may have resulted from women in the West Indies taking over an African male role, or it may be a local invention stemming from a vision whose original stipulations were lost except that the role is that of a woman. One further possibility is that it may come from the masquerade bands of Carnival. Abrahams (1970:169) reports that "Warrior" was an office in a "speech band" in Tobago in the 1960s.

The sources of the Indian tribes in the spiritual city of India are easier to trace. It is clear that they are taken from the portrayals of American Indians in film and television. The Indian, appropriately called "Prairie Indian" by Pollack-Eltz (1970: 830), in the Converted spiritual city of India is almost always hostile, attacks in large groups, and lives in the desert. The inhabitants of the spiritual city of India are usually referred to as Indians, but sometimes as "Wild Indians." One Converted person who had been to (the spiritual) India told me, "Apaches is one of the tribes."

However, the American Indian as a symbol has an important history throughout the West Indies. Plays about hostile American Indians have been part of the traditional "Christmas sports" on Nevis since at least the 1930s. Abrahams (1970:174; 1983:14–17) points out that the Nevesian models derive from popular novels and from Hollywood films of the time. Huggins (1978) reports that "Wild Indians" was a traditional Carnival group in the Company Towns in Trinidad (populated by the descendants of American Blacks). Wild Indians carried "a sword called a lance, a shield on the hand, and a crown [made from a] bamboo frame decorated with beads, small mirrors and feathers" (65). The Wild Indian in the West Indies was both a play and a dance in which the Indian fights with White men (Abrahams 1983:16; Mills and Jones-Hendrickson 1984:55–57). In 1968, the "Wild Indian" was one of the traditional characters portrayed during Carnival in St. Vincent (Abrahams 1983: 104). I did not see this at the Carnival I attended in St. Vincent in 1995. But I did see the appearance of "Wild Indian" behavior in almost every Converted church I regularly attended.

The American Indian as a symbol extends even further back in time. Steele (1996) described a dance performed by African descendants in Grenada in the last century that was called "Wild Indians." It is not clear if North American Indians were portrayed, but it is certain that imitation of Amerindians was the goal. The appeal of North American Indians to subject peoples is obvious. The Indians were belligerent, fierce, and proud in their defiance of the colonizing White man. By identification with the Wild Indian (untamed by colonial society), local Black people could symbolically express their dissatisfaction with the colonial order.

The Converted are not alone. Other groups under oppression, like the New Orleans Black Spiritualist Churches, "have incorporated Native Americans, Old Testament characters, and figures from popular culture as part of the churches' hagiography" (Jacobs 1989:65).

Christmas/Carnival

In many ways, Converted religion is a cognate of such groups as the Carnival bands. However, Converted religion offers a permanent alterity. Whereas the Carnival masquerade ends after a short season, the Converted person is reminded daily of her status by the wearing of the headtie. She must always wear her headtie, not only in church, and it is worn by no other women in the island. During Carnival, groups called "bands" performed selections from various classic works, including *The Pilgrim's Progress* and Shakespeare (Abrahams 1983; cf. Fayer and McMurray 1994). The incorporation of John Bunyan's popular work into Converted cosmology likewise may be an extension of the temporary Carnival condition into a permanent state.

Dirks (1987) tells us that of Christmas and Carnival, Christmas was more important in the British West Indies. In St. Vincent, as late as the 1960s, Carnival was considered the children's Christmas—"pickaninny Christmas" (Abrahams 1972). The calendar has been altered now. The government changed Carnival from a two-day event in February or March to a 10-day event in July. At the time of my study, Carnival was the more important event, economically and socially. Vincentians made more money at Carnival and invested more money for Carnival than at Christmas. Vincentians talked about Carnival much more than they talked about Christmas.

However, Christmas in St. Vincent is still of great importance to the local population. There exists in St. Vincent a traditional Christmas celebration called "Nine Mornings" (mysteriously missing from Dirks' [1987] study of Christmas in the British West Indies, and from Abrahams' [1972, 1983] study of Christmas in St. Vincent).[3] Vincentians told me that no other islands celebrate the Nine Mornings. I was told that the tradition began during slavery when the slave owners would go to church on the nine mornings before Christmas. As soon as the White people left, the Black people would have a party.

As it is practiced today, Nine Mornings is a carnival-like party beginning about two or three o'clock in the morning and lasting until shortly after dawn. The partygoers then go to work and repeat the process for each of the nine mornings. Like Carnival, the Nine Mornings is a time of license. A local proverb goes, "Nine Mornings, nine months," because many women get pregnant at that time. Soca and Calypso music, both equated with licentiousness, are played and danced to, but Christmas caroling contests are also held. Because Christmas is seen to be a celebration about Jesus, it is more respectable among Converted and other Christians than is Carnival. Some sort of celebration around the Nine Mornings has been practiced at least since 1820. The slave laws of that year expressly prohibit owners from giving their slaves any time off during the nine days preceding Christmas (St. Vincent 1823:162).

Although his seasonal ecological argument is less valid for the Converted because their activities are relatively aseasonal, Dirks' view of Christmas in the West Indies may provide an explanation for the activities of the Converted. According to Dirks

(1987:xi), Christmas brought normally invisible conflicts into the open. Converted religion makes conflict ritually visible to the initiated in the church service. Outsiders like myself, other anthropologists, and colonial administrators may not see the conflict that is being acted out. Although the conflict was only ritually portrayed, Converted religion was still a threat to colonial society—the Africanness of Converted religion representing a feature that was out of the control of the colonial administrators—and was eventually made illegal. Converted religion may be seen as an extension of the Christmas inversions.[4]

Converted religion is a dramatic, performative, and imaginative response to colonial oppression. One reason it developed on St. Vincent and not elsewhere may be that the Christmas saturnalia lasted 12 days in St. Vincent compared with three days in the other islands. As in the other islands, the Christmas holidays were legislated for three days (Dirks 1987:169), but the slaves in St. Vincent, while working on the previous nine days, would attend parties and celebrations in the predawn hours and then go to work. The work itself was light in the month of December due to the nature of cane cultivation (26).

Converted religion also may be seen as an extension of the Christmas and Carnival festivities during slavery in another way. As Taussig (1982) points out for Afro-Colombians: whereas European religion was imposed on the poor Black workers, religious festivals were under their control. The festivals of the religious calendar implied license to immorality but also license to temporary freedom.

Abrahams and Baumann (1978:195) indicate that festivals of license and disorder do not represent the "antithesis of behavior" in societies such as St. Vincent, where disorder and license prevail throughout the year, but that festivals like Vincentian Carnival are "the antithesis of behavior called for by the *ideal* normative system, which is a very different thing." According to Abrahams and Baumann, Carnival is a time when disorder and order are brought closely together. The Converted ritual inversion is outside of the normative system of St. Vincent; it is a deviant system (as the attitudes of many Vincentians attest). However, like the ritual inversion of Carnival, it does unite order and disorder in the form of the unpredictability of spirit possession and the predictability of the liturgy.

Inversion

At least three things are going on in the Converted experience of the spiritual world: creation, constraint, and inversion. By the creative inspiration of the poetic imagination (Eliade 1982:138), Converted religion is different from other religions in St. Vincent. Yet, cosmological creation is constrained by the experience of the Converted; their daily lived experience is as much a part of the cosmology as the spiritual world. Inversion is a way of addressing the restrictions of colonially structured experience. In other words, the Converted work with what they have to make a vehicle that moves them far from where they are.

Constraints on creation do not mean that people cannot imagine what they have not experienced, only that they are unlikely to do so. The spiritual lands are not considered by the Converted to be different from the physical lands of which they are a counterpart. When Converted people go on spiritual travels about St. Vincent, it is the same St. Vincent they experience in their daily lives. The other spiritual lands should not be expected to be any different than the spiritual aspect of St. Vincent. Frequently, when Converted gave me descriptions of the spiritual cities, information about the individual's experience in the spiritual world was supplemented by material taken from books or television shows. One may travel to the spiritual lands by airplane as well as by ship. Every one of my respondents who did travel in the Spirit on an airplane had been on airplanes in their "carnal" life. One Converted man told me he had been on a rocket ship in the Spirit and had gone to outer space where he saw aliens in their own spacecraft. Although a Vincentian, he had lived most of his life in New York and had had more exposure to such things.

I have already mentioned that Africa, India, and China (the sources of British colonial labor) are part of the spiritual world. However, Europe is not. America is, only inasmuch as Converted have been there physically. America is never visited in the Spirit by people who have not been there. I repeatedly asked if any of the European countries or cities were part of the spiritual world. Most people had never thought that they could not be, but everyone was certain that they had never heard of anyone traveling there. The excision of Europe from the spiritual earth (and especially Great Britain, which has such a strong presence in St. Vincent) is a wonderfully creative inversion. Europeans, who created the world in their own fashion, moving populations hither and yon and drawing the boundaries of Earth in geographically impossible straight lines, are not a part of Converted cosmology. The British, who debated so long about whether or not African slaves should be Christianized and allowed into heaven (and freedom), are denied all spiritual reality in the Converted world.

Converted Cosmology in Vincentian Life

Many things in the spiritual world were presented by my respondents in a frank way, unburdened by mystical language. When I had difficulty understanding the function of the spiritual gift of *matron*, the Converted who had just mentioned it to me said that surely I had been to a hospital. Only by further questioning was I able to learn that matron is a common occupation in British-style hospitals—roughly equivalent to the American "head nurse." It had not occurred to my respondents that hospitals anywhere, carnal or spiritual, would be set up any other way (cf. the discussion about Robert A. Monroe in chapter 8). Most things in the Spirit display this same quality.

Ryle (1988) argues that the emphasis on African elements in Candomblé has obscured the Brazilian nature of the religion. Likewise (and maybe more so), Converted religion is a religion of a uniquely Vincentian nature. Most items in the religion are readily traceable to an immediate event or feature of colonial society.

Nurses, for instance, were a common feature of slave life in St. Vincent (Sheridan 1985:271). Dirks (1987:112) notes that in St. Vincent, "nurses" took care of children beginning two weeks after birth when their mothers returned to work in the fields. Plantation practices did not change during the period of development of the Converted religion (up to the 1850s), and plantation nurses may be related to the custom of Converted nurses remaining with the mourner while the pointing mother and/ or pointing father attend to other things. In any case, people who lived in a society where nurses took care of children would find it natural for spiritual nurses to take care of spiritual children.

The celebration of the nine mornings preceding the birth of Christ has a mirror in the nine days of liminality of the Converted after mourning. The nine-day pattern of both may have had something to do with the ninth-day celebration of a newborn infant noted by Dirks (1987:108–109) for Jamaica and West Africa. The child was not bathed during the nine days nor were wrappings of the umbilicus changed. Similarly, during the nine days following mourning and baptism, the Converted are prohibited from bathing and they cannot remove their bands.

Lane (1988) contends that an American sense of placelessness generated an emotional investment in the creation and discovery of sacred places in American religions (as in, for instance, the Mormon Deseret). It is possible that the difficult access to land during the development of Converted religion (in the postemancipation plantation days) engendered a spiritual investment in spiritual lands to which they could "belong" and in which they had freedom of movement and association. Halifax (1979: 233) writes of myths: "They are the cartographies that give coherence and direction to the people's lives." Well, myths are really just indigenous versions of history. Colonial history becomes the cartography for the Converted.

Conversion to a religion is an acceptance of explanations that fit one's experience and one's "antecedent beliefs" (Proudfoot 1985:102). That is why the Converted are so successful. They already fit into Vincentian culture. Spiritual Baptists comprise a minimum of ten percent of the Vincentian population (St. Vincent 1993:27), although most of my respondents say the percentage is at least twice that. Glazier (1993) estimates Trinidadian Spiritual Baptists at 10,000, and Houk (1995:77) calculates 11,000 out of a Trinidadian population of over one million. If these figures are even close to the actual numbers, they point to the far greater integration of the Converted into Vincentian society compared to the same (or very similar) beliefs in another society in which Spiritual Baptists are less important to the majority of the population.

Other Liberating Cosmologies

Colonialism always requires a metropolitan ego and a colonized alter. Colonial histories (especially British ones) have produced similar societies wherever the hand of

Progress has rested. Fisher (1985:248), who studied mental health in Barbados wrote, "Barbadian history has been hardened into nature, into an immutable self-justifying and self-perpetuating social order." He viewed madness as a way of coping with colonial oppression.

There are other ways. Religion does provide hope for the hopeless. The hope, however, usually comes from the gods introduced by the colonial masters. The Tshidi Zionists of Southern Africa have reacted in a similar way as the Converted to Anglicized Christianity in a colonial setting: "Even while their practice stems from a felt desire to cast off the shackles of domination, their structural predicament condemns them to reproduce the material and symbolic forms of the neocolonial system" (Comaroff 1985:261). The Tshidis, though far away, dress like the Converted, have titles like the Converted, and structure their religion like the Converted. Like the Tshidi Zionists, Converted religion is not merely

> apolitical escapism but an attempt, under pitifully restrained circumstances, to address and redress experiential conflict. Far from being a liminal refuge, the movement was an integral part of the culture of the wider social community, drawing upon a common stock of symbols, commenting upon relations of inequality both local and more global, and communicating its message of defiance beyond its own limited confines. (Comaroff 1985:262).

The Papuan Mansren movement featured a like re-creation of colonial norms (titles, uniforms, organization) in a religious setting (Worsley 1957:140–141). It was not a re-creation in a spiritual world, however, but in the physical only, in preparation for a soon-to-come supernatural restructuring of the world. The Converted, though millenarian like the Pentecostals, are not, like the cargo cults, looking for a speedy earthly end to their troubles. Converted religion is a religion that provides its followers with a way of coping with the troubles of continuing oppression: by denying its eternal validity and providing escapes from the secular oppression by giving access to a spiritual world where the dominant position in the unchanging temporal structures are now occupied by the Converted themselves.

TEN

Comparative History of the Converted Religion

BY THE 1850S, POLICE REPORTS indicate that the Converted religion was established in St. Vincent (Fraser 1995, April 19). It is one of the oldest surviving religions on the island, but it has had to struggle against persecution for most of its history. The religion was outlawed from 1912 to 1965. It was called Shakerism back then, and it still is by some people, but usually derogatorily.

From my first days in St. Vincent I was encouraged to seek out Bishop Sam. He had been imprisoned for Shakerism during the days of prohibition and was widely regarded as an exemplar of the religion. One Sunday, on a visit to a church in the countryside, I did meet Bishop Sam. He was an old man, but strong. When he preached his style was courteous persuasion, and he emanated an almost supernatural sweetness. As I shook his hand, I could feel the whole history of Converted religion in his grip. All together, he seemed to me to be the very embodiment of the Converted religion—both the man and the religion persevering whatever the hardship because of the essential persuasiveness of the spiritual experience and each maturing over the years to become a fixture of Vincentian religious history.

Prohibition

The legal persecution of the Spiritual Baptists in Vincentian history is a symbol of colonial intolerance. In several public speeches during my stay, local politicians blamed the Shakerism Prohibition Ordinance on the colonial White government, but the law remained on the books for 14 years after universal adult suffrage and the beginning of local Black rule. Maintaining the status of the Spiritual Baptists as illegal suited the needs of many in St. Vincent. The colonial attitudes remain among many in the population today. Agitation by the established religions initiated the Shakerism Prohibition Ordinance and their influence kept it in force until 1965, even though efforts had been made to revoke it since the 1930s.

Converted ritual has remained essentially the same since the early 1900s. A police report prepared in 1905 described much the same process that I observed 90 years later. I quote from transcripts of Vincentian historian Dr. Adrian Fraser's radio program, "From Whence We Came," airing on the 20th of April 1995:

> Mr. Griffith's report also contained a description of certain aspects of the Shaker ritual as told to him by Mr. T. W. Clarke, a teacher at the Troumacca Government school. It stated that and I quote: "After hymns and prayers comes the part which is called rejoicing. This consists of songs set to dance music which cause them to shake and jump about in the most awful manner possible. In their frenzied state, they make use of words which indicate the meaning, but which they call the unknown tongue, said to be known and understood by them alone." . . . The acting chief of police ended his report stating that no measures of repression had been used outside of preventing meetings in any of the towns. He felt that great care had to be taken in dealing with it since it was "a matter which has its roots in one of the few distinct hereditary traits of African barbarism which still remains to the black race of St. Vincent." Mr. Griffith then predicted that Shakerism would die a natural death. The general report was prepared in 1905 and, as I have indicated before, its main aim was to set the stage for the making of the practice of the Shaker religion illegal.

The religion was made illegal. The text of the ordinance appears at the end of this chapter. Its wording and the powers granted to the police by its provisions may seem shocking. But we should not forget that laws in most of the world's countries grant the police similarly broad authority in dealing with habits thought to be "pernicious." [1]

In argument for the passage of the law to make Shakerism illegal, the colonial administrator made a speech on July 12, 1912. "The administrator felt that the practices of the Shakers were relics of barbarism and, as he put it, 'a blot on our civilization and a stain on the history of the colony' " (Fraser 1995, April 25). The view that Converted religion is a relic of barbarism is still widely held in St. Vincent. The roots of that attitude can be seen in the history of Christianity in the island.

Christianity in St. Vincent

The first record of Christianity in St. Vincent involves the death of two visiting Jesuits in 1654. They had been on the island less than two weeks and were killed in retaliation for the death of a Carib man who was shot by a French trader (du Tertre 1978:441). A Jesuit missionary was present among the Caribs in St. Vincent, on a more permanent basis, from the latter part of the 17th century (Labat 1970). Gonzales (1991:25) reports that many Caribs had become Catholics from their association with the French. The French had thousands of slaves in St. Vincent before the Treaty of Paris and they may have baptized and instructed their slaves in Catholicism as was the custom in French colonies, but there is no record of this.

Whatever the state of Christianity during the Carib rule of the island, the British, once in possession of St. Vincent, took steps to prevent the Christianization of slaves. Methodist missionaries had been active in St. Vincent from 1787.[2] The House of Assembly in St. Vincent passed a bill in that same year against preaching to negroes, the maximum penalty for an infraction of the ordinance being death. The bill was later overturned by the Crown after a Methodist missionary was arrested and imprisoned. Even after the repeal of the bill, the Vincentian government continued to attempt to restrict the efforts of the missionaries, calling the Methodist doctrines "baneful and pestilent" (Watson 1817:12). The homes and meeting places of the Methodist missionaries were regularly raided and destroyed by local soldiers and planters. Yet, by 1812, St. Vincent had the largest Methodist population in the West Indies after Jamaica: 14 Whites and 2926 Blacks, who all worshipped together. One reason for the persecution of the Methodists may have been that John Wesley "had boldly denounced slavery and the African slave trade on grounds that they were contrary to the will of God" (Morris 1995:33). The apprehension about Methodists and their support of abolition was widespread in the region. A novel published in 1827, *Hamel, the Obeah Man*, featured as its villain a Methodist missionary in Jamaica. In the novel, the immoral Methodist missionary, an obeah man, and a maroon plot the overthrow of the plantation system represented by a gentle, wise planter and his family (*Hamel* 1827).

According to Ferguson (1993), the British just would not believe that conversion did not imply emancipation and thus were adamantly opposed. "The colonial bureaucracy [including the state church] feared that ideas of spiritual equality generated a vocabulary about rights that jeopardized white society" (Ferguson 1993:39). The British opinion contrasted sharply with the view in the French islands, where all slaves were baptized into the Roman Catholic church and slavery was justified by the ability to convert otherwise damned souls (L'abbé Rigord in Schoelcher 1847: 189).

The British were not very active in keeping up their own religion either. There had been an Anglican church on the island, but when it was destroyed in the hurricane of 1780, it was not rebuilt until 1820, with funds from the sale of Carib lands expropriated after the Second Carib War. In 1793, there was not a church building in existence of any denomination in the island, and only one (Anglican) clergyman in the entire island, serving only two of the five parishes. By 1825, the number of church buildings had grown to two, one Anglican and one Methodist.

The revision of the slave laws in 1820 made some religious provisions. As the slaves were no longer to be considered chattel, but were changed in status to real estate, they were required to be baptized by Anglican clergy. They were also exempt from service to their owner from 7 P.M. on Saturday to 4 A.M. on Monday. Presumably, that would have allowed some freedom to attend church. However, Sunday was the slaves' market day and the day they worked their provision grounds.

The Converted people I talked to all said the religion originated during slavery, and some of the practices of the Converted do appear to be referred to by the slave laws. Clause 42 of the Slave Laws of 1820 prohibited any assembly of slaves after the hour of 10 o'clock. The playing or blowing of "drums, horns, and shells" was prohibited at any time by a slave, the owner who permitted such an act getting six-months imprisonment. Clause 45 provided that slaves administering oaths or found at any secret meeting be punished with death or transportation for life. Clause 50 of those slave laws required that "slaves preaching [be] punished" by whipping or imprisonment for preaching or teaching any religious subject.

Some practices from neighboring islands bear a remarkable similarity to Converted practices today, and it is reasonable to assume that they either had a presence in St. Vincent at the same time or were a later influence. Dirks (1987:153) described an obeah ritual bath in Barbados from 1750. Just like the Converted washing ritual, the washer used two basins of water with different kinds of leaves placed in them. As in current Converted practice, the leaves themselves were used to clean the body of the patient. Bell (1970:32) described a dance in Grenada in the 1870s that is identical to the Vincentian Converted "Number One" doption. He wrote that it was only practiced by old "Congo negroes." [3]

Labor practices and the attitudes of plantation owners to laborers remained the same after emancipation, and the disillusionment may have fostered the growth of the Converted. During the 1862 riots in St. Vincent, some of the rioters were connected with a group called the "Wilderness People" who held middle-of-the-night meetings in "prayer-houses" (Marshall 1983:101). If the Wilderness People were not the Converted, then they may have been a precursor to the Converted.

Apart from the Converted, the only denominations operating among Black people in St. Vincent in the 19th century were the Anglicans and the Methodists. Henney (1971:230) wrote, "Shakers say that John and Charles Wesley were the originators of their religion." It is possible that the term "The Converted" originated with Methodism. Dr. Coke referred to Christian slaves in St. Vincent as "the converted negroes" (Coke 1810:269, 283).[4] Converted churches are sometimes known as "praise-houses," but other churches on the island are not. A Methodist missionary resident in St. Vincent in the 1840s reported that each plantation had a "prayers-house" (Moister 1866:319). As well, most Converted today use the Methodist order of worship.

By the twentieth century, Methodists and Presbyterians saw the Converted religion as a threat, as did the Anglican church. The Rev. E. A. Pitt (1955), an anthropologist and Methodist minister in St. Vincent, did not consider the Converted or other Caribbean religions to be Christianity. Others, though, put Methodism and Converted religion on a continuum of spirituality. One of his parishioners told him that she attended communion in the Methodist church, but when she wanted to go to "Higher Heights" she went to the "Shaker" church.

Religious affiliation in St. Vincent has changed dramatically since the Shaker religion was made illegal. In the census of 1911, the four main religions were Anglican, Methodist, Roman Catholic, and Presbyterian. In, 1991, the four main religions were Anglican, Methodist, Pentecostal, and Spiritual Baptist, with Roman

Catholics making a close fifth (St. Vincent 1993:14). From 1911 to 1991, the numbers of Presbyterians fell from 1033 to 120, while the population rose from 41,000 to 106,000. Cox (1994:209) put the number of Shakers (Converted) in St. Vincent at 400 in 1911, but in the 1991 census, 10,264 people identified themselves as Spiritual Baptist (St. Vincent 1993:6).

For 53 years, until 1965, the Converted religion was illegal. The first Converted denomination, known as the Organization, was incorporated in 1978 (Spiritual Baptist Organization of Saint Vincent Incorporation Act 1978). In 1983, the Archdiocese denomination was incorporated: Archbishop and Primate (Spiritual Baptist) of St.Vincent and the Grenadines Incorporation Act. These two denominations cover one third to one half of the current Converted churches. The remainder are "unregistered."

Although many of the various religious denominations in St. Vincent had been around for a while before they were incorporated, in recent years groups have incorporated shortly after entering the island. Dates of incorporation of some of the churches are able to give us an idea of when the religions came to St. Vincent. A few, like the Salvation Army (since 1905) have never incorporated. The Anglican church was incorporated in 1926. The Seventh-Day Adventists had a presence in the island since 1903 and were incorporated in 1938. After 1938, no churches were incorporated until 1966 when two Pentecostal-type groups (Streams of Power and the Evangelical Church of the West Indies) were incorporated. Next came the Apostolic Faith Mission (a Pentecostal body) in 1976. Then two more Pentecostal bodies and one fundamentalist (Church of Christ). The next church to be incorporated was the Spiritual Baptist Organization in 1978.

From 1978 to 1983, when the Spiritual Baptist Archdiocese was formalized, 11 churches were incorporated, only two of which were not Pentecostal-type churches. From 1984 through 1995, 15 more churches were incorporated in St. Vincent, seven of which were Pentecostalist. In the whole history of the island up to the first Spiritual Baptist denomination in 1978, there were only eight churches incorporated (plus three more that were already recognized: Methodists, Roman Catholics, and Gospel Hall). In the past 20 years, 30 churches have been incorporated, most of them with no presence on the island before the very recent past. Of these, competing in ecstatic worship with the Spiritual Baptists, 19 are Pentecostalist bodies. Before I looked at these figures, I had difficulty understanding the frequent, almost daily, distancing the Spiritual Baptists make from the Pentecostals. They say, "Just because you do [this or that trait common to Converted and Pentecostals] doesn't make you a Pentecostal." Pentecostals compete with Spiritual Baptists for membership and are a threat. By sharing some traits with the Spritual Baptists, Pentecostals are also a threat to the Converted sense of a unique Christian identity.[5]

Gullick, however, calls the Shakers a "Pentecostalist sect" (1985:20). Apparently, the Spiritual Baptists in some parts of the island were also called "Jumpers" by their detractors (Stone 1973:151). Other names Vincentians use to refer to the Converted are "Tieheads," "Clap Hands," the "barefoot religion" and the "candlelight religion." These are impolite terms, but not as impolite as "Shaker." [6] When speaking politely, Vincentians usually say "the Converted" (or "Converted people"). The Converted refer to themselves as Spiritual Baptists, Converted, Believers, or the Penitent, but most often as "the Baptists."

This last name has aroused the vituperative attention of the Southern Baptists, who feel that the term "Baptist" should apply only to them, even though the first Southern Baptist missionaries did not enter St. Vincent until 1976 (Hazell 1994:61–62, 66–67). In the 1990s, a campaign was launched to distance Southern Baptists from Spiritual Baptists—the "Baptist Identity Campaign." Many Spiritual Baptists, rather than being affected by these efforts, view the Southern Baptists as failed imitators of the Spiritual Baptists.

Twenty-four different North American Protestant bodies are active as missionaries in the Windward Islands (Hazell 1994, 61). The Christian missionary endeavor often appears as a contemptuous patronization or "compassion as contempt" (Bruckner 1986); that is, an invidious sort of Eurocentrism (or Euro-Americo-centrism) exemplified by the Peace Corps in St. Vincent as well as the North American missionary groups. The goal of the Christian and government missionaries is to make the people of St. Vincent like themselves. The contempt that the messengers of enlightenment feel for the locals is unmistakable. An experienced Peace Corps worker in St. Vincent told me with some exasperation, "We're trying to teach them to be on time." Some of the groups are able to gain adherents because of the attraction of gifts of money, food, or clothes. For example, I was told by a group of Mormon missionaries in St. Vincent, "They want our clothes and our food, but they don't want to stay in the church." The Mormons also told me that they have had several hundred converts in the past 20 years, but they had to excommunicate most of them for "immorality."

In the history of Christianity on St. Vincent, Black people were first told they were incapable of being Christians. From 1820, they were forced to be Christians (to be baptized in the Anglican Church). After 1912, they were told they could be any kind of Christian except for their one indigenous Vincentian type. The fact that Converted distance themselves from Southern Baptists and Pentecostals is an assertion of their own (Black Vincentian) worth in the face of the same sort of (White) European- and American-centered conversion efforts Vincentians have faced since the slave laws of 1820.

Persecution

The Shakerism Prohibition Ordinance was not an idle law. The police did enforce it. Converted religion today is a loud, colorful, visible presence in St. Vincent. People who remembered the days of prohibition told me the practice was very different before 1965. They said that the Converted sang very softly, were unable to use the bell, and had to hold meetings in the woods or in a swamp. Mourning was done in one's own bedroom. Banning was performed by a pointer or pointing mother alone; church members seldom assisted. If the police heard any singing at all, I was told, they would break in and arrest all present. The Shakerism Prohibition Ordinance gave them this right. The usual sentence was three months, but the law provided for six months of hard labor at the judge's discretion.

Edward Cox (1994) describes several prosecutions for Shakerism in the first year of the ordinance but the official police report for 1913 does not list any (St. Vincent 1913). The Report of the Chief of Police for the year 1916–1917 recorded 19 people convicted of Shakerism, 6 cases dismissed, and 28 cases withdrawn (St. Vincent 1917). After that year, the format of the annual police reports (the ones that were sent to London and could be viewed by those authorities who might disapprove of the infringement of religious rights) was changed and it cannot be determined from them how many Shakers were arrested or convicted. The arrests and imprisonment continued in spite of official subterfuge. Cox suggests that between 1914 and 1920, colonial administrators concealed prosecutions of Shakers because they wanted to show the effectiveness of the law in eliminating the practice of Shakerism from St. Vincent.

According to Cox, between 1923 and 1935, court action against Shakers ranged from zero convictions up to 35 per year, whereas prosecutions ranged from none to 94. These figures show that many Converted people were willing to attend the meetings but denied their affiliation with the religion in court. In St. Vincent today, many Converted are reluctant to disclose their religion, preferring instead, when asked, to name the denomination in which they were christened as an infant. Cox indicates that after 1935 government prosecution eased, but Converted individuals told me that persecution was heavy right up to universal adult suffrage—the granting of the franchise to poor people in 1951. Converted pastors and pointers were denied marriage officer licenses and marching permits until after the 1965 repeal (Fraser 1995, May 22). Cox (1994:235) concludes that the authorities misunderstood the nature of the religion, that Shakerism "was drawing on a distinctly Caribbean folk tradition to alleviate problems generated by an outmoded political, economic, and social system." The religion still does.

The prohibition and persecution of the Converted religion was upheld by popular opinion throughout the existence of the Shakerism Prohibition Ordinance. "The law itself reflected the contempt in which the colonial authorities and the planter class held the black population" (Ryan and Williams n.d.:33). In April 1939, George McIntosh, a champion of the poor, tried to get the ordinance repealed, but the administration was set against it because "the leaders of the recognized churches were up in arms" (John 1979:12). McIntosh said that the ordinance was a "deliberate attempt to impose hardship on the Shakers, merely because they were poor" (12). Finally, the repeal of the Shaker prohibition passed the parliament on May 25, 1965. A law preventing freedom of religion was seen as incompatible with the colony's approaching independence.

Comparison with Trinidadian Spiritual Baptists

Trinidadian Spiritual Baptists have had an important effect on Vincentian Converted practice and identity. Sometime in the early 1900s, Vincentian migrants had carried the religion to Trinidad, where it acquired the name Spiritual Baptist, altering in the process. When the Converted were struggling against their prohibition, a Trinidadian Spiritual Baptist denomination, the West Indian United Order of Spiritual Baptists, held a large service in St. Vincent in 1952 which several hundred Converted attended. Like their Vincentian counterparts, the Trinidadian Spiritual Baptists had been illegal from 1917 under the Shouters Prohibition Ordinance.[7] The law was repealed in Trinidad on March 30, 1951. As a legal religious body, the Trinidadian Spiritual Baptists were allowed to conduct the service while the illegal Vincentian Converted were not. Converted in St. Vincent began calling themselves Spiritual Baptists about that time (although many Vincentians still do not use that name).

The Vincentian Converted and the Trinidadian Spiritual Baptists are different in many ways. However, the Trinidadian influence is so strong in the recognized Spiritual Baptist denominations in St. Vincent that even though the Converted were not made legal until 1965, they celebrate their National Spiritual Baptist Day (or Spiritual Baptist Emancipation Day) from the Trinidadian date. On May 21, 1995, I attended a celebration in honor of the 45th anniversary of the legalization of the religion in St. Vincent and the Grenadines.[8]

The Trinidadian Spiritual Baptists are affected by the Vincentian Converted as well. The Trinidadian Shouters Prohibition Ordinance of 1917 was patterned on the Vincentian Shakerism Prohibition Ordinance. Debates in the Trinidadian legislature regarding the law expressly linked the religion to St. Vincent (Herskovits and Herskovits 1947:343). As late as the 1970s, individual Spiritual Baptists in Trinidad indicated that the religion came to Trinidad from St. Vincent (Parks 1981:24). As well, migration from St. Vincent to Trinidad continues to the present time, including some Converted in the count.

However, St. Vincent has negative connotations in Trinidad (Basch 1987:189). By the time of my study, Trinidadian Spiritual Baptists I met in Brooklyn found it important to distance the (now positive) religion from St. Vincent. A Trinidadian bishop in Brooklyn said that the religion has its roots in West African Aladura, which came to Trinidad with Yoruban laborers in the nineteenth century. Thomas (1987) also lists a Yoruban origin. Eric Williams (1962:39) claimed they "have come to Trinidad straight from Africa." The Trinidadian "Archbishop Raymond Oba Douglas, D. D. in his book 'The Bible and the Spiritual Baptist Church' claims that the Spiritual Baptist Faith, also called 'Shouters' existed thousands of years before the advent of Jesus Christ" (Hackshaw 1992:14). Hackshaw holds to a Trinidadian origin (79) as does Jacobs (1996). Glazier (1984:153, fn. 1) allows that the Spiritual Baptists originated in St. Vincent and extended to Trinidad and Tobago around 1900. However, he writes that "their origins go back to missionary efforts on the part of North American Baptists who proselytized in the Caribbean region"

(153, fn. 1, translation mine).[9] Mervyn Williams (1985:27), Pollack-Eltz (1972:141), and M. G. Smith (1962:10) agree with him. I have been unable to find any evidence of American Baptist missionary activity in St. Vincent until the arrival of the Southern Baptists in 1976, but it is certain that Trinidadian Spiritual Baptists prefer an American or African origin to that of denigrated and backward St. Vincent. The prevailing view among Trinidadians, St. Lucians, and Grenadians I met was that nothing good can come from St. Vincent, the poorest country in the Eastern Caribbean. When the religion was bad and a symbol of barbarism, it was said to come from St. Vincent to encourage its prohibition. Now that the religion is a source of indigenous pride, it cannot be conceived by those on neighboring islands to have come from inferior St. Vincent.

Differences between the practices of Trinidadian and Vincentian Spiritual Baptists are discussed at length in chapter 12. The main differences are that the Trinidadians rely more on visual symbols (e.g., steel swords, brass snakes, statues of saints, etc.) and borrow more from other Trinidadian religions, especially Shango (Orisha) and Hinduism (see Glazier 1985c; Houk 1995).[10] Some Trinidadian practices are found in St. Vincent—for instance, the use of the Hindu *lota* (see chapter 3). It also may be true that the Vincentian Converted did not practice baptism by immersion before contact with Trinidadians as Hackshaw (1992:82) claims, even though immersion is now a central tenet of the faith. I asked an older Converted mother if it was possible that the Converted did not practice baptism at the turn of the century. She said it might be true because she remembered a pointer in his 80s some 30 years before who said that he had never been baptized and that he had to do so before he died.

Some practices of the Trinidadian Spiritual Baptists appear to be nearly opposite to Vincentian Converted practices. Goldwasser (1996:162) described a Spiritual Baptist leader in Trinidad who interpreted mourners' visions by the use of books, astrology, and numerology. This sort of thing was seldom mentioned among my respondents, but when I brought it up, it was roundly denounced as indicating someone who did not know what he was doing in the Spirit and who should not be pointing souls. I was told the pointer who got his knowledge from books rather than from the Spirit could do damage to his mourners. Goldwasser (1996:161) as well as Simpson (1966:544) indicate that "signing" of bands and "sealing" of bands mean, respectively, writing the designs in chalk and dripping wax on the cloth. This is exactly reversed from the meaning in St. Vincent. I had always associated the word "sealing" with wax and the meanings of the Converted terms *sealing* and *signing* were something I verified numerous times. Furthermore, many of the Trinidadian meanings and usages of terms seem to be more common-sensical than the Vincentian meanings. For instance, Trinidadians in Brooklyn often refer to doption as "adoption" (cf. Simpson 1966:542). The Trinidadian Spiritual Baptist use of the terms "pilgrimage" and "mission" seems to agree with the usual standard English usage (Glazier 1988; 1992), while in St. Vincent a pilgrimage is more or less just a trip and a mission is merely something one is sent to do.

Despite the differences, the Converted feel themselves to be the same denomination as the Trinidadian Spiritual Baptists. Most of the differences are minor and appear to have become exaggerated over time, especially as the Spiritual Baptist religion in Trinidad has become more affected by Shango and other religions. The descriptions of the Shouters the Herskovitses studied in the 1930s as well as Lovelace's (1982) fictional account of Trinidadian Shouters of the same period seem nearly identical to current Vincentian Converted practice.

One thing that sets Spiritual Baptists apart from other religions, both in St. Vincent and in Trinidad, is the importance of each member to the group. The observation of Herskovits still holds:

> When the Shouters are compared to other groups in Toco, they are equated not so much with churches as with 'orders,' and they are often referred to as a lodge . . . some of the more obvious reasons being the internal organization, the intense feeling of unity . . . the canons of mutual aid, the discipline, the ritual handshake, and the ways in which at funerals of adherents, the group takes charge. (Herskovits 1966:329)

Comparison with Other Caribbean Religions

There are African survivals in Caribbean religions to be sure, just as there are Saxon survivals in American culture or Roman Catholic survivals in the Pentecostal religion. The African nature of the religions should not be highlighted to the point of obscuring the Caribbean nature of the religions (cf. Glazier 1983:xvii; Raboteau 1995:154).[11] In this section, I mention selected elements of various religions in the Caribbean that match up with Converted practices. The similarity may be due to a common African origin, a shared colonial history, or merely human experience. As Chevannes (1978) notes of the spiritual journey in Jamaican Revivalism:

> The concept of a journey in the course of which one struggles with and overcomes evil in the final analysis owes its origins to a view of the world which is determined by man's struggles against nature and by the historical limitations on man's contacts outside his social grouping. The dangers from these include both known and unknown, a river to cross, a cross-road, a "strange and foreign land." (14)

The two groups who bear the strongest resemblance to Spiritual Baptists outside of the Windward Islands are the Revivalists of Jamaica (Revival, Revival Zion, Pukkumina) and the Jordanites of Guyana (cf. Bryce-Laporte 1970; cf. Barrett 1974: 116–124). I mentioned above the probable connection between Kongo religion, Pukkumina labouring, and Converted doption. Although Revival Zion churches also practice labouring, only to the Pukkumina adherents does it signify travel in a spiritual landscape. It is slightly possible that a direct connection exists between Pukkumina and Converted religion. After the eruption of the Soufriere volcano in St. Vincent in 1902, some of the people from the devastated region (the area of highest

Converted concentration) were resettled in Jamaica (Nanton 1983:225). Morrish (1982:52) claims that Pukkumina (or Pocomania) began in Jamaica in the 1920s.

Revivalist offices are similar in name to Converted offices: shepherd, captain, father, wheeling shepherd, warrior shepherd, hunting shepherd, rambling shepherd, cutting shepherd, mother shepherdess, queen-dove, bible-pointer (Morrish 1982:57; cf. Simpson 1956). Beckwith studied the Revivalists in the 1920s. She wrote, "The women (called *mesdames*) dress in white and carry wands. They march, sing and pray in the streets at night. They hold their service about a table with a white cloth on which they set a glass of water, flowers and a Bible" (Beckwith 1923:32). Like the Converted, they practice baptism by immersion, Holy Spirit possession, and wear turbans and long garments. The Jordanites of Guyana similarly baptize and become filled with the Holy Spirit, have special garments, and wear turbans and headties (Bisnauth 1989:183–184).

Haitian Vodou also resembles Converted religion. In the previous chapter, I discussed the connection between the Converted center pole and the Haitian *poteau-mitan* and between the *veves* and the Converted seals. The two religions correspond in other ways as well. Converted flags are similar to some of the Vodou flags of the early part of the twentieth century (Polk 1995:326). Like mourning, the *kanzo* (ritual seclusion) is the "core" of the initiation into Vodou priesthood (K. Brown 1991:76; Bourguignon 1970), although it must be said that seclusion is common as part of initiation rites throughout the world. The feelings of discomfort and spatial and temporal disorientation described by Planson (1974:157–175) of his own *kanzo* are similar to the descriptions Converted give of mourning. Like the Converted, Vodou initiates spiritually travel to other lands, including Africa and *Nan Ginin* under the sea (Planson 1974:167; Laguerre 1980:183). The Haitian *Lavilokan* is described by Cosentino (1996) as a spiritual city—the City of Camps—whose representations may be found throughout Vodou and Haitian society. Similarly, the visitors to the numerous Converted spiritual cities are commanded by God to make, hold, and operate artifacts related to the cities they have visited. More than souvenirs, among the Converted these flags, uniforms, and tools are emblems of citizenship.

Converted religion and Vodou are responses to similar structural instruments. Vodou ceremonies, like Converted rituals, always begin with a standard prolog—Catholic for Vodou, Methodist for the Converted. For both, the words to sacred songs act as canonical scripture (Laguerre 1980).

The parallels, however, diverge when it comes to the nature of the gods and the spiritual world. Like most religions in the African diaspora, Vodou emphasizes the manifested presence of the spirits in the physical world at the service. Converted religion, however, emphasizes the presence of the worshippers in the spiritual world (although spirits coming and believers going occurs in both religions). In Vodou, each *loa* has its own drum beat that accompanies the approach of the loa to the setting of the ceremony. Each spiritual city of the Converted has its own beat that attends and assists the arrival of the travelers, in doption, to each location in the spiritual world. Likewise, in Vodou, the gods express "colonial social roles," for example general, admiral, baron (Cosentino 1995:33), whereas the Converted attain the colonial positions in their own (spiritual) right. The separate paths of Vodou and Converted religion owe something to the different histories of the nations with which they are identified.

All religions in the Caribbean share a colonial past and European as well as African influences. Similarities between the religions on different islands should not be seen as deriving from a single tradition. The culture in each island made of its own history the religions found there. There is a native sense of this fact. In Brooklyn, I described the Converted to a Haitian woman. She replied, "Each island practices its Vodou in its own way."

Indian Shaker Religion

Throughout the text, I have stressed the origin of Converted religion as a response to the colonial structures in which poor Vincentians found themselves. I would like to emphasize here one religion with which the Converted have very little historical connection, but with which they share a strong structural similarity. These are the Shakers of the Northwest Coast.

The Converted were called Shakers by their opponents, as were the Shakers of the Northwest Coast and the American Shakers originating in England. All three were named Shakers by others, and although they may have preferred other names, Shaker is the one that persisted. The Shakers (all three groups) were so called by their detractors because of their Holy Spirit possession behavior that could be described as shaking. In 1912, in encouragement of the prohibition of the Converted religion, the Presbyterian minister Dr. McPhail gave a lecture on the origins of Shakerism, asserting that the Shaker religion in St. Vincent was the very one begun by Mother Ann Lee in England in the 1770s and that was later established in the American Northeast (Fraser 1995, April 26). Several writers have taken care to establish that the Converted of St. Vincent are not related to the Shakers in America (Gullick 1971:8; Henney 1974:23; Houk 1995:73; V. Young 1993:162; Cox 1994: 236). However, the practices of the Converted bear such strong similarity to the Shakers of the Northwest that one cannot fail to notice.

The Indian Shaker Church was founded in the nineteenth century by a Coast Salish man, John Slocum, who experienced a sudden and terrible illness.[12] He said that he died, that he traveled in a spiritual landscape, and that God brought him back to life. When he returned, he began a church. One of the purposes of the religion was healing, and one thing that set the Shakers apart from Salish shamans was that all in the church worked together to effect a cure. However, like the practices of the Converted, the Indian Shaker practices imply a type of shamanism on their own (Smith 1954).

The symbol of the Shakers is a flag that has on it the images of a cross, a candle, and a hand bell. Like the Converted, curing involves shaking and spinning, bells rung over the body, and prayers said while holding candles in the hand. Conversion involves brushing and spinning of the candidates. They believe in the travel of the soul and in spirit helpers. The Indian Shakers have two kinds of songs, "In one there are no words, but only nonsense syllables" (Barnett 1957:236). Like the Converted, they wear a special uniform called a "garment." They raise their right hands when they pray. They also practice a ritual handshake at several times in the service. They said that "everyone should shake hands with fellow members when they met inside the church and before they left it, for the church, like heaven, was a different place from the outside world" (230). Like the Vincentian religion formerly known as Shakerism, the Indian Shaker church has flourished in its region.

When similarities are detected among groups that have a phylogenetic connection, as in the Caribbean examples just illustrated, they are often assumed to be related by diffusion and cultural survivals. When groups have little or no historical connection, structural similarities must be related to similarities in biology or in a common lived experience. The two groups of Shakers (the Spiritual Baptists of St. Vincent and the Indian Shaker Church) share subjugation under colonialism.

The Text of the Shakerism Prohibition Ordinance

AN ORDINANCE TO RENDER ILLEGAL THE PRACTICES OF
"SHAKERISM"
AS INDULGED IN IN THE COLONY OF ST. VINCENT.
Ordinance No. 13 of 1912.
(1st October, 1912.)

WHEREAS there has grown up a custom amongst a certain ignorant section of the inhabitants of the Colony of St. Vincent of attending or frequenting meetings from time to time at houses and places where practices are indulged in which tend to exercise a pernicious and demoralizing effect upon the said inhabitants, and which practices are commonly known as "Shakerism";

AND WHEREAS it is expedient in the best interests of the said Colony of St. Vincent and its inhabitants that such meetings and practices should not be permitted.

1. This Ordinance may be cited as the "Shakerism" Prohibition Ordinance.

2. In this Ordinance:—

"Shakers meeting" shall mean a meeting or gathering of two or more persons, whether indoors or in the open air at which the customs and practices of Shakerism are indulged in. The decision of any Magistrate in any case brought under this Ordinance as to whether the customs and practices are Shakerism, shall be final.

"Shakers house" shall mean any house or building, or room in any house or building which is used for the purpose of holding Shakers meetings, or any house or building, or room in any house or building, which is used for the purpose of initiating any person into the ceremonies of Shakerism. The decision of any Magistrate in any case brought under this Ordinance as to whether a house or building, or room in any house or building, is a Shakers house shall be final.

"Manager" shall include Town Wardens and any person having control or charge of any land whatsoever in the Colony.

3. It shall be an offence against this Ordinance for any person to hold or to take part in or to attend any Shakers meeting, or for any Shakers meeting to be held in any part of the Colony, indoors or in the open air, at any time of the day or night.

4. It shall be an offence against this Ordinance to erect or to maintain any Shakers house, or to shut up any person in any Shakers house, for the purpose of initiating such person into the ceremonies of Shakerism.

5. (1) If it shall come to the knowledge of the owner or manager of any estate or land in the Colony that a Shakers house is being erected or maintained, or that Shakers meetings are being held on the estate or land over which such owner or manager has control, he shall forthwith notify the Chief of Police of the erection or maintenance of such Shakers house, or of the locality, or place at which such Shakers meetings are being held.

(2) The manager or owner of any estate or land in the Colony who fails so to notify the Chief of Police, or who knowingly permits the erection or maintenance of any Shakers house, or the holding of Shakers meetings, on any estate or land over which he has control, shall be guilty of an offence against this Ordinance.

6. It shall be an offence against this Ordinance for any person at or in the vicinity of any Shakers meeting to commit, or to cause to be committed, or to induce or to persuade to be committed, any act of indecency or immorality.

7. (1) It shall be lawful for any party of police, of whom one shall be a commissioned or non-commissioned officer, without a warrant, to enter at any time of the day or night any house or place in which such commissioned or non-commissioned officer may have good ground to believe or suspect that any person or persons is or are being kept for the purpose of initiation into the ceremonies of Shakerism, and to take the names and addresses of all persons present at such Shakers meeting or Shakers house.

(2) It shall also be lawful for any commissioned or non-commissioned officer of police, or for any police or rural constable, to demand the names and addresses of any persons taking part in any meeting in the open air, which he has good reason to believe is a Shakers meeting.

(3) Any person refusing to give his name and address to any commissioned or non-commissioned officer of police, or police or rural constable, when asked to do so under the authority of this section, shall be liable to be

arrested and to be detained at the nearest police station until his identity can be established.

8. Any person guilty of an offence against this Ordinance, shall be liable, on summary conviction, to a fine not exceeding fifty pounds, and in default of payment thereof, to imprisonment with or without hard labour for a term not exceeding six months.

ELEVEN

Going to Brooklyn

BROOKLYN IS A LONG WAY FROM St. Vincent. But it appears in the conversation of Vincentians almost daily. Not only because their relatives may live there, but it is the source of fashion, and music, and money. "I thought the streets were paved with gold," more than one Vincentian told me in Brooklyn. Hardship was found at the end of those streets for most of my respondents. But money too, and so they stayed. Migrants to the United States from many countries have the same story. Vincentians, like the others, continue to be attracted to Brooklyn, and they continue to go.

This chapter looks at the core of Vincentian Converted religion by contrasting it (and looking at how it contrasts itself) with other religions in New York. The close contact with like religions in Brooklyn forces a self-definition that is not required in St. Vincent, where the religion is readily defined by its social context.

Henney (1971:219; 1974:23), who studied the Vincentian Spiritual Baptists, described them as a form of fundamentalist Christianity. Glazier (1983:4; 1992:143), who has written more than anyone else about the religion, identified the beliefs of the Spiritual Baptists in Trinidad as polytheistic. While these two views seem irreconcilable, they do in fact reflect the wide variation that occurs in Spiritual Baptist belief and practice.

This chapter examines what happens when the (more) fundamentalist Vincentian Converted meet up with the (more) polytheistic Trinidadian (and other) Spiritual Baptists in Brooklyn, New York. Trinidadians and Vincentians and people from every Caribbean nation have migrated to Brooklyn. Converted practices in New York change in response to contact with others. Beside religions from the Caribbean, the Converted also have interaction with American churches in Brooklyn, who present further inducements to change.

Vincentians abroad remain in close communication with the home island and maintain a Vincentian identity by a variety of means; St. Vincent is prototypically transnational (Basch, Shiller, and Blanc 1994). As we saw in chapter 1, the history of St. Vincent has been characterized by massive migration (voluntary or involuntary), into and out of, from its first settlement. The British imported scores of thousands of slaves from Africa. They also deported thousands of Garifuna to Central America. After emancipation, many former slaves began migrating to Trinidad and Guyana where wages were higher than in St. Vincent. That pattern continued into the twentieth century with Aruba, Panama, and Trinidad, and then London, Canada, and the United States as the major destinations. Since the 1830s, Trinidad has persistently drawn Vincentian workers. In chapter 10, we saw some ways the relationship between Trinidad and St. Vincent influenced the interaction between Spiritual Baptists in the two islands. A similar relationship holds in New York.

Converted in New York

Population movement under colonialism (that is, by the slave trade and indenture) is a chief historical factor in the development of Caribbean cultures. Currently as well, migration is the major factor in the creation of societal norms in the Caribbean. Not only are Vincentians part of the larger African diaspora, but they sometimes refer to the dispersal of Vincentians to other parts of the world as a "Vincentian diaspora." At least one-seventh of the entire Vincentian population lives outside of St. Vincent (North and Whitehead 1990:5).[1] An important focus of the Vincentian diaspora is Brooklyn, New York. Vincentians have lived in New York at least since the early 1900s, some going to the United States after working on the Panama Canal. It is estimated there were about 5000 Vincentians living in New York City in 1980 (Basch, Shiller, and Blanc 1994:56). By 1996, the number had certainly increased, including large numbers of illegal immigrants and long-term visitors from St. Vincent. A Vincentian reporter I interviewed, who had lived most of his life in Brooklyn before returning to St. Vincent in 1995, estimated the number of Vincentians resident in Brooklyn at 40,000. The Vincentians I checked with in Brooklyn agree with the 40,000 number—if American-born children of Vincentians are included in the total.

According to Gearing (1992:1279), two factors tend to push people out of St. Vincent: the colonial preference for all things foreign over things Vincentian and emigration as the "preferred response of the Vincentian people to harsh economic conditions and political control." The pressures for emigration from St. Vincent are increasing. To look at only one factor, unemployment in St. Vincent rose gradually from 13.5 percent in 1960, 13.8 percent in 1970, 23 percent in 1980, to 44 percent in 1990, and 52 percent in 1995. The outmigration further affects the economy of St. Vincent. Because of the emigration of skilled and semiskilled health workers (the most common job for a Vincentian in New York is "home attendance," taking care of bedridden people), St. Vincent has suffered a decrease in its ability to provide adequate health care.

In New York, there are between 400 and 800 Vincentian Converted.[2] The percentage of Converted among Vincentians in New York is probably around 3 percent. In St. Vincent, the ratio of Converted to the larger population is a minimum of 10 percent. Nearly everyone I talked to in St. Vincent, from a Roman Catholic priest to ministers in government, told me that there are far more Converted than are reported in government records. The reason for the lower rate of Converted among Vincentians in New York is simple. Converted religion is a religion of the poor. Vincentians who travel abroad, especially to America, tend to be those with the most money and the most contacts. They are not the poorest in the island.

This factor affects the congregational makeup of the Converted in Brooklyn. Converted in New York are better off financially than those in St. Vincent; they can afford to mourn more often and receive more spiritual gifts. In St. Vincent, many Converted told me they had a call from the Spirit to mourn, but that they could not afford either the time or, more often, the price for candles and food for two weeks of mourning. Many put off mourning for over a year while they found the resources. Consequently, there is a higher number of mothers, teachers, and pointers in the Brooklyn Converted churches compared to those in St. Vincent. (On the other hand, despite the generally higher spiritual status of Converted in Brooklyn, once in America, whether as home attendants, as nannies, or as housekeepers, they are often servants to Whites [cf. Silvera 1989].)

There is a focal point to Vincentian identity, in New York for Converted and non-Converted, and it lies in St. Vincent. Converted churches are a symbol and a reproduction of that core in the alien place. The fact that many of the Converted in Brooklyn joined the faith only after moving to Brooklyn may be an expression of that feeling—of the need for a connection with home. Chaney (1987:4) writes that "Caribbean migrants do not appear to leave their homelands definitely, even though they may never return except for visits. Their insertion in New York City retains a provisional quality."

In a way, all of Spiritual Baptist locality is provisional. This stems from the frequent relocation of meeting places necessitated by (former) state persecution, the requirement that spiritual work must often be done in people's houses (e.g., wakes), and the spiritual emphasis of the religion (the physical world is not as important as the spiritual world). As Glazier (1992:143) indicates for other Spiritual Baptists, it is the presence of the Converted that makes the site sacred. They carry the sacredness with them. The site is far less important than the fact that the Converted are there. As an example of this, every service, whether in the church, at a home, in the market square or beside the road, requires a fresh consecration of the ritual space.

The provisional quality of Vincentian life in New York can be detected in a typical Converted service in Brooklyn.[3] The church is usually in a basement or a storefront. The service begins with the *consecration*, or *surveying*. It accomplishes the same end as physical surveying, establishing boundaries, in this case, of a sacred space. While the congregation sings a hymn, designated members proceed to the four corners of the church, making a cross by their movements. Each *surveyor* is in charge of one element used in the consecration. One person has a bell, one a glass of water, one a bottle of perfume, one a calabash of grain. Sometimes, milk, honey, and wine are added. (Note the difference from St. Vincent, where only a bell and water are used; the multiplication of elements follows the Trinidadian example.) At each corner, a prayer is said, the bell is rung, and the water, the perfume, and the grain is spilled on the floor. Then a trail is made of rung bells and spilled water, perfume, and grain from the doors of the church to the center, where the surveyors shake hands.

In St. Vincent, the heat evaporates the water quickly, but in Brooklyn the water tends to stay on the floor. In some churches, the poured water is mopped up after the consecration. One church has done away with the rite entirely. Another concession to the climatic differences between St. Vincent and Brooklyn is that the bare feet required at services in the tropics may be covered with slippers. I was present one night when a pointer denounced this practice. Those under his charge, however, were allowed to wear socks as protection from the cold concrete floor.

The service is opened by the *leader* or *leadress* who recites the liturgy of the Order for Morning Prayer, which is used both morning and evening. Most people in the church carry (British) *Methodist Hymn Books*, from which the majority of hymns are taken. The words to the hymns are still called out by the leader, as they are in St. Vincent, where few can afford hymnals. The congregation recites together the General Confession, the Lord's Prayer, the Apostle's Creed, Psalm 23, Psalm 121. In some churches, the Magnificat is then sung.

The liturgy ends with the *greeting*. The hymn "And Are We Yet Alive" is sung. Each member of the congregation greets every other member of the congregation, usually shaking hands, but sometimes performing the complete greeting—holding hands outstretched, touching chest and side of the head on the left, then right, then left sides, and finally holding hands overhead while dipping slightly. The full greeting can take a long-time and the hymn is repeated for as long as it takes for everyone to acknowledge everyone else. After the liturgy is performed, a few members are invited to offer prayers, which they sing to tunes they have been given in the spiritual world. The rest of the congregation joins in the prayers by singing antiphonal responses. Those who have prayed again greet or shake hands with all in the congregation.

After the prayers, the leader turns the service over to the pointer or the pointing mother. The pointer may make announcements or invite members or visiting Converted to speak. At some services, everyone present is expected to say something. *Visions* (dreams containing a message for the congregation) are reported at this time by the pointer or other members. The pointer is likely to preach, as in St. Vincent, although in the island, some churches rarely have a sermon. Singing is the most important part of the service, and that is emphasized over speaking.

If an important ritual is called for (relating to mourning or baptism), it is commenced and occupies the rest of the evening. A *thanksgiving* may be given at this time as well. A thanksgiving is an offering of thanks from an individual for a particular grace from God. The person giving thanks (the thanksgiver) is required to supply a table covered with food and candles that are distributed to the congregation afterwards. The congregation is also usually fed a full meal by the thanksgiver. A thanksgiving is expensive, and I only saw two in St. Vincent. In some Brooklyn churches, they occur almost weekly.

Whether the occasion is an important ritual or a normal service, *doption* is a usual part of the service, as in St. Vincent. Doption, the special rhythmic movements accompanying journeys to spiritual lands in the church service, is contrasted with the journeys during mourning in which the person is usually lying down. The captain takes over the service at this time, guiding those doing doption to whichever lands the Holy Spirit directs him. Not everyone can do doption. There are different doptions for different cities, and one may only do the doptions for the cities to which she belongs (that is, the cities to which she has traveled during mourning). The rest of the congregation sings choruses and hymns to help the travelers along. Doption is the same in St. Vincent and in Brooklyn, but each congregation has its own tradition regarding the meaning of specific doptions. Doption may occur at different times in the service depending on inspiriation by the Holy Spirit, but it often signifies a climax to the meeting.

To end the meeting, the entire congregation recites a series of doxologies. In St. Vincent and in Brooklyn, church services usually last five hours. Many last longer.

Despite of numerous pressures for change, there is a close correspondence between rituals and ideas in St. Vincent and those in Vincentian churches in Brooklyn. In large part this is due to a high level of contact between Brooklyn and St. Vincent, including a yearly pilgrimage to St. Vincent for one Brooklyn church.

Changes in Vincentian Converted practice between St. Vincent and Brooklyn relate primarily to differences in economic and environmental conditions as well as the influence of culture contact. However, the relative wealth does not necessarily make it easier to be a Converted. All who had something to say on the matter told me it is harder to be a Converted in Brooklyn than in St. Vincent. One reason is the lack of a sense of place in the larger community. Another is the different lifestyle required in New York. These changes affect all Caribbean religions. The difficulties negotiated by Haitian Vodounists in Brooklyn, "[w]ork pressures, distance, the problems of late-night travel in New York City, even a different sense of time" (K. Brown 1991:47), apply equally well to the Converted. Although many of the differences between Converted life and worship in New York and St. Vincent stem from the differences in secular life in the two places, exposure to other religions motivates the greatest changes in the practice of Converted religion in Brooklyn.

Other Spiritual Baptists in New York

Although New York contains over one million West Indians (van Capelleveen 1993: 132–133), those from Trinidad affect the Vincentian Converted the most. Many

Vincentians in New York have spent time working in Trinidad before moving to America. Vincentians in Trinidad find a stigma attached to their nationality. "The Vincentians and Grenadians are small islanders. . . . In Trinidad they are viewed as clients, a status tinged with an aura of inferiority" (Basch 1987:189). This association carries over to the relation between the Vincentian Converted and the more numerous Trinidadian Spiritual Baptists in New York.

Trinidadian Spiritual Baptists offer some confusion to the Vincentian Converted. The term "Spiritual Baptist" originated in Trinidad. In St. Vincent, the official government name for the Converted is Spiritual Baptist. This changed from Christian Pilgrim or Pilgrim Baptist two decades ago. The two ordaining denominations in St. Vincent (the Archdiocese and the Organization), covering about half of the churches there, have Spiritual Baptist in their full denominational name and nearly every Converted church is known as Spiritual Baptist. In St. Vincent, however, and among the Vincentians in Brooklyn, "Converted" is the word that evokes the most passion and identity. The problem with names is more complex, however, as the Trinidadians will also sometimes refer to themselves as Converted. I do note that for the Trinidadians in Brooklyn, the name Spiritual Baptist carries more emotion, probably because that name is deeply rooted in Trinidad (and less well-rooted in St. Vincent). Whereas terms of reference can be superficial in other circumstances, for the Converted in Brooklyn the subject is vital. Discussion of these matters takes up large amounts of their time (cf. Hackshaw 1992:77–98).[4]

The Spiritual Baptists in Barbados and Grenada (and Tobago and Venezuela) originated with sojourners in Trinidad returning to their home countries. Some Vincentian presence is found among the Spiritual Baptists in other islands, but the influence is small. Every Vincentian Converted has been told since childhood that the religion emerged in St. Vincent and traveled to wherever else it is found. Many, maybe most, of the Trinidadian pointers and bishops discount the idea of a Vincentian origin, although some do admit to me that the Vincentian tradition is well grounded in the Spirit. Vincentians, coming from a small, poor country with few resources, already have to contend with strong prejudice from Trinidad. To claim their country as the birthplace of one of the important religions in the Caribbean, a position of which they could be rightly proud, is difficult to do when confronted with assertions to the contrary from large, rich, better-educated Trinidad. Added to that is the fact that the Spiritual Baptists in all of the surrounding islands are practicing the Trinidadian tradition. Vincentians have been told that slaves in secret prayer and fasting in the Vincentian mountains established the techniques that make the Spiritual Baptists special among all Christians. In the face of Trinidadian denials, Vincentians may be inclined to wonder if their religion is not after all a species of African Christianity (Aladura) rooting itself in Trinidad and spreading to St. Vincent as a Trinidadian bishop in Brooklyn announced in his church when I visited one day (see also Brathwaite 1982b:45).

Trinidadian rituals differ mainly in access to and acceptance of elements of ritual goods and symbols from other religions, notably Shango and Hinduism, although any observable tradition is fair game (e.g., Buddhism and Confucianism [see Glazier

1983] and Freemasonry, sources that do not yet have a notable presence in St. Vincent). This does not make the Trinidadian Spiritual Baptists any less Christian; non-Christian elements are simply additional routes of power and knowledge given to the Spiritual Baptists by God. Elements taken from Shango/Orisha and other religions among the Trinidadians vary by congregation and denomination (among at least eight Spiritual Baptist denominations in Trinidad [Hackshaw 1992:24]), but generally amount to a greater use and variety of physical symbols and ritual goods than in the Vincentian churches. Every physical item in the church has a spiritual counterpart. Moreover, many spiritual items in the church are only visible to those with "spiritual eyes." A steel sword that one might find in a Trinidadian church would be considered too strong a reliance on a physical symbol in St. Vincent, where the spiritual sword for which the physical stands should only be seen by those who have spiritual eyes to see it.[5]

The Trinidadian Spiritual Baptist churches I visited in Brooklyn exhibit a greater emphasis on the presence of spirits at the church meetings than do Vincentian churches. Spirits other than the Holy Spirit may come to a church service in St. Vincent and be entertained (in some churches) by the lighting of candles, pouring of water, and waving of specific flags on occasion. However, the interaction with spirits that is so prominent in the Trinidadian churches in Brooklyn—and some of the Vincentian ones there—is at least secondary in the Converted churches. In St. Vincent, the primary spiritual activity is travel in the spirit, either in journeys to the spiritual lands or by *gazing* (the ability to see people and places in the spiritual world without traveling there). In other words, the Trinidadian churches participate in the Caribbean-wide pattern of spiritual beings "coming to" the believer rather than the Vincentian pattern of believing practitioners "going to" the spiritual beings, wherever they may be. Spirits do come to the Converted churches, but the emphasis is different.

Trinidadians travel, too, through gazing or doption as well as by mourning, but the emphasis on the presence of spirits, with the very same saint names as those found in Shango, makes many of the Trinidadian churches feel ideologically different from the Vincentian ones. Furthermore, the syncretic influences from other Christian denominations are mainly Roman Catholic, Trinidad being primarily a Catholic country, including saints' images (in five of the seven Trinidadian Spiritual Baptist churches I visited in Brooklyn). This, visually at least, puts the Trinidadian churches at odds with the Vincentian ones, who, coming from a Protestant tradition, tend to eschew images of saints as idolatry. In the 17 Converted churches I visited in St. Vincent, only two had any representation of saints: One had a six-inch statuette of St. Francis, and one, whose pointer had spent many years in Trinidad, had two 18-inch statues on the altar. Acknowledging the saints is fine to the Vincentians—they see and converse with saints in the spiritual world frequently, and each Converted person usually has one saint who they work with closely. Keeping a statue of a saint, however, seemed improper to most of the Converted who voiced an opinion. That said, one Vincentian shrugged her shoulders when I asked if she was offended at Trinidadians praying to saints. She said, "Everybody has a saint they work with, why shouldn't you ask them for something?"

In addition, many of the Trinidadian churches in Brooklyn also have Hindu images, and in two I was able to observe a statue of the Happy Buddha, representing the spiritual city of China. Some of the ritual movements and spiritual dances among the Trinidadians are too different for the comfort of my Vincentian respondents; the influence of Shango, they said. A further Shango influence is found in that some of the Spiritual Baptist churches in the Trinidadian tradition will at times sacrifice a pigeon or dove.

Drums, never found in the Spiritual Baptist churches in St. Vincent, are present in most of the Trinidadian churches. Although this is apparently a Shango influence, it does not bother the Vincentians as much as other differences. In their own churches, the Vincentians "play the drums" spiritually; that is, they imitate the instrument with their voices. The Trinidadian Spiritual Baptist churches I visited do not consider themselves Shango and for the most part will not even acknowledge the term *Shango Baptist* (colloquially applied to all Spiritual Baptists by non-Spiritual Baptist Trinidadians I met in Brooklyn and to all Trinidadian Spiritual Baptists by many Vincentians). Those who the Vincentians consider Shango Baptist are sometimes called merely "Shango" and shunned as such by the Vincentians, even in churches where those same Trinidadians told me they would have shunned Shango or Orisha religion themselves.

Despite some differences, the Trinidadian church service corresponds, in most respects, to the Vincentian norm. Vincentian respondents with whom I visited the Trinidadian churches explained the Shango-like variances as errant knowledge on the part of the Trinidadians. Shango (Orisha), like voodoo (Vodou), is often conflated with obeah by the Converted. The perceived connection of obeah with Shango and Shango with the Trinidadian Spiritual Baptists forms part of the apprehension some Converted feel in approaching a Trinidadian church. Trinidadians are believed by many Vincentians to be potential workers of obeah.[6] Pointers in New York make frequent reference to this belief, and the belief in obeah in general, in their sermons, trying to convince their congregations that the misfortunes they experience are the result of their own shortcomings, not from someone applying the powers of "bad" to them. The pointers' common aphorism: "You say somebody do you; but you do yourself."

Despite a belief that there are some bad individuals among the Trinidadians, the Trinidadian Spiritual Baptists are seen as "fellow workers in the vineyard," trying to do good spiritual work for Christ. They are considered to be part of the same communion and denomination as the Vincentian Converted.

To make matters more confusing, Trinidadian Spiritual Baptists are not the only Spiritual Baptists in Brooklyn. While most of the Spiritual Baptists from the Caribbean appear to have historical connections to the ones from St. Vincent, the "Spiritual Baptists" from Jamaica and Guyana have an independent development and seem to have taken (or had ascribed to them) the name out of a sense of affinity, as the Converted themselves did (Hackshaw 1992:78–82; cf. Pitt 1955:386). The identification of the Jamaican (Revival Zion) and Guyanese (Jordanite) religions with Spiritual Baptists is natural. They are each religions of the poor in their own countries; they are perceived as strange in their own countries; they wrap their heads with cloth and work with spirits. They rejoice in a lively "pentecostal" fashion, and keep good fundamentalist doctrine: emphasizing the grace of Jesus Christ and justifying their actions with Biblical references. They are considered Spiritual Baptists by the Vincentians I was with. Again, the features that distinguish them from other churches in their home country—baptism by immersion and working with spirits, following the command of Christ in the third chapter of the Gospel of John that one must be born of the water and the spirit—make these a natural ally of the Vincentian Converted and Trinidadian Spiritual Baptists. Given the red-letter injunction to baptize, it is not surprising that disparate Christian groups sensing in themselves a greater spirituality than others would use the words "Spiritual Baptist" as an identifying marker. Yet the Jamaicans are different from the Converted. Tellingly, the Vincentian pointer I was with told me in a low voice as we entered a Jamaican church in Brooklyn, "They don't mourn."

Several of the Trinidadian churches have Vincentian heads (pointers or pointing mothers), but they practice the Trinidadian traditions and learned their ways in Trinidad (that is, the individual migrated from St. Vincent to Trinidad and then, eventually, to the United States). Some do return to St. Vincent, but on return, the least Vincentian of the traits are deemphasized or are not practiced at all. A pointer in New York who had noticed this explained the reason for the conformity by saying, "The people wouldn't like it [the Trinidadian rituals]." The pressures to change abroad are countered by pressures for conformity at home.

Other Caribbean Religions in Brooklyn

Caribbean religions besides the other Spiritual Baptists have little influence on Converted practice. Language differences account for some of this as does the visibility of other religions. Vodou is confused with obeah because *voodoo* and obeah are synonyms in St. Vincent. Even though Converted in St. Vincent are aware of Haitian Vodou (as voodoo), it is little talked about in New York. When I asked why, I was told that Vodou is not an issue, because Haitians are generally avoided because of their association with voodoo. The same is true of Santeria from the Spanish-speaking Caribbean.

Converted also have little contact with Shango/Orisha. Both Shango from Trinidad and Pukkumina from Jamaica are avoided because of their practice of sacrifice. Because Shango is practiced by English-speaking West Indians, Vincentians show a rather high awareness of it. Many of the traits of the Shangoist (head-tying, working with spirits, Africa-orientation) are shared by the Converted. "Catching spirit," the shaking behavior of spirit possession, for both looks nearly the same. However, the Shango practice is diabolical because they catch *a* spirit, whereas the Spiritual Baptists catch *the* Spirit (a distinction made much of by the Spiritual Baptists). The *orishas* personified as saints are seen as powerful spirits able to affect the Converted. Shango spirits are avoided. One Vincentian pointer, explaining why Converted should not attend Shango or Shango Baptist meetings, told me that one should not associate with "that part of the spiritual world."

The Converted in St. Vincent have no opportunity for contact with Shango practices, except for those individuals who might go to Trinidad or Grenada to work. Even then, prolonged direct contact with Shango is unlikely. In New York, the situation is the same. The Shango ceremonies tend not to be community affairs open to all but are accessible only by invitation. Nonetheless, the Shangoists in Trinidad and Grenada are associated more with the Spiritual Baptists than with any other religion. Shango does influence Vincentian Converted practice in that effort is sometimes expended by Converted to distance themselves from possible identification with Shango.

American Influence

As in St. Vincent, American religions in Brooklyn are influences for change. Although the Converted note with interest the big churches, flashy preachers, and radio and television exposure of the Euro-American and African-American churches in New York City, the Caribbean churches are more or less invisible to the Americans. In the recent book *The Black Churches of Brooklyn* (Tylor 1994), there is not one mention of a West Indian church or of the Caribbean at all, despite the presence of hundreds of thousands of Black Caribbean churchgoers in Brooklyn, and that Brooklyn in the 1990s is essentially a Caribbean colony. In fact, some of the Caribbean churches with a presence in New York were founded by American missionaries in the West Indies (such as the Caribbean-wide New Testament Church of God, a part of the Church of God, Cleveland, Tennessee). The West Indian religions, whose appeal is limited to West Indians, represent no threat to the American churches. The overwhelming presence of the American churches does present a challenge to the West Indians, however.

Once Vincentians enter the United States, multiplied varieties of Pentecostal and Baptist sects introduce themselves with features approaching more closely the Spiritual Baptist norms than do the Pentecostal and "American" Baptist versions in St. Vincent. Many of the Black Baptist churches in Brooklyn have similar singing rhythms (not found in any of the other churches in St. Vincent) and some, referring to the spiritual baptism believed to accompany water baptism, describe themselves as "spiritual baptists." One can see that people coming from a small island, trying to find their place in the world, and believing themselves to be a part of a larger religious communion, may be tempted to conform to the predominating forms as an attempt at legitimacy in a foreign country.

Responses to Change

The outward symbols that make the Converted special in St. Vincent are shared by many religious groups in New York, by whom they are sometimes drawn in admiration, sometimes repulsed in antipathy. The influx of ideas and images from other religions are accompanied by pressures for change. The motivators arise from the need to fit in to the new place as well as to preserve the sense of connection to St. Vincent.

The dual nature of Converted identity—Spiritual/Baptist (African/Christian)—is a natural divider. Alterations in practices and in outward symbols depend on who the Converted, as individuals and as congregations, consider themselves most to be and most not to be. Bases on which the changes are made can be found in St. Vincent and in the pattern of Vincentian imagination about the world. St. Vincent suffers the stigma of being seen as "backward" by other Caribbean nations, an unpleasant label for a developing nation. The Vincentians, especially those who have been to Trinidad, feel the sting of being "small island." On top of that, other Vincentians criticize the Converted as "backward." Those who make it to Brooklyn tend to be the most mobile, the most forward-looking Vincentians, a large number having worked in Trinidad before traveling to the United States. One common response in Brooklyn is a tendency to present one's self/congregation as less "backward," less African, more like the American churches in style and form, although the essential Converted elements of mourning and work in the Spirit are not given up. Reflecting an appeal to urban sophistication, the pastor of one Converted church explained his lack of candles and lack of spiritual flags, absence of a bell, and use of the hymnal of an American denomination in his church as preferred because they are "more modern."

Although acknowledging itself as Spiritual Baptist, this particular church had removed "Spiritual" from its name, the sign indicating only that the storefront church is one of any scores of "Baptist" churches of any nation or denomination in Brooklyn. Converse to this, many Converted churches drop "Baptist" from their name. The signs over their church doors read "Spiritual Temple" or "Spiritual Church," stressing difference from the American churches that carry the name Baptist. As in St. Vincent, many churches have no signs at all, members knowing which building to go to (or, more likely in Brooklyn, which basement). Selection of which symbols to accent is situational. Stressing "Baptist" or "Spiritual" is not an abnegation of either. The pastor of one of the more "Spiritual" churches told me that when people ask him what he is, he just says, "West Indian Baptist." If people respond, "Shango Baptist?" He replies, "No, Vincentian Converted Baptist."

Experimentation is another response to the proximity of similar spirit-oriented religions from the Caribbean. The Converted recognize the sharing of African and/or spiritual traits in their religion with other Caribbean religions and may adopt practices that will enhance their knowledge and power to do the work of Jesus. Most Vincentians, at the very least, are wary if not outright afraid of the Trinidadian churches—so dangerously close to Shango, with statues of saints and representations of Indian gods (perceived as saints). Despite the potential danger, the Converted are skilled spiritual experts. They are able to detect good and combat evil. For the Converted churches that selectively accept foreign practices, some qualities change, but the substance of the religion remains the same. That does not prevent "purer" Converted from complaining about Shango, Orisha, or Hindu influences.

Individually, some members, directed by vision or by personal inclination, turn completely to the Trinidadian styles or even to working with the orisha spirits— who, according to my few Vincentian respondents who work with them, are seen as powerful helping spirits serving the cause of Christ, not seen as possessing deities. Those Vincentian Spiritual Baptists who follow the Trinidadian tradition or practice the Shango Baptist rites (that is, praying to saints and sacrificing doves) are usually those who have spent time in Trinidad and have had direct contact with Shango/Orisha in its Trinidadian setting.

Resistance to change is a third strategy. Some congregations shield themselves from the challenges offered by contact with other religions by reducing the amount of visiting they do with other churches. This represents a major change. In St. Vincent, visiting between churches is a cherished and joyful institution. One pointer in St. Vincent told me, "You hardly stay home a Sunday." Visiting is a mixing of different church families, a time to see how different churches perform certain rites, to learn new songs, to see new faces, and it is one of the means by which Converted churches in St. Vincent stay fresh and vibrant in a way that the conventional churches cannot approach. For churches in New York, not to visit with other Spiritual Baptist churches is different, but protects the members from confusing influences. A Converted church, already a refuge of Vincentian homeliness in the chilly and foreign social atmosphere of New York, can become a fortress of spiritual immunity from dangerous forces.

The history of Converted religion is one of rapid response to changes. In Brooklyn, this pattern continues. Even though the changes vary by congregation, the religion remains substantially intact. Despite the colonial effort to eliminate Africanisms from the descendants of Africans, a sense of African-ness has remained in St. Vincent in the form of Converted religion. In spite of the buffets of in-island prejudice as well as out-island prejudice, legal persecution, lowly origins, and challenges from other religions in Brooklyn and elsewhere, the Converted remain spiritual workers dedicated to their Christian purpose. The relatively simple spiritual equation in St. Vincent—with the Converted poor and powerless in the physical world but rich and powerful in the Spirit—is more complex in Brooklyn. Other religions are rich in the spirit as well. American Pentecostals and Baptists as well as Spiritual Baptists from other islands force a sharper definition of Converted religion than in St. Vincent. Vincentian Converted, individually and as congregations, address this problem variously by speedy adaptation to external influences, by the alteration of external symbols, by adaptation of useful strategies for power, and by reclusion for protection.

TWELVE

Conclusion

WHEN I ARRIVED IN BROOKLYN IN October 1995, I had never been there before. Although I was in my own country, Vincentians became my guide in the city nicknamed "America's Home Town." I began my study in one of the poorest countries in the Western Hemisphere; I ended it in the capital of the world. I went to Brooklyn thinking I would find out how the religion changed in a place that is opposite to St. Vincent in so many ways. I found out that the religion had largely stayed the same. Vincentians in New York need it to stay the same. The religion represents home. The main point of this study is that Converted religion is a part of that home; it is Vincentian culture.

Part One demonstrates that the Converted are spiritual workers of a type usually associated with shamanism. Part Two shows the spiritual experiences of the Converted to be derived from the local context. Part Three indicates the comparative context of the religion and explains how Vincentian culture and Converted religion are both constituents of each other. In chapter 11, I have presented a sort of summary of the religion by contrasting it with like religions in New York. In this chapter, I focus on lessons to be learned from the Converted and on suggestions for research for which data from the Converted are especially promising.

By demonstrating similarities that the Converted bear to many different religious styles, I have intended to show that they are not necessarily tied to other Caribbean spirit-possession religions. I emphasize shamanic aspects because of the work that is done in a spiritual landscape. However, by pointing out similarities to other religions such as Haitian Vodou and the Indian Shaker Church, I stress that they are not shamans of the sort normally encountered in the ethnographic literature. What the Converted do, though, fulfills all the criteria usually required for an identification of shamanism. Not only are shamanistic experiences common in the world and able to emerge spontaneously (as in the case of Wesselman), but they can develop quickly into complete religions (e.g., Monroe). Although the Converted may have derived from an existing shamanistic tradition, it is just as likely that their practices developed gradually over the years from the spontaneous experiences of individuals. The religion would have gained adherents as people discovered a much better world away from plantations and colonial authorities. Even though the Converted are similar to other religions in the African diaspora, the evidence suggests that many and maybe most of the features of the religion are the result of local invention.

I have discussed colonialism in terms of its effects on the poor people of St. Vincent and their reactions to it. This work follows others that contextualize and localize colonialism in a relatively small population (e.g., Taussig 1980; Comaroff 1985). The Converted spiritual world is a reproduction of the colonial experience. Not only do Converted encounter and become colonial authorities in the spiritual landscape—inspectors, surveyors, soldiers, nurses, and for one Converted man, a knight commander—but the spiritual world itself is the British colonial world. Zion and the Valley (heaven and hell or life and death) are the most important places. Next in importance are the sources of colonial labor (Africa, India, China). It is as if the originators of the religion entered the mind of the people who enslaved them. The Converted supposition that all are sinners and no one sin is worse than another could just as well be a justification for slavery. The people who became the Converted could not enter the colonial world; they were already the foundation of it, with no possibility of changing that status. One way of addressing the inequalities, of continuing to live in a colonial situation that degraded their humanity (before and after emancipation) was to make themselves symbolically masters of it.

On other islands, symbolic inversions are the norm. Carnival bands that mock the European and the Rose and Marguerite societies that put local people in the place of Europeans (kings, queens, magistrates, etc.) may help to release the tensions of plantation society. Converted religion is a permanent form of those same sorts of ritual inversions and rites of license, with license to subvert the normal order of things. Dirks (1987) has shown that temporary freedom in the form of scheduled festivals does not necessarily lead to peace, that the festivals may even foster rebellion. Riots in St. Vincent in 1862, 1879, and 1935 follow patterns throughout the region. The Converted or a group very like them was associated with the 1862 riots in which White people were singled out for violence. The 1879 riot in which policemen were killed was labeled a "masquerade riot" (Anderson 1938:179). The same man who championed the 1935 rioters led the fight to legalize Shakerism (Ryan and Williams, n.d.). Symbolic means to reverse oppression only go so far, but may provide a model for physical action. The leader of the 1862 riots was known on the plantation as George Bascom, but during the insurrection his followers called him "King Bascom" (Marshall 1983:99).

Converted religion has more to offer the world than a history lesson. The experience of their spiritual world (that to them it is tangibly real) is potentially very important. The experiences of the Converted show that imaginal (as opposed to physical) landscapes can be experienced by large numbers of people. A pointer can send a pilgrim to a specific spiritual land and she is able to go there. A pointer may travel to a spiritual land without apparently altering consciousness. A number of Converted may travel together to a spiritual city, see the same things, and experience unique events. Converted individuals may learn practical tasks by which they may earn a living or otherwise materially improve their lives. I have shown that all of these features exist in other shamanic cultures. The way the Converted have put them together makes them easily observable.

Furthermore, that Converted religion is an indigenous Western Christian shamanism makes the concepts of the religion accessible to a Western observer. The metaphors they use are familiar Western ones. The phenomenology and quite possibly the physiology of possession experience and other altered states may be easier to discover in a group of people whose culture is both Western and shamanic.

The description of the Converted contained in this study should be welcome in some circles. Much of Converted religion seems to be a twin to Kilton Stewart's Senoi Dream Theory. It is clear that "Exceptional abilities develop most fully in cultures that prize them" (Murphy 1992:160), and the Converted appear to make greater use of the creative faculties available to everyone. Those desiring to develop human potentials may learn from the Converted. As Murphy wrote:

> We live only part of the life we are given. Growing acquaintance with once-foreign cultures, new discoveries about our subliminal depths, and the dawning recognition that each social group reinforces just some human attributes while neglecting or suppressing others have stimulated a worldwide understanding that all of us have great potentials for growth.

Besides the useful altered-states models the Converted might provide, their story is an example of the creativity possible under harsh and uncertain circumstances.

Glossary

Africa	A spiritual location. The spiritual aspect of the physical Africa.
African warrior	A spiritual gift. The African warrior (a female) enlivens the worship with her energetic movement and singing.
air	The tune to a song.
anointing	A ritual. A *pilgrim* or one who is ill is anointed on the head and limbs with olive oil.
apron	Part of a spiritual *uniform*.
assistant leader	A spiritual gift. The assistant leader (a male) assists as needed in the liturgical part of the service and aids in other rituals.
assistant mother	A spiritual gift. The assistant mother (a female) is qualified to assist in the *banning* and in other rituals.
assistant nurse	A spiritual gift. The assistant nurse (a female) assists the nurses in the *washing* and in tending to the *pilgrims* during *repentance* or *mourning*.
assistant pointer	A spiritual gift. The assistant pointer (a male) assists the pointer in the *banning* and other rituals.
bands	Blindfolds inscribed with *seals* to assist the *pilgrim* on her spiritual journey.
banning	A ritual. The banning is the ritual where the *bands* are placed on the *Pilgrim* to prepare her for *mourning*.
baptism	A ritual. The baptism is by immersion in a stream or in the ocean. It is one of the chief rituals of the Converted.

bark	To give a *spiritual bath*.
bath	A spiritual bath given by a *pointer* to a client.
bell	The brass hand bell of the Converted churches.
bell ringer	A spiritual gift. The bell ringer rings the *bell* to call people to church and at other times throughout the service.
belt	The wide belt worn on the outside of the garment by mothers and pointers. A symbol of authority.
bench of repentance	The bench on which the baptismal candidate sits during church services. Also called the *mercy seat* or the "bench."
Bethlehem	A spiritual location. The spiritual aspect of the physical Bethlehem where Jesus is considered to have been born.
Beulahland	A spiritual location. A pleasant spiritual city as described in *The Pilgrim's Progress*.
blowing	A ritual. Blowing is delivering a message (whether by song or by speaking) that one has been commanded by God to give.
Bramble Picker	A saint.
Brother Cutter	A saint.
calabash	A *calabash*, the fruit of the calabash tree (*Crescentia cujete*), dried and cut in half to make a bowl of from 6–12 inches, filled with water, flowers, and a lighted candle. Represents the *spiritual city* of Africa.
Canaan	A spiritual location. The spiritual aspect of the Canaan described in the Bible; a land of milk and honey.
candlelighting	A ritual. A celebration where hundreds of candles are burned.
captain	A spiritual gift. The captain (a male) directs the singing in the church.
catching Spirit	Another term for *shaking* (Holy Spirit possession).
center	The center of the church. May be marked by a pole or a *seal*.
center pole	The center of the church. May have a *lota*, a *calabash*, a Bible, a *bell*, and a candle at its base.
centurion	A rare term for a prayer that is sung.
chanting	Humming or low singing that is carried on while people are speaking in church. May also be done when no one is speaking.

China	A spiritual location. The spiritual aspect of the physical China.
chorus	A short song, usually of one verse. May be repeated dozens of times.
christening	A ritual whereby a name is given to a person, a place, or an object.
"cleaning" of a house	A ritual. Removes evil influences from a house or apartment and protects against future evil.
communion	A ritual. The Eucharist or Lord's Supper. The Converted ritual is as it is commonly performed in Methodist churches.
consecration	A ritual. The process of establishing a sacred space for ritual use.
cord	A colored cord worn around the waist or neck as part of one's uniform.
court	Another term for a Converted congregation.
cross-bearer	A spiritual gift. The cross-bearer (a male) carries the cross when required during Converted rituals.
crowned	A prefix to a spiritual gift denoting the method in which the gift was obtained, e.g., crowned *shepherd*.
crowning	A ritual. Lighted candles are placed on a plate and a *pilgrim* at a *shouting* must balance the plate on his or her head.
current	The flow of the *Spirit* in the church service.
diver	A spiritual gift. The diver (male or female) encourages and warns worshippers during the service.
doctor	A spiritual gift. This gift is an adjunct position for many pointers and indicates an enhanced ability to heal.
doption	A ritual movement. One means of entering into and of journeying through spiritual lands.
dragon	The dragon plant (*Dracaena spp.*).
dying away	Falling down under the power of the *Spirit* and *traveling*. Occurs during the church service. Also called *dying off*.
fasting	A ritual. A time of prayer and a seeking of *visions* that is less structured than *mourning*.
flag (spiritual)	A flag representing a location or quality in the *Spirit*.
flag waver	A spiritual gift. The flag waver (a female) waves her *flag* when motivated at any time during the service

	and also stands behind those knelt in prayer at the altar or *center pole*.
florist	A spiritual gift. The florist (a female) cleans the church and decorates it with flowers in preparation for services.
forty days	A ritual. A wake held on the fortieth night after a death.
foundation	The chief scripture text read at the church service.
funeral	A ritual. The main feature of a Converted funeral is the joyous *marching* accompanying the casket from the home of the deceased to the grave site.
garment	The spiritual *uniform*.
gazing	Seeing into the *Spirit* without traveling there.
get lash	To be whipped by the *Spirit*.
gown	The long cassock worn by some Converted men.
greeting	The special greeting Converted give to each other. Hands are held straight out to the sides, right chest touches right chest while sides of head touch. This is repeated on left side, then right. May also refer to shaking hands.
hailing	A singing call to the spiritual lands.
headtie	The female headdress. Covers the top of the head.
headwrap	The male headdress. Does not cover the top of the head.
house blessing	A ritual. The same as the *"cleaning"* of a house.
house christening	A ritual. This is the same ritual done for the christening of a child or the *"cleaning"* of a house, except that to the latter is added the bestowal of a name and the choosing of godparents.
humming	Singing without words.
hymn	A song that comes from a hymn book.
India	A spiritual location. The spiritual aspect of the physical India.
inner room	The *mourning room*.
inspector	A spiritual gift. The inspector (male or female) "drills the troops" and keeps them in line.
Israel	A spiritual location. The spiritual aspect of Israel as described in the Bible.
Jericho	A spiritual location. The city of Jericho as described in the Bible.

jump Spirit	Another term for *doption*.
key	A song. It is the key to gain entry to a spiritual city.
king	A preface to a spiritual gift, e.g., king *shepherd*.
lash	A whip or the stroke of a whip (spiritual).
laying down the pilgrim	The last part of the *banning* rite. At this part of the rite, the pilgrim is left to begin journeying on her own.
leader	A spiritual gift. The leader (a male) opens the service, recites the liturgy, and assists the pointer.
leadress	A spiritual gift. The leadress (a female) performs all of the same tasks as the *leader*.
licks	Strokes from a spiritual whip.
lock up	To be locked up in the *Spirit*.
lota	A brass vase filled with water, flowers, and a candle. Sometimes represents spiritual city of *India*. Also spelled *luther* or "loter."
low grounds	Another term for the *mourning room*. Also called the "low grounds of sorrow."
luther	The *lota*.
marching	A ritual. A procession of the Converted in the church setting or in a public place.
matron	A spiritual gift. The matron (a female) directs the actions of the *nurses*.
meditation	Entering the spiritual world by quiet intent.
mercy seat	The *bench of repentance*.
messenger	A spiritual gift. The messenger (a male) delivers messages from God to the church or to the community.
memorial	Another term for a *wake*. A service the Converted provide to the larger community.
mission	A ritual. Usually a service held in a public place, but may refer to any task God commands one to do.
mother	A spiritual gift. The mother is the highest female rank in the church.
Mt. Zion	A spiritual location A high mountain that the pilgrim must climb.
mourner	The person undergoing the ritual of *mourning*.
mourning	A ritual. The chief Converted manner of experiencing the *spiritual cities*.
mourning room	The small room in which *mourning* and spiritual travels take place.

the Nations	A spiritual location. A place with people of all nations resident.
nine days	A ritual. For nine days after *mourning*, the *pilgrim* is considered to be partly in the spirit world and must adhere to certain codes of behavior.
nine night	A ritual—see appendix under *memorials*.
nurse	A spiritual gift. The nurse (a female) attends the *pilgrim* during repentance, during the *banning*, and during *mourning*.
Nurse Dinah	A saint.
nurse matron	A spiritual gift. The same as matron.
obeah	The West Indian term for sorcery.
open air mission	A ritual. A service held in a public place, usually a crossroads or a market square.
opening of the service	The opening liturgy of the church service. The process of performing the liturgy.
palm	Any palm frond used to represent Christ or Jerusalem. Often the sago palm (*Cycas revoluta*).
pass	The secret word used to gain access to places in the spiritual world or to save oneself from harm in the *Spirit*.
password	The *pass*.
pilgrim	The *mourner*.
pilgrimage	A trip with the congregation to another part of the island.
pilgrim journey	The *mourning* experience.
pointer	A spiritual gift. The highest rank of spiritual gift. The pointer (a male) sends pilgrims to the spiritual lands.
pointing	The *banning*. Also called "pointing on" or "pointing down."
pointing mother	A spiritual gift. The female equivalent to the pointer.
pointing parents	One's *pointer* and *pointing mother*.
pole	The *center pole*.
praise	A ritual. The ordinary church service.
proofs	Randomly selected scripture verses used for guidance.
prover	A spiritual gift. The prover (a male) searches members of the church and visitors for hidden sin.
proving	Seeing into the soul of someone.
putting down the pilgrim	The last part of the *banning* rite.

queen	A prefix to a spiritual gift, e.g., queen *mother*.
reading	Seeing into someone's past and personality.
rejoicing	Another term for *doption*.
repentance	The ritual of baptismal candidacy.
rising	A ritual. Occurs on the third day of mourning and symbolically raises the *pilgrim* from the dead.
road	A tune. It is a road to a spiritual location.
robing	A ritual. An investiture of a spiritual *uniform*.
rod	A stick carried by a *pointer, mother*, or *teacher* to represent authority.
the room	The mourning room.
sankey	A solo sung in church. Also called a "song key."
sash	A part of the spiritual uniform.
school	The church, especially in reference to *mourning*.
Sea of Glass	A spiritual location. The bottom of a transparent sea.
Sea of Tingeling	A spiritual location. The bottom of a sea full of metallic sounds.
seal	A spiritual symbol that imparts power. Usually drawn in chalk.
to seal	To draw *seals* on.
sealing	A ritual. *Seals* are drawn on pilgrims' clothing and body for protection and education.
seeing	Seeing items or events in the *Spirit*.
shaking	The shaking behavior of Holy Spirit possession.
shepherd	A spiritual gift. The shepherd (a male) acts as a peacemaker and as an assistant to other leaders.
shepherdess	A spiritual gift. A female shepherd.
ship	A tune. The tune is a ship that carries one (or the congregation) to a spiritual location. Sometimes used to refer to the church itself.
shouting	A ritual. The joyful return of the pilgrim from the *mourning room*.
shuttling	A vocalization related to *doption*.
to sign	To drip candle wax on something in a pattern. Normally done by pointers on *bands*. May be done to individuals (as at the end of a *banning*).
signing of bands	A ritual. The preparation of the *bands*.
sing pray	A prayer that is sung.
Sister Clearer	A saint.

smoke	A type of spiritual cleansing.
Spirit	Has three meanings often combined into one: 1) The Holy Spirit, 2) one's spiritual self, 3) the entire spiritual world.
spiritual bath	A ritual. A cleansing from sickness or sin.
spiritual city	Any specific location in the spiritual world, whether rural or urban.
spiritual eyes	That part of one that is able to see into the *Spirit*.
spiritual fighting	Ritual fighting in which the hands are held as swords and the participants circle each other in a kind of dance.
spiritual gifts	Spiritual tasks or offices.
spiritual names	Another term for *spiritual gifts*.
spiritual school	A Converted church. Refers specifically to the teachings and guidance of the *pointer* or *pointing mother* of the church.
strap	A *pointer*'s belt that is used for discipline (to beat church members). It is often an old belt that has been cut to a smaller size to better serve as a beating tool.
swaddling bands	*Bands* made of pieces of cloth that are long (up to eight feet) and rectangular instead of triangular (as are the other bands). Swaddling bands are rolled around the head of the *pilgrim* at the *banning* rather than tied. They are held on with other bands or a *headtie* tied on top.
surveyor	A spiritual gift. The surveyor (male or female) consecrates the church or other space at the beginning of each service.
sword fighting	Another term for *spiritual fighting*.
teacher	A spiritual gift. The teacher (male or female) is able to explain events in the spiritual world.
thanksgiving	A ritual. A service and a meal is sponsored by someone giving thanks to God.
tracking	Watching someone with *spiritual eyes*. May watch that person on their spiritual travels or in their physical activity. *Pointers* must track their *mourners* on their *pilgrim journey*.
tracks	The spiritual journeys of the *pilgrim* during *mourning*.
traveler	The *mourner*.
trumpet blower	A spiritual gift. The trumpet blower (a female) delivers messages from God to the congregation or to the community.

uniform	The clothing that one has received on one's *pilgrim journey*. Must be worn during church services.
upper room	The *mourning room*.
the Valley	A spiritual location. The "Valley of Dry Bones" or the "cemetery," a place of death and rejuvenation.
Valley dogs	Watchdogs in *the Valley*. Converted individuals bark like dogs to indicate danger in *the Valley*.
veil	A supplement to the spiritual *uniform* worn by women at a *banning* and during *communion*. It is nearly identical to the Anglican confirmation veil as used in St. Vincent.
vision	A dream that contains a message.
wake	A ritual. The memorial service held to commemorate a death.
washing	A ritual. A pilgrim or a person who is ill is washed with consecrated water.
watchman	A spiritual gift. The watchman (a male) keeps a spiritual guard over the church.
water carrier	A spiritual gift. The water carrier (a female) sits or stands near the front of the church and passes a cup or *calabash* of water to anyone who indicates he or she is thirsty.
wheel	The most common *seal* used by pointers. Sometimes used to refer to the *center*.
working spirit	Another term for *doption*. To "work spirit" is to perform doption.
Zion	A spiritual location. Sometimes equated with heaven, sometimes with the city of Zion as described in the Bible.

A P P E N D I X

Converted Ritual Classifications

ALTHOUGH THE CONVERTED HAVE several types of ritual classifications, which I have detailed in the text, the different types of rituals and the different kinds of spiritual offices are the most complex. I present here a complete list of the items in the two categories.

Types of Converted Rituals

The following rituals are the ones identified as separate rituals by the Vincentian Converted with whom I had contact. Some events, like the various doptions, that have a ritual form but are not identified as separate rituals by my respondents are not included in this list. The rituals are arranged in alphabetical order.

Anointing.   The rite of anointing is consecration by the rubbing of olive oil on the person to be consecrated. It is performed by those in a teaching position in the church (pointer, mother, teacher, assistant pointer, assistant mother). The oil is rubbed on the body in this order: face, eyes, ears, nose, mouth, neck, hands up to shoulder, feet up to knee, the top of the head. For each body part, an exhortation is given (e.g., "I am anointing your feet so you will be able to stand"). Anointing almost always follows washing, but it may be done alone if that is all that is called for by the Spirit. One may be anointed for healing from sickness or for help through a difficult time. One may be anointed if about to go on a long trip. The pilgrim is always anointed in preparation for her journey in the mourning room (at a banning) and on return from the mourning room (at a shouting). Anointing signifies the presence of God and the setting apart of the individual for special action. The

189

scriptures read for anointing are usually I Samuel 6 or Psalm 23. An anointing is described in chapter 5.

Banning.   Banning is the ritual blindfolding of an individual about to enter the mourning room for a spiritual journey. It comprises several parts and incorporates washing, anointing, sealing, taking proofs, as well as the rituals of the ordinary praise service. The most important part of the banning is the "placing of the bands" (also called "laying [the pointer's] hands on," "placing [the pointer's] handwriting on the head of") where numerous waxed pieces of cloth are placed on the pilgrim to blindfold her. The scripture most often cited in reference to the putting on of bands is Ezekiel 3. A banning is described in chapter 5.

Baptism.   Baptism by immersion is a defining ritual of the Spiritual Baptists. The actual baptism may be preceded or followed by time in the mourning room. A person going on her "baptismal journey" usually goes into the mourning room for three days, but some churches do a full mourning prior to baptism (9–15 days). Others follow with a full mourning. Baptism may be done in a river or in the ocean (usually on the calmer leeward side of the island). The church's cross, staff, and rod are planted in the sand, and the area is consecrated as in a church. The service is opened while the candidate kneels in prayer (with a lighted candle as always). The pointer, the leader, and the cross-bearer enter the water and consecrate the water where the baptism will take place. The cross is lifted out of the water and dropped in four directions. The bell is rung in four directions. Petals of flowers and colorful leaves are scattered all about. A nurse leads the candidate into the water. She is reminded by the pointer of the seriousness of her action. Her bands are lifted temporarily so that she may see the witnesses to her baptism. She is given one last opportunity to back out. When she says she wishes to continue, the pointer pushes the bands back down and immerses her three times (in the name of the Father, the Son, and the Holy Spirit). As the pilgrim goes under the first time, she releases her candle and it floats away as a symbol of her old life. The nurse leads her out of the water and several women take her to change into dry clothes. The pilgrim is then returned to the mourning room to await the shouting later that day. The scripture references most often cited regarding baptism are John 3 and Mark 16:16.

Blowing.   Any reporting of a message from God in church or elsewhere may be called blowing. However, blowing usually refers to the action of a trumpet blower going about her village or other areas calling out the message. Blowing was most often described to me as occurring in the middle of the night in response to a vision. The messages are often about someone going to die (if they don't change their ways) or about an imminent eruption of the volcano.

Candlelighting.   This is a type of thanksgiving where the table is not covered with food but with candles (although in some churches the food is present as well). In St. Vincent, candles are very expensive and a candlelighting is rare. The one I attended in St. Vincent had the members of the church and the visiting congregations (about a hundred people in all) march from the main road into the church carrying their candles, which each then set on a table and all about the church. The candles generated a lot of heat and light, and the effect was quite beautiful. In Brooklyn, candlelightings are fairly common. Of about ten I witnessed in New York, none involved marching. Most involved food. Like other thanksgivings, candlelightings were given as a thanks to God, to ask for a special favor, or in response to a vision instructing one to do so. The most common chorus sung during the lighting of the candles is, "Light your Light, Light your Light, Angels Watching Over You."

Christening.   A christening of any kind is a consecration to God as well as a naming. The christening rite is read from the Methodist *Book of Offices* (included at the back of the *Methodist Hymn Book*). In some churches, the christening rite is read from the *Book of Common Prayer*. The same rite is read whether the christening is for a child, a church, a house, or any spiritual item.

———— of a baby   Before the christening, the baby has no name. All in the congregation lean forward, eager to hear the name spoken for the first time.

———— of a church   A church, likewise, has no name before a christening. Apart from the required ritual goods (candle, calabash, etc.), the church is not decorated until it is christened. Like a baby, a church has godparents—usually one for each corner.

———— of a house   A house is also given a name at a christening, but it is not called by a name in daily life. A house has godparents as well.

———— of other items   Other items may be christened. For instance, on one occasion I observed the christening of a new bell for a church. The bell was given a saint's name and had four godparents as would a child, a church, or a house.

Consecration (or surveying).   The consecration is part of the opening of the church service. It is the establishment of a sacred space. The consecration is performed for every kind of Converted service, whether it be in a church, a house, in the market square, or at a crossroads. Each corner of the space is consecrated in turn, the surveyors making a cross by their movements (e.g., NE corner, then SW corner; NW corner, then SE corner). If the consecration is done in a house or church, all doorways are consecrated after the corners. The center pole and the altar are done next. A minimum of two items are required for the consecration, a glass of water and the bell. A prayer is said at each corner and the bell is rung, then the surveyor with the water says a brief prayer and pours some water into the corner. Most churches in St. Vincent use only the bell and the water. In Brooklyn, churches may have several surveyors. Corn, farine (casava flour), perfume, milk, oil, and/or wine may be spilled in the corners and thrown in several directions around the church during the consecration. The pattern of consecration in Brooklyn is similar to the practice of the Trinidadian Spiritual Baptist churches there. A description of consecration is given in chapter 3.

Communion.   This is the Eucharist as practiced in most Christian churches. The communion service is read from the Methodist *Book of Offices* in the *Methodist Hymn Book*. In some churches, communion is always given at a shouting. In most churches, communion is given on the first Sunday of each month. Both bread and wine (or grape juice) are given to the communicants.

Crowning.   If a pilgrim has received a crowned gift in the Spirit, a crowning must be performed at her shouting. It is not done if one merely receives a crown in the Spirit; the crown must accompany a spiritual gift (office) for a crowning to take place. A ring of five to nine candles (with one in the center) are placed on a plate. The plate is then set on the head of the pilgrim and she dances with the plate on her head. The effect of the candles moving about suggests a crown of light. A single hymn is sung during the crowning. The first verse is: All hail the power of Jesus' name / Let angels prostrate fall / Bring forth the royal diadem / And crown Him Lord of all / Bring forth the royal diadem / And crown Him Lord of all. A crowning lasts less than 10 minutes.

Fasting.   Fasting is prayer in the mourning room while eating little or no food. Sometimes mourning is referred to as fasting. A ritual called a *fasting* (or a *fast*) is a reduced form of mourning—usually for one night only. Bands may or may not be placed on the head, but all who are fasting are washed and anointed (from Matthew 6:17). Eight people participated in one fast I attended in St. Vincent. See chapter 6.

Funeral.   A Converted funeral is usually in three parts: the *churching*, the *marching*, and the *burial*. The churching is the service said over the body, usually in the home of the deceased, but it may be in a church. The family is expected to maintain silence during the churching. The marching is the funeral procession from the home or church to the graveyard. A funeral marching is a joyous, and sometimes raucous event. The Converted are happy that the deceased is "going to meet his maker." Ordinary people in the village come to the road to watch the singing, dancing, and the movement of the colorful uniforms. The churching is a solemn, sad event. The marching is happy and joyous. The burial is again sad. As the coffin is lowered into the ground, many cry. The pointer says a few prayers and the gravediggers cover the coffin. A mound is raised on top of the grave, on which are placed lighted candles and flowers. At the one Converted funeral I attended in St. Vincent, the immediate family stayed by the grave while the rest of those in attendance began to go home. The family posed next to the grave for a photograph and then they too left the site. The candles were left to burn on the grave.

House blessing (or cleaning of a house).   This is a ritual that may be performed for Converted people or non-Converted people. When one moves into a new house, it is blessed so that prosperity may come to those who live there. If particularly bad luck befalls long-time inhabitants of a house, the house may be blessed to remove evil influences. The pointer draws seals at each of the furthest corners of the house (or apartment) and above each door. Then each room has at least one seal drawn in it by the pointer. Each corner of the house, each door, and each room is consecrated as in the consecration ritual. The house is then considered cleaned or blessed. At some house blessings, a regular service is then held in the main room. The pointer may bless a house alone, but usually members of the church help him. The site of a house may also be blessed prior to construction (cf. Herskovits and Herskovits 1947:216–217). When a house is being constructed, the Vincentian custom is to put a peg (a clove) of garlic or some money under the corner post so that the house will bring prosperity.

Laying of cornerstone for a church.   This is the same ritual as the blessing for a house site. The Converted say, "You have to pay the church," by putting money under the cornerstone.

Marching.   A marching of the Spiritual Baptists is an interesting sight to the whole village. People come out of their houses and stand alongside the road to watch the colorful procession. Usually several churches participate. Each Converted is supposed to wear his or her full uniform. The leaders march in the front calling forth the choruses to sing as the marching proceeds. Everyone is supposed to dance— actually to "jig"—as they move down the road. Several hundred Converted may march at once and the singing is quite loud. The most frequent occasion for a marching is a funeral. Some churches march their candidates from the mourning room to the baptism site. A candlelighting in St. Vincent calls for a marching. At other times, a marching will be held when the Holy Spirit directs one or more important church members to organize one.

Memorials (nine night, forty days, and one year).   These are the traditional Vincentian (and West Indian) wake nights, held on the ninth night, the fortieth night and one year's anniversary of a death (cf. Hill 1977:351; Williams 1984). A wake is sometimes held on the night of the death and some Vincentians hold a memorial on the *third night* or *rising night* (when the spirit of the deceased is said to leave the body). A memorial in St. Vincent is often conducted by Spiritual Baptists whether or not the deceased or the family are Spiritual Baptists. The Baptists are believed to be especially efficacious in dealing with spirits. A memorial is described in chapter 8.

Missions (to specific places or churches).   A mission is any task that one is directed to do by God. Most often it is the result of a vision to hold a service in a specific place—which may be a church, a house, or a street corner. It may also be a call by God to deliver a message in a certain place or in a series of places. For example, while I was in St. Vincent, a pointing mother had a mission to deliver a message to the neighboring island of Bequia: Bequia would sink if the people of the island did not begin to pray for mercy. In the Converted churches, a mission is rarely, if ever, a proselyting effort as the word is commonly used by Christians. In Brooklyn, a group of Vincentian Converted have started a missionary society. The aim of the group is not to find converts, but to promote Christian unity by visiting different churches.

Mourning.   Mourning is the period of ritual seclusion in the mourning room during which the pilgrim traveler journeys in the spiritual world. In the mourning room, one grieves (or mourns) for one's sins. As the pilgrim is forgiven, she is taken by the Holy Spirit on various tracks (journeys), which may be in St. Vincent or in the various spiritual cities. The most commonly cited scriptural references regarding mourning are Daniel 10 and Matthew 5:4. Mourning is described in chapter 7.

Nine days.   For nine days after coming out of the mourning room, the pilgrim must leave the bands on her head. She is believed to be "still partly in the spiritual world" and continues to go on journeys and to receive visions for the nine days. During the nine days, she may not touch a knife, soap, money, or fire. She may not cook for herself and she must abstain from sex. She must pray with a candle four times a day—at six in the morning, at noon, at six in the evening, and at midnight. The pilgrim is said to "be in her nine days" or to "be doing her nine days." A further discussion of the nine days is provided in chapter 7.

Open air missions (or open airs)   An open air is a church service that is held in the market square or at a crossroads. The space is consecrated as in a church service. The main spatial difference between the church and the open air mission is that the altar table is set at the center of the space and the altar acts as the center—a condition never found in the church buildings. The entire rest of the service is as usual. The "open air" acts as a bridge between those who regularly go to Converted churches and those who sympathize with the Converted. Sometimes a collection plate is set on the altar table and money is contributed by passers-by. However, even if there is no collection plate, the entire table is likely to be covered with donated money. Most of those who give money are not Converted. Quite large sums may be collected at an open air service. One congregation used the money from a single open air to repaint their church building.

Opening the service.   Every meeting of Converted, whether it is the normal praise or a special ritual, must be opened by the leader of the church. The leader greets the congregation. The church is consecrated. The liturgy is recited (for most churches, the Methodist "Order for Morning Prayer"). The opening prayers are sung or said. All sing the greeting hymn and everyone in the church shakes hands with everyone else. After the greeting, the leader turns the service over to the pointer, who continues the service in whatever fashion is called for that evening.

Praise (Sunday morning worship and/or evening praise).   The praise is the usual church service. The main difference between a praise and other services is the absence of additional ritual. After the opening of the service at a praise, the remainder of the service is usually occupied with testimonies, rejoicing, and sometimes preaching.

Repentance (or baptismal candidacy).   The period of baptismal candidacy is characterized by begging for mercy from God. The candidate must sit on the *bench of repentance* (also called the *mercy seat*) in constant prayer. Candidacy usually lasts from six weeks to three months. If a candidate is on the bench, most of the speaking in church is directed to her. The candidate must sit on the bench with eyes closed (if a man) or eyes covered by the headtie (if a woman). The candidate must keep her feet marching in time whether she is sitting or standing. The candidate must also keep her palms up in supplication. The arms are bent and swing back and forth. Like the marching of her feet, the movements of the arms symbolize the candidate's forthcoming pilgrim journey. The candidate must always have a leaf or a flower or a candle in her right hand while she is sitting on the bench. A nurse always sits by the candidate, sometimes on the bench, sometimes in an adjacent seat. The nurse takes care of all of the needs of the candidate during the church service. If the candidate is a woman, the headtie that she wears to church is loosened and retied by the nurse to cover her eyes. During the service, the nurse wipes any sweat from the candidate's face. The nurse must bring the candidate water to drink and must clean the dripped candle wax from the candidate's hand. The nurse must accompany the candidate to the lavatory. After each service, the liminality of the candidate is set aside until the next church service. She may behave as normal outside of church until her baptism. After baptism she must behave as a Converted. If no candidate is on the bench, a candle or a sago palm leaf is placed on the bench to indicate its sacredness (or the bench may be kept in the mourning room).

Rising.   Rising is a ritual performed in the mourning room. On the third day after the banning, the rising is performed. At the banning, the pilgrim had been put down "like she is dead" and she is raised back to life at the rising. The pilgrim is laid down with a stone on her belly or chest. John 11 (the story of Lazarus' resurrection) is read. The stone is removed; the pilgrim is raised up and church members dance with her. The bands are retied by the pointer, and the revealing band (the one under the chin) is removed. The mourning room is usually ritually cleaned at this time. The floor may be scraped of candle wax and swept. The candles may be removed and new ones put in their place. The ritual goods (flags, calabash, lota, etc.) are usually rearranged. The floor may be washed with florida water (a perfume). In one church, the florida water is set on fire and the pilgrim is made to walk through the fire. The pilgrim's spiritual journeys often become more intense and vivid after the rising. A rising is described in chapter 7.

Robing.   A robing is a ritual investiture of spiritual clothing. It need not be performed for every item of spiritual clothing one receives, but it is a common ritual after a mourning. The spiritual clothes that the pilgrim received in the Spirit are blessed by the pointer and placed on the pilgrim. The items of clothing are placed on a cross as tall as a person (sometimes as if the cross is wearing the clothes, sometimes draped over); the bell is rung over all articles of the uniform—dress or gown, headtie or headwrap, apron, sash, or cord. The clothes are then put on the pilgrim. The pointer may say something like, "This uniform means work. When I put this uniform on you it means you have to work." If the clothes fit, it is taken as a sign of spiritual preparedness for the task associated with the clothing. Spiritual clothing is discussed in more detail in chapter 3.

Sealing.   Sealing is the placing of seals (pointers' seals) on a person. The sealing may be done for any sacred reason, but it is usually seen at a banning and at the time that candidates come forward "to accept Jesus" at a church service. When Converted say *a sealing*, they refer to the ritual used to seal individuals for baptismal candidacy. *Sealing*, without the indefinite article, is any sealing ritual. In sealing for baptismal candidacy, the candidate kneels and the pointer uses chalk to draw seals on the individual (head, hands, feet, shoulders, chest, and back) while Revelation 4 is read. Sealing during a banning is usually performed while the pilgrim is seated but in other respects is identical to the sealing for candidacy. Sealing is further described in chapter 5.

Shouting.   This is the return of the pilgrim from the mourning room. The main feature of the shouting is the ritual telling of the pilgrim's tracks (her journeys). The shouting comprises the following parts: the pilgrim is marched from the mourning room to the church; she is welcomed into the church; she is marched around the inside of the church; she is washed and anointed; words are given to the pilgrim; she receives gifts of candles; she tells her tracks. A shouting is among the most joyous of Converted events. A shouting is described in more detail in chapter 2.

Signing of bands.   This ritual is normally done by the pointer alone and in private. The pointer cuts cloth of different colors into triangular shapes and folds each of these into an elongated trapezium. These are the bands. Each band is then sealed with seals specifically selected for the pilgrim. The bands are then signed by the dripping of wax onto the cloth in a pattern that has been revealed to the pointer by the Holy Spirit. Most bands are nubbled with candle wax over their entire surface. Ten to 20 or more bands are prepared for each pilgrim. Pointers sign their bands in a variety of ways. The way that one pointer signs his bands is described in chapter 6.

Spiritual baths.   Spiritual baths are private rituals similar to the washing done in church. Spiritual baths are usually given to non-Converted who suffer spiritual or physical afflictions. Converted who experience suffering are more likely to seek a solution by mourning (communing with God directly). Spiritual baths are prescribed by the pointer to individuals who come to him (or her, if a pointing mother) with feelings of oppression or with illness that cannot be healed by secular doctors. Spiritual baths, along with dream interpretation, are the main private rituals that pointers perform on behalf of clients. A pointer who may give a spiritual bath is also called a *doctor* or a *spiritual doctor* or may be referred to by his specialty as a *bush doctor* or *bark doctor* (use of leaves, bark, and roots) or *chemical doctor* (use of perfumes and oils). The process of giving a spiritual bath is sometimes called *barking* someone. Some pointers may perform a ceremony known as *smoking* that uses the smoke of rosemary or other aromatic herbs. The Vincentians who told me about smoking indicated that it is only used to cleanse a baby from sickness caused by covetousness (that is, someone loving the baby too much). The baby is held over the smoke and the sickness goes away.

Taking a proof (or Bible proofs).   Converted individuals may take a proof at any time they feel they need spiritual guidance. At a banning, it is always done. The pilgrim kneels and opens the Bible with her thumbs. The verses indicated by her thumbs (and the two verses following) are read out loud to the congregation. It is a form of bibliomancy that "helps the pointer know where the pilgrim is at" spiritually. At home, a proof is often taken without kneeling. The individual crosses himself with the Bible and opens it with his thumbs, reading the verses to himself. Taking a proof is described in chapter 5.

Thanksgiving (or giving a table).   A thanksgiving is a ritual that may be performed at someone's home or in a church. It is given by a person who is thankful for a specific grace from God or in anticipation of such a grace. A thanksgiving is often given for one who is going away (for instance, from St. Vincent to Brooklyn or from Brooklyn to St. Vincent). A table is dressed with food, candles, flowers, and sometimes wine. The pointer may put seals on the table before it is dressed. After the service is opened, the thanksgiver says why she is giving the table. She sits beside the table while members of the church and visitors give her words of encouragement. The candles on the table are lit by different people in the congregation indicated by the thanksgiver. Usually dancing and rejoicing follows. When the church service is closed, the items on the table are distributed to the congregation to take home.

Washing.   A washing signifies spiritual cleansing and may be performed on various occasions. It is done at every banning and shouting. It may be done for one who is sick. Two basins of water are used, one for the feet and one for the rest of the body. Two towels are used, one for the feet and one for the rest of the body. At least five church members are required to wash each individual. Two nurses hold the basins and two hold the towels while the pointer or mother washes the person. A washing is described in chapter 5.

Spiritual Gifts

Spiritual gifts (or *spiritual names*) are the ritual roles or offices that individual Converted receive in the spiritual world. Converted are expected to perform the tasks associated with their spiritual name at appropriate rituals in the church service.

The following spiritual gifts are listed in roughly hierarchical order, low to high. The exact ranking varies by *spiritual school*. Most are not thought of as being in a specific order of rank, although a Converted individual generally is able to say if one gift is higher or lower than another. Broadly speaking, those roles that require more spiritual experience and knowledge have higher status.

The clothing for each gift varies with the individual's experience in the Spirit. Where the clothing is standardized, I indicate the standard. Usually, the higher one's rank, the more sashes, cords, and outer clothing are worn.

Bell Ringer (male or female).   In Converted churches, the bell is a tool of invitation to church members, to the community, and to the Spirit. The job of the bell ringer is to ring the (hand-held) bell at ritually prescribed times during church services—to call people to the service, at consecration, at a marching, and in greeting a visiting church. In addition to the times when everyone knows that the bell should be rung, the bell ringer responds to the Spirit. This is the defining feature of the bell ringer. Anyone may be pressed into service as a bell ringer when it is required by visible ritual, but the true bell ringer is one who is able to hear the bell ringing in the Spirit. When the bell is heard, the bell ringer is to go to the center pole (or wherever the bell is usually kept) and ring it in precisely the manner he or she hears in the Spirit. The manner is usually vigorous, but may be done softly on occasion.

Florist (female).   She is responsible for making sure the church is clean and full of flowers. She may respond to visions in deciding which flowers and plants to put in the church, but the choices are fairly standard. Crotons, dragon, sprigs of green plants, and white flowers of any sort are the main plants found in Converted churches in St. Vincent. Some plants are ritually prescribed. If the bench of repentance is empty, the place that would be taken by a candidate should have a "palm" (cycad) placed. While florist is a spiritual gift, some churches have no florist. Even in those churches with a florist, it is usual for a group of people (to keep each other company) to go together to clean and dress the church. Whereas in St. Vincent, flowers and colorful plants grow almost everywhere and may be picked without cost, in Brooklyn the church must purchase flowers from a secular florist. In Brooklyn, the tendency is less toward tropical plants and more toward temperate ones.

Water Carrier (female).   Converted services are long affairs, usually lasting five hours or more. The responsibility of the water carrier is to be alert to who in the church is thirsty and to carry or pass a glass or calabash of water to that individual. She is usually seated next to a large container of water at the front of the church so that she can observe the congregation and so that those who are thirsty can catch her eye.

Cross-Bearer (male).   The cross is the symbol of the sacrifice of Jesus Christ for the redemption of mankind from the eternal consequences of sin as well as the symbol of the sacrifices the Christian must make in the form of persecution and spiritual service. The cross is used as a symbol at transitional points in the life of Converted individuals (at banning, baptism, shouting, robing, and sometimes at sealing for baptism). At baptism, the cross-bearer carries the cross into the water. At a shouting, the cross-bearer precedes the pilgrim on her entry into the church. The cross-bearer carries the cross before the congregation at a marching. At other times, the cross-bearer is responsible for holding and carrying the cross from one place to another, but the pointer often takes the cross himself for use in whatever action is required.

Flag Waver (female).   Each Converted church has a number of flags hanging from the rafters, standing in corners, arranged on the center pole. Each of these are spiritual flags and are present in the church according to visions received to place them there. Many of the flags represent spiritual cities. Many represent Biblical themes (Victory, Truth, Faith). Others represent specific lessons learned in the Spirit, and some may have pointers' seals. Individuals who have been given a flag in the Spirit are required to make or have that flag made physically and then to wave that flag in every church service (in fact most do not, but they know that they should). Waving of the flag is both an invitation to the Spirit and a protection of the members from evil influences. At times when members are praying on their knees, flag wavers stand behind them, waving their flags to support them spiritually. The flag waving has the additional benefit of providing circulation in the dense tropical heat.

Trumpet Blower (female).   A trumpet blower (or *blower*) is an individual who receives messages from God and then must go about the town (or to wherever the message is directed at whatever time the message is directed) shouting out the message, frequently a prophecy, but usually an admonition. One blower passing my house in St. Vincent, arrayed in full spiritual clothing, had walked about six miles starting at five in the morning when I saw her. She was singing the hymn, "Christians Awake," stopping to deliver her message at villages along her route. I asked her the message and she called back, "Matthew 5" [the Sermon on the Mount]. The trumpet blower may also receive and deliver messages from God in the church service. Members will call out to anyone who has a message to give (even to those without the spiritual name of trumpet blower), "Blow your trumpet!"

Messenger (male).   The messenger is the male version of the trumpet blower. I never met one, but several Converted assured me that they exist.

Watchman (male).   This individual is responsible for spiritually guarding the church building. Every item in the church (the center pole, the bell, flags, etc.) has a spiritual reality more vital than its physical reality. Those with spiritual skill are able to enter the church and steal (spiritually) whatever they find there. The physical item is not stolen, only its spiritual efficacy. Several instances of this happening were related to me. Those whose spiritual tools have been stolen are unable to "go anywhere in the Spirit" and must apply to the individual who took them or else engage in a spiritual fight with that individual to get them back. Often when the item is taken, it is for instruction—a reminder to the church to take greater care of its spiritual assets—and the items are quickly returned, usually after a didactic spiritual fight. Sometimes the theft is with the intention to harm the congregation by luring away members from the church which has become spiritually ineffective. The watchman stands at the door (or sometimes sits), usually holding a rod (reminiscent of the eighteenth century constable's staff), scrutinizing the spirits who arrive (with his spiritual eyes), as well as keeping an eye on visiting Converted, especially ones unknown to the congregation. In Brooklyn, I did meet one female watchman (but I was informed that was rare).

Shepherd (male).   The shepherd is responsible to "tend his flock." He must watch that church members are properly attired and living right. I have seen shepherds intervene if two people were known to be feuding, forcing them to shake hands and make up. Shepherds will also encourage members to attend church who have fallen away. A strong spiritual discernment is required of the shepherd, but his activities are mainly in the physical world. In some congregations, the shepherd is a role for young men only. Others give it a very high status, seating the shepherds at the front of the church with the pointers and leaders.

Shepherdess (female).   The female version of the shepherd.

Surveyor (female or male).   Either a male or a female can be a surveyor, but it is usually a female. The surveyor "marks her line." She is responsible for the consecration of the church. At the consecration, she is the one who takes the water and the bell from the pointer and hands one or the other to whomever will assist her that evening. In St. Vincent, two people perform the consecration (ringing the bell and pouring water with prayers) at the four corners, the doors, the center post, and at the altar. In Brooklyn (probably reflecting Trinidadian influence), the churches frequently have up to six people doing the consecration, each with a different item (farine, perfume, oil, etc.).

Inspector (female or male).   The gift of inspector has a different status according to one's spiritual school. Inspector in this relative rank (relatively equal to shepherd, surveyor, and nurse) is someone who will "keep the troops in line." In St. Vincent, there is no army; the police take that role. The police inspector is a sergeant who drills his troops. In some churches, an inspector is one rank of pointer, higher than an ordinary pointer. In churches with lower-ranking inspectors, the role of inspector is to keep the singing lively. The inspector, in this or the higher rank, wears khaki with a sergeant's chevron on the sleeve.

Nurse (female).   The ranking of nurses is *Assistant Nurse, Nurse, Nurse Matron*. The term of address for assistant nurse and nurse is "Nurse," for nurse matron is "Matron." The nurse is responsible for the well-being of Converted who are in the mourning room. She will sleep with the mourner either inside the mourning room or in a room adjacent for the entire length of the mourning experience. She will escort the mourner to the toilet or latrine, she will give water to drink and food to eat. She reminds the mourner when it is time to pray. During candidacy for baptism, the nurse for the candidate sits on or beside the bench of repentance, tending to the needs of the candidate. She escorts the candidate from the mourning room to the baptismal site, attends the physical requirements of the candidate at baptism (providing dry clothing, etc.), and sits beside the candidate throughout the shouting. The nurse is integral to the mourning experience. The assistant nurse helps, but the nurse does the bulk of the work. The nurse matron directs the work.

African warrior (female).   The African warrior (or *warrior*) is one who fights the spiritual fight (by lively singing and dancing in the church setting). It is said that one can always tell an African warrior because she cannot keep still in church, she always "goes all about the church." African warriors are among the easiest of the roles to detect. In St. Vincent, the only warriors are African warriors, but in Brooklyn, some Vincentians recognize Indian and Chinese warriors as well (possibly due to Trinidadian influence).

Diver (male or female).   The diver is one who, during the church service, is able to see with spiritual eyes the status of each worshipper. The diver is (supposed to be) very active in the service, going about to different members in the congregation, encouraging them in a spiritual way (to sing more lively, to give up sin that is holding them back, to answer a call to mourn). The diver is the beginning of a series of spiritual names with enhanced spiritual power.

Captain (male).   This is another of the gifts that in some churches has a very high status that one matures into and that in others has a rather lower status believed to be most suitable to young men. However, every gift from God is respected as sacred. All agree that the job of the captain is to steer the ship. One of the primary organizing metaphors for Converted life is that of the church as a ship. The captain steers the ship by directing singing and doption. In churches where the captain has a high status, he will be seated at the front of the church with the other ministers. The role of the captain, whether it is exercised by a captain, a leader, or a pointer is one of the most important jobs in the church setting. The whole spiritual experience of the service may depend on the skill of the captain at steering the boat through the spiritual lands.

Prover (male).   This is a person with great spiritual power. He can see into the hearts of individuals. In fact, his job is to search the souls of those in church and to warn them of dangers he finds there (normally, sin that will bring the chastisement of the Holy Spirit). Sometimes the prover, to do his job better, sits at the back of the church so that he can see everyone, that some will not hide from him, as they often do.

Leader (male).   The job of the leader is to open the service and to direct the prayers and opening hymns. The leader is also responsible for keeping the service lively (sometimes taking the role of captain, sometimes assisting the captain in that role). Ranks of leader are *assistant leader* and *leader*. The leader must have an excellent memory to keep the liturgy in the right order. Although some leaders read the liturgy out of the Methodist *Book of Offices*, most recite it from memory. The leader is responsible to call out the words of hymns. Leaders have hundreds of tunes and their words memorized. The leader is second in authority only to the pointer (and/ or pointing mother) of the church, though his role is primarily liturgical.

Leadress (female).   The female version of the leader. Usually this is a *mother leadress*, but she may be a leadress without being a mother.

Mother (female).   All Converted agree there are several kinds of mothers. Some insisted that there are seven kinds of mothers, but no one was able to name all seven for me. (I think this relates more to the mystical importance of the number seven than to the existence of seven kinds of mothers.) Three ranks of mother that all agreed on are: *mother, assistant mother, pointing mother*. If we add "mother leadress," "teacher," Henney's (1974:31) "queen mother" and "nurse matron," that would make seven, but I think it is more significant to note that the type of mother is flexible and not categorically fixed. The mother's role is one of instruction and correction. The mothers assist in every aspect of the spiritual work in the church.

An essential accoutrement of the mother is the belt. This is a wide article, seldom less than two and a half inches, fastened on the outside of the clothing, ready to come off if necessary to give someone a strapping. The universal reason given for the meaning of the belt was chastisement. The mother is a general rank of authority and service in the church. The assistant mother aids in the banning. The pointing mother has the ability to sign bands and to point pilgrims on to the Spirit. The pointing mother frequently has a church of her own. She is, in essence, a female pointer.

Teacher (male or female).   This is a high rank that has variable meaning according to spiritual school. In some churches, the gift of teacher is equated with a pointer. In others, it simply means an individual with deep spiritual knowledge to which one can turn for advice or spiritual instruction. Another one of the main organizing metaphors for Converted life is that the church is a school. A teacher usually carries a stick, like one a "carnal" teacher will use to point to lessons on a chalkboard. The teacher, if not a pointer, may stay in the mourning room with the pilgrim, helping the mourner to make sense of her journeys. The teacher is someone to whom one turns for dream interpretation or other advanced spiritual tasks. The Spiritual Baptist Archdiocese denomination (consisting of 40 churches or approximately 20–25 percent of the Vincentian Converted churches) discourages use of the term *pointer*, which does not occur in the Bible, preferring *teacher* instead (Ephesians 4:11).

Pointer (male).   The pointer is the head of the church. The role of pointer also requires a belt. The belts are of the same type as those of the mothers, some thicker than others. The main job of the pointer is to baptize converts and to mourn pilgrims. The *Assistant Pointer* (whose term of address is also "Pointer") aids the pointer in placing the bands on the pilgrim's head and with anything else his pointer directs him to do. The pointer's role is larger than merely baptizing and pointing, and there are a number of additional gifts that are found only in pointers (namely, various types of healing abilities, such as *bush doctor* and *chemical doctor*). A pointer may also be an *inspector* of a different order than that described above. The inspector is a pointer whose role is to guide other pointers. The inspector is generally a mature pointer with several spiritual children who have gone on to become pointers themselves. Any of the additional gifts unique to pointers may also be acquired by women. It is not uncommon to meet pointing mothers who are high-ranking inspectors.

Notes

1: Introduction

1. On the other hand, Caribs were often Christian. Many of the Caribs had been converted to Catholicism during their hundred years of association with the French (Gonzales 1991: 25). By the 1850s, Davy (1971:195) reported that all of the Caribs that remained on St. Vincent were Christians and had their children baptized in the Established (Anglican) Church.

2. Caribs in St. Vincent are apparently rather different from the ones on Dominica, the Vincentian ones having become completely "West Indianized" (Banks 1955). Gullick's (1985) data show that a sense of identity is all that separates the Vincentian Caribs from the rest of Vincentian society.

3. I was unable to elicit the word "Creole" from my respondents (except as a language spoken in St. Lucia), even though that word is applied to Black people in St. Vincent by several researchers (Lowenthal 1967; Abrahams 1983; V. Young 1993). Rubenstein (1987) and Gullick (1985) use the term "Afro-Caribbean," but my respondents most often used the term "Black" if they needed to differentiate between groups on the island.

4. In the 80 years after 1834, only 5,610 indentured workers were introduced into St. Vincent: 2,470 East Indians (of whom 1,050 were repatriated at the end of their indenture), 2,100 Portuguese from Madeira, and 1,040 Africans (Byrne 1969:155). From the early 1860s, poor White Barbadians started migrating to St. Vincent. By 1870, 300–400 people had settled at the still predominantly White area of Dorsetshire Hill (Sheppard 1974:86). Their descendants are today called "Coolies" or "local Whites" or, pejoratively, "Bajans." Lowenthal (1967:593) wrote that they "are not part of the elite, but are close in culture and status to the black peasantry." They are perceived by the (Black) people I knew as manual laborers. The local Whites are the people one would hire to help with harvest or other farmwork.

5. More information on whaling in Bequia can be found in Adams (1970; 1971) and Thomsen (1988). Curiously, there are no studies of whaling on St. Vincent itself.

6. In 1995, when I was in St. Vincent, the per capita Gross Domestic Product was 1,700 U.S. dollars (EIU 1996:47). Of course, the people with whom I had the most contact controlled only a portion of that figure. The number was skewed by the small government and business elite, many of whom had income counted in millions of dollars. The figures also do not represent the large volume of gifts sent in barrels, especially around Christmas, from the United States, Canada, and England by Vincentian expatriates to their families.

7. Those studies (e.g., Said 1978; Bhabha 1984; Fabian 1986; R. Young 1990; Thomas 1991; 1992; Stoler 1992; Taussig 1993), in turn, follow from debates on colonialism set in larger questions of power (e.g., Wallerstein 1974; 1980; Bourdieu 1977; 1990; Foucault 1980; de Certeau 1984; Scott 1985).

8. Local religious expression in colonial societies has sometimes been viewed as a way of creatively engaging the structures of domination (Taussig 1980; 1982; 1987; Lan 1985; Comaroff 1985; Dirks 1987; Ong 1987; Comaroff and Comaroff 1991; Stoller 1995; and less directly, Bourguignon 1973; Lewis 1989; Boddy 1989; 1994). Comaroff (1985), for instance, shows how a religion similar to the Converted reproduces colonial constructs in its organization, and Taussig (1980) demonstrates how the terrors of capitalism are met by a colonially structured religious response.

9. For general works, see especially Herskovits 1966; Bastide 1978; Raboteau 1978; 1995; Sobel 1979; Simpson 1980; Thompson 1984; Pitts 1993; Murphy 1994.

10. I use the terms "shamanism," "shamanistic," and "shaman" to describe the practices of the Converted. I detail why I think the Converted are best compared to shamans in chapter 8. Briefly, though, I use the terms to refer to all of the traits usually associated with shamanism in small-scale societies. For a concise definition of shamanism, I use: the practice of spiritual work on behalf of the community by ecstatic means. Much of the debate on shamanism has revolved around what should and should not be described as such (see Atkinson 1992 for a review of the literature). Mostly, though, the category "shaman" has been applied to those whose religious practices resemble the Siberian shamans from which the name derives. I continue that custom by terming the Converted shamans. Whether or not the Converted or any of the hundreds of groups who have been described as practicing shamanism actually do the exact same thing as the Siberian groups is not as important as recognizing that the complex of traits we have called shamanism is a widespread human tendency. I continue this discussion in chapter 8.

11. At least 12 researchers have looked at the religion in Trinidad (in order of the number of pages dedicated to the Spiritual Baptists are: Glazier 1980; 1983; 1984; 1985a; 1985b; 1985c; 1986; 1988; 1992; Simpson 1966; Houk 1992; 1995; Parks 1981; Herskovits and Herskovits 1947; Ward and Beaubrun 1979; Williams 1985; Taylor 1993; Littlewood 1993b; Hackshaw 1992). Other studies have been done on Spiritual Baptists in Grenada (Pollack-Eltz 1970; 1972), in Tobago (Nagashima 1985), and in Barbados (Griffith and Mahy 1984; 1985; Griffith, Mahy, and Young 1986).

12. The research of other anthropologists in St. Vincent and the Grenadines is available in books (Fraser 1973; Abrahams 1983; Gullick 1985; Rubenstein 1987; Price 1988; Thomas-Hope 1992; V. Young 1993), dissertations (Henney 1968; Jackson 1972; Landman 1972; Ciski 1975; Hourihan 1975; Betley 1976; Fraser 1979; Glesne 1985; Toney 1986; Gearing 1988), and articles (Pitt 1955; Fraser 1975; Beck 1985; Gearing 1992). Besides the anthropological works, Spinelli (1973), Punnett (1984), Ishmael (1988), and Stewart (1993) have written dissertations related to Vincentian culture. Other scholarly articles related to St. Vincent are by Hadley (1973), Austin (1989; 1996), Brittain (1991), and Thomas-Hope (1992). A neocolonial metropolitan view of St. Vincent (partially fictionalized) appears in two of the stories in Shacochis' *Easy in the Islands* (1985) and in his novel *Swimming in the Volcano* (1993).

13. I respected the wishes of those who told me not to put certain things "in the book," but if I received the same information from other people without that stipulation, I have included it. I repeated over and over that I did not want to know any secrets. While I did not miss much, I am lacking detailed knowledge of the private rituals the Converted do for clients (e.g., cleansing from sickness and feelings of oppression). Some information of a potentially sensational nature I will reserve for a later publication. I do not include illustrations or photographs with the text. I took very few photographs in the field. Even though the Converted would have let me take as many as I wanted, it was more respectful not to do so at the time. Likewise, I do not provide drawings of the beautiful *seals* (chalk drawings)

produced by the Converted. They are believed by the Converted to be endowed with spiritual power and misuse and/or misunderstanding of the symbols are thought by many to be dangerous to the uninitiated. Examples of Converted seals may be found in Henney (1974) and Thompson (1984).

3: Spiritual Workers

1. The relationship of Converted religion to shamanism is discussed in chapter 8.

2. Jesus and God the Father are as important to one's salvation, but the Holy Spirit is most important to the accomplishment of work. Converted frequently meet Jesus in the spiritual world. Less frequently, they meet God the Father. Sometimes they meet someone in the form of a man who is described as the Holy Spirit. All three are united as one God in the Trinity. One who has met any one of the three has met God. God the Father, God the Son, and God the Holy Spirit are prayed to separately or all together as "God." Although the Trinity may be confusing to one who is recently introduced to it, most Converted, and most Christians in the world, accept the concept as normal. The human ability for spiritual travel is sometimes explained as analogous to the Holy Trinity. The human, like God, has a body, a soul, and a spirit. It is the spirit that travels in the spiritual lands while the body remains in the mourning room or in one's bed.

3. See the appendix for a description of each of these.

4. Herskovits and Herskovits (1947:194–197) identified 19 offices among the Spiritual Baptists they studied in Trinidad: preacher, teacher, prover, leader, divine healer, healer, captain, pastor, shepherd, shepherdess, pumper, diver, prophet, apostle, queen, fortune-teller, surveyra [sic], judge, nurse.

Glazier (1983:52–54), also in Trinidad, listed 22: prover, preacher, shepherd, captain, pointer, bell ringer, water carrier, postman, healer, diver, watchman, surveyor, nurse, teacher, leader, mother, sister, brother, warrior, commander, inspector, and judge.

Parks (1981:69) found six: nurse, teacher, mother, captain, shepherd, leader.

Henney (1974:30–31) noted 13 among the Vincentians she studied: pointer, leader, captain, king captain, preacher, mother, pointer mother, assistance mother, mother matron, mother helper, queen mother, nurse, and warrior.

5. A description of each of the spiritual gifts may be found in the appendix. Some gifts included in the lists of the other ethnographers were recognized as existing by my respondents. Since I was unable to elicit them independently, I do not include them in my list of general spiritual gifts available in St. Vincent at the time of my study.

6. In Brooklyn, a highly respected individual had the spiritual name of "Missionary Janey" by which she was addressed. While anyone may be sent on a mission (any spiritual task in another location or church) by the Spirit and are thereby missionaries, the specialization of this gift in this individual was recognized. She described the responsibility associated with the gift of missionary as "going from church to church" for the purpose of goodwill. The spiritual gifts of bell ringer, cross-bearer, messenger, florist, water carrier, trumpet blower, and flag waver do not carry with them terms of address. These individuals are called Sister or Brother (as are those who have not gained any spiritual task) and visiting strangers (such as myself), who may or may not be Christians. I was commonly known as Brother Wally.

7. The pole may extend from floor to ceiling or only partway. It may have a stepped "wheel" constructed at the base or have one drawn in with chalk. In some Trinidadian churches I visited in Brooklyn, the pole, ascends only three to four feet, with a rotating horizontal wheel placed atop, which is attended by the captain of the church. Some Trinidadian churches had no center pole. In Vincentian churches, the captain steers the ship of the church by his voice (see chapter 4).

8. Occasionally, the pattern or the number and gender of participants in the consecration varied. In Brooklyn, consecrations accomplish the same task with quite a bit more variety.

9. In Brooklyn, the lota represents India and is always set in its accompanying brass plate, the *taria*. In St. Vincent, where the lota is a recent introduction, I was unable to elicit a connection with India. In St. Vincent, the taria is separated from the lota and is used in most churches as a collection plate.

10. One pointer added scissors to the list of tools one is required to possess in the Spirit before becoming a pointer. The scissors are necessary because one must know how to cut the bands.

4: Music

1. Some of these ideas are discussed by Eliade (1982:103), Stoller (1984), Hart (1990), and Spickard (1991).

2. On only one occasion in St. Vincent did I observe a man play an actual, physical, flute in church. I assumed this was because of some direction from the Spirit. On later occasions, he did not bring his flute.

In Trinidadian churches in Brooklyn, musical instruments were sometimes present, usually drums. Trinidadian Spiritual Baptist music is different from the Vincentian Converted musical tradition, but it may provide some correspondences. I refer the reader to Glazier (1997) and McDaniel (1995). After I had been fairly well socialized into the Vincentian Converted musical patterns, I was often frustrated (as were Vincentians I was with) by the difference in styles, words, and meanings given to songs in churches in Grenada and in non-Vincentian Spiritual Baptist churches in Brooklyn. Nonetheless, the majority of the songs themselves are the same or very similar. The meanings ascribed to individual songs vary between the islands, by congregation, and according to individual understanding.

3. Drury (1982:8) writes of the shaman's drum that "its rim is invariably made of wood from the world tree." Although I am skeptical of that statement, it does have a Converted parallel. The Bible—the word of God—is the main axis of Converted belief. The Converted use the Bible as a percussive instrument, sometimes trying out several borrowed Bibles to get the right tone.

4. The definition of overtone singing is that one person sings in two voices (Klingholz 1993:118). Michael Vetter (1983:6) describes the effect of hearing vocal overtones on the listener: "At first the innocent listener can scarcely believe his ears: out of the single-toned sound of one voice a second voice unfolds, and over the unchanging ground tone there develops a melodic line whose ethereally pure tonality and harmony seem removed from all things human." The fundamental (the lower tone, also known as the drone) and the overtone (the separately perceived higher tone) sung together are sometimes known as a "chord chant" (Bloothooft et al. 1992:1827), because the single person, in effect, sings a chord. An important difference between the overtone singing I have heard in other contexts (recordings of Tuvan singers and Gyuto monks) is that the drone (as well as the overtone) of the Converted overtone singing is composed of quarter notes, while the drone of the Asian style is held for several seconds. The Converted overtone singing, in other words, conforms to African rhythmic patterns. A possible corollary may be found in St. Lucia, where "[s]ome of the male singers are adept at *gundé* (French *gronder*) singing, giving a throaty rattling effect to their tones" (Crowley 1957:9). I did not notice the overtoning technique in the few Trinidadian churches I visited in Brooklyn, nor does Mervyn Williams (1985) mention it in his study of Spiritual Baptist music in Trinidad.

5. Glazier (1983:45), in his study of Trinidadian Spiritual Baptist leadership, identifies uses of Spiritual Baptist songs in terms of power relations. Later, he refers to these as "battles in the spirit" (Glazier 1997). I did not find power struggles between leaders played out in songs in St. Vincent or in Brooklyn. Introduction of songs in St. Vincent is a way to lay claim to a turn at speaking.

6. The Caribs still resident in St. Vincent are identical in culture to other Vincentians, retaining only some phenotypical differences (Crawford and Comuzzie 1989) and a sense of Carib identity (Gonzalez 1991). A delegation of Black Carib (Garifuna) from Belize (whose culture originated in St. Vincent) made a tour of the island while I was in St. Vincent. I was able to view several of their dances and to hear many of their songs. Apart from a general African nature, I detected no similarity to Converted songs or dances.

7. Pitts (1989; 1991; 1993) analyzes African American church song styles as consisting of two frames, a "soporific first frame" (deriving from European structures), and a more lively, more vernacular, "ecstatic" second frame (with an African or African American origin). For the Spiritual Baptists, the slower songs are as ecstatic as the faster ones. I was even told by several Converted that the slower songs help them to "go through" (into the Spirit) faster than the songs with a quicker tempo. Although some of the slow songs did seem soporific to me, the meaning applied to the song was more important to the Converted than the tempo. Unlike the American Afro-Baptist churches described by Pitts (1989), where only songs exhibiting African traits may induce trance, every song in the Converted repertoire (European-like or African-like) is conducive to trance (or entry into the Spirit). Likewise, in St. Vincent, there is not a temporal separation between lined hymns and choruses as he finds (Pitts 1993: 145–153). The Converted have transformed African and European sounds and meanings into their own.

8. I did not find the tune recorded for this hymn by Herskovits and Herskovits (1947: 211) in current use in St. Vincent or in Brooklyn. Glazier (1997) notes alterations of (or experimentation with) tunes of hymns in Trinidadian Spiritual Baptist practice. The tunes for hymns that I recorded in St. Vincent as well as in Brooklyn among Vincentian Converted are nearly always the original tunes used by the Methodists (and sometimes as compiled by Sankey, n.d. The disparity between this apparent conservatism on St. Vincent and the experimentation on Trinidad may have something to do with the presence of greater pressures for cultural change on the larger island.

9. Many Converted choruses are similar in structure and tune to sea shanteys. I have been unable to identify any Converted tunes as belonging to specific shanteys, but shanteys are commonly sung in St. Vincent both on sea and land (Abrahams 1974), and the style would have been familiar to Converted during the development of the religion. Shanteys, like many of the Converted songs, are used to coordinate the actions of a group of workers.

6: Pilgrim Travelers

1. Information on the spiritual world is compiled from information gathered at 16 *bannings* (of 29 people) and 14 *shoutings* (of 28 people) in nine different Converted churches as well as scores of interviews with individual Converted regarding their spiritual travels. One third of the pilgrims in the bannings and shoutings I observed were men. This contrasts with the church services themselves, where men usually make up about 20 percent of the congregation. I also attended two bannings (of five people) in Trindadian churches in Brooklyn and a shouting of three individuals in a Spiritual Baptist church in Grenada. While the expectation of travel in these churches was similar, the traditions of what to expect appeared to be different.

A number of individuals sat down with me and detailed every place they traveled in the Spirit. Some of these respondents were new to the faith. One had only one experience; others had several journeys. Experienced Converted have had hundreds of journeys. By those, I was given an overview of their travels. In addition, in most church services, mention is made of events and locations in the spiritual world.

2. I feel I must reiterate that to the Converted, the most exciting part of their cosmology is salvation through Jesus Christ. Praise of Christ takes up the major part of every Converted

gathering. Converted, however, do express excitement that they get to travel in the spiritual lands.

3. The Valley dogs are watchdogs. They are watching on behalf of God. In reference to sleeping watchdogs, some pastors admonish their children not to be "dumb dogs" (Isaiah 56: 10) that cannot bark. Dogs, common to human experience, are to be expected to find their way into metaphors that organize experience. The Dominicans were known as "Domini canes," the watchdogs of God. (Harvey 1995:46). In St. Vincent, dogs, like death, are dangerous (and both are associated with bones). In Desana and related cultures, the shaman and the jaguar are connected by the fact of both being, respectively, the most dangerous of animals and the most dangerous of humans (Reichel-Dolmatoff 1975). The most powerful shamans turn into jaguars. In St. Vincent, the most dangerous animal is the dog. (I was often asked, in relation to my tendency to walk about alone at night, "Aren't you afraid the dogs will get you?") The most common animal the Converted become is a dog, though I have seen them become snakes as well (and among non-Vincentian Spiritual Baptists, lions). Snakes in St. Vincent are not dangerous. Although an extremely poisonous species of snake, the *fer-de-lance*, exists on the neighboring island of St. Lucia, it is not found in St. Vincent, and, apparently, cannot survive there (Kingsley 1910:40).

4. Jericho is not associated with horses in the Bible. However, Joshua, the conqueror of Jericho and one who is forever associated with Jericho in song, is connected with horses in Zechariah 6. No Converted referenced Zechariah in relation to Jericho. They said one had to enter Jericho on a horse but they did not know why.

5. The nature of God is problematic in the analysis of Converted religion. God is too multiform for me to give a concise description of how the Converted relate to him. The Converted themselves do not seem to have problems with his many forms and characteristics or with his many demands. The name of Jesus is sometimes used as a talisman, sometimes in discussion of historical material, and sometimes to refer to a person they met in the spiritual world. God the Father and the Holy Spirit are equally variable. Except for the expectation that it is possible to see and converse with God in the spiritual world, the Converted perceive him in much the same way that he is treated in Pentecostal churches.

6. Allegorical names given to spiritual beings is not restricted to the Converted. Among the Haitian loa recorded by Rigaud (1985:56–57) are Madame Travaux (Mrs. Works) and Maître Cimitière (Master of the Cemetery).

7. Converted spiritual fighting is similar to descriptions of *ladiya (ladjia, agwa)* fighting in the French Antilles (Desch 1994). The photographs in Michalon's (1987:62–73) book about ladjia could have been taken (with different costuming) in Converted churches in St. Vincent. Converted sword fighting is also similar to performances of Ogun dancing that I have seen in Brazilian Candomblé. Converted spiritual fighting is only done in the context of the church. Nonsacred ritual fighting (like ladiya or the stick-fighting of Trinidad) is not found in St. Vincent. Like many of the Converted dances, we find in spiritual fighting the curious survival of a no-longer-practiced secular event in the sacred setting of the church.

8. Like other churches that have a Pentecostal experience, Converted glossolalia displays much "routine in the group's spontaneity, a recurrent limited vocabulary" (Bateson 1994: 123). In fact, American Pentecostal groups who speak in tongues do have denomination-limited patterns, contrary to their insistence that God is enabling them to practice xenoglossia (the speaking of actual foreign languages unknown to the speaker). That the patterns in Converted glossolalia are standardized and limited (contrary to the findings of Henney 1974: 59–78; 1980) is not a problem to the Converted. They are speaking a spiritual language, and it cannot be expected to adhere to the same rules as a "carnal" language. Languages for most of the spiritual cities have a mere four or five morphemes (e.g., Africa: ga, ge, gi, gong; China: ching, chong, see, saw; the Valley: skop, kip, kop, skip, kik). We cannot rule out the possibility of diffusion. The Wesleys spoke in a similarly alliterative glossolalia (May 1956:75–76)—And they are one of the sources of Converted religion (see chapter 11; Henney 1971:230). On the

other hand, Converted glossolalia may be an extension of a regional linguistic stereotype. Trinidadian Earl Lovelace (1988:41), in his story, "The Fire Eater's Journey," writes about a calypsonian who "went on stage without a clear tune or thorough lyrics, just a theme, just a chorus: *Chong chiki chong chong*. It was a song about a Chinese man."

9. The doctor's shop is the same name used during slavery (Sparling 1970:59). Perhaps the term is still used in the countryside, but the people I knew were more likely to say they were going "to the doctor." "Doctor's shop" seems to be reserved for the spiritual lands.

10. "Dans le cas de l'ébéniste, de la couturière, les témoignages concordent. Il s'agit de réaliser un objet à partir d'un modèle; or ces personnes, étant analphabètes, déclarent: «je ne pouvais pas laisser partir cet argent. J'ai donc accepté le travail. En allant me coucher, je me suis demandé comment j'allais m'y prendre. La nuit, en dormant, quelqu'un m'est apparu et m'a indiqué comment faire. Le lendemain, je réalisais très bien l'ouvrage demandé. Depuis, j'opère de cette façon et je peux réaliser n'importe quel modéle.«"

11. Persinger (1983) hypothesizes that religious and mystical experiences are derived from electrical microseizures in the temporal lobe. Although this work does not deal with the physiology of Converted experience, the Converted are able to provide information about the physiological nature of spirit possession and of mystical states. I am inclined to agree with Persinger when I consider the remarkable similarity of Converted and other Pentecostal-type possession "shaking" to epileptic seizures and also to many of the behaviors in Tourette's syndrome. Both epilepsy and Tourette's are sometimes disorders of the temporal lobe (Cytowic 1993:134). And possession is sometimes known as "theolepsy," being seized by a god (Price-Mars 1980:203). Although it is probably unrelated, I must note here that the bands worn during mourning are often tied about the temples so tight as to lacerate the ear (where the edge of the bands rubs against the ear) and permanent scars are often left. Checking the ear for scars is cited by Converted as a way to confirm someone's identity as a Spiritual Baptist. The tightness of the bands on the temples may produce effects on the temporal lobe of the brain.

12. The spelling of *doption*, as with all of the words significant in Converted experience, was elicited. A few Converted preferred the spelling *duption*. That spelling, in fact, appeared in print in Richards (1965:18). Whenever I asked for spellings, Converted protested that they did not write the words that I was asking about, but they obliged when I told them I would rather have their guess at a spelling than my guess at a spelling. One woman said to spell it "doption" because it is related to adoption. Trinidadians I met in Brooklyn often called it "adoption." Glazier (1980:95) wrote it (for Trinidad) as "adoption" and referred to it as "a form of hyperventilation."

13. In Jamaican Pukkumina, "labouring" denotes travel (Seaga 1982:8). It appears to be similar in concept to Converted doption. However, in Pukkumina, a number of people perform specific tasks during the journey, while in Converted doption, journeying is the task. Although travel in a doption-like event occurs in Jamaican religion and seems to direct the origin of both Converted doption and Pukkumina to an African source (probably Kongo [Brathwaite 1982a; Bilby and Bunseki 1983]), we cannot assume it. Similar travel is reported for the Wana of Sulawesi, the Yamana of Tierra del Fuego, and the Salish of the Northwest Coast—all cultures remote from one another. A more likely explanation is one based on human physiology. On the other hand, the content of the journeys is clearly culture specific.

14. "Seeking" (conversion) in African American churches in South Carolina and Georgia took place alone, under the guidance of a spiritual parent and "typically involved visions and dream travel. Required to pray at dawn, noon, sunset, and midnight, often in the midst of a wood or thicket, seekers were supposed to follow wherever the Spirit led and to report all dreams and visions to their guides" (Raboteau 1995:154–156; cf. Sobel 1979:108–128, 139–149; C. Williams 1982; Creel 1988:285–290. Brown 1994;). Glazier (1985a) proposes that the similarity points to a historical connection between the Afro-Baptists of the American South

and the Spiritual Baptists of Trinidad (cf. Raboteau 1978:29). However, similar events are found in many parts of the world.

In the Daime religion in Brazil, revelations attained on spiritual journeys occasioned by ayahuasca use become a second "New Testament" in addition to the Bible (Chaumeil 1992; cf. Monteiro 1988). The collective revelations become a source of inspiration for the entire congregation. The Spirit Dance of the Salish of the Northwest appears to be remarkably like Spiritual Baptist mourning, with days of seclusion in darkness, blindfolds, being attended to by "baby-sitters," learning songs and dances from spirits, rhythmic chanting, and a celebratory coming-out ceremony (Jilek 1992). Lushootsheed Salish shamans conduct an important rite of healing by means of a collective spiritual journey through a culture-specific spiritual landscape (Miller 1988; cf. Jilek 1992). Miller (ibid., 175) calls it "co-officiating." It is significant that the ritual requires the shamans to journey together and to stop at each of several specific locations along the way (like doption).

15. Dying away may have changed over time. Gullick (1971:9) wrote that "going dead away" was interpreted as a spirit attacking the worshippers. Sinners in the congregation collapsed from the attack. However, when revived, the person who went "dead away" was described by Gullick as recounting an experience with a spirit—as in the case of the nonsinners among my respondents who died away.

16. Winkelman (1992:93–97), in a cross-cultural survey of shamanism, lists techniques to induce shamanic states: auditory driving, fasting and nutritional deficits, social isolation and sensory deprivation, meditation, sleep and dream states, sexual abstinence, excessive motor behavior, endogenous opiates (e.g., dancing), hallucinogens, and alcohol. The Spiritual Baptists do all of these, short of hallucinogens and alcohol. The Converted do not use hallucinogens or intoxicants to achieve their altered states, but both tobacco and alcohol are occasionally present in the church setting in an auxiliary way—and consumed when directed by the Spirit.

17. Like Rokeach's (1964:208–209) *Three Christs of Ypsilanti*, the Converted know that experiential facts with social support are less controversial than those without. That does not, however, make them less likely to believe their experience, but it does affect how they report it. A number of the tales told to me in private of travels in the spiritual world would not be told at a shouting. Some of them, my respondents told me, they did not even tell to their pointer. The sensations are physical, even though the travel is spiritual. Rokeach (Ibid., 286) found that suggestions produced actual somatic effects in the three Christs, as did Griffith, Mahy, and Young (1986) in relation to Spiritual Baptist mourning.

8: Work and Travel

1. In this chapter, I draw on general works on shamanism with only a few quotations from case studies. The intention is not to debate the nature of shamanism but to indicate that the Converted may be profitably compared with shamanism to show both something new about shamanism and to show Converted religion as an example of a basic human ability.

2. Cox (1995:224–228) uses the terms "pentecostal shamanism," and "Christian shamanism" to refer to Pentecostal churches in Korea, where a long tradition of shamanism exists. He names, as evidence that Christian shamanism is operating in the Pentecostal churches, the presence of "shamanic trance, demon possession, exorcism." These three elements are present in every Pentecostal church in the world. Pentecostals, following good biblical precedent (e.g., Luke 9:42) recognize the presence of demons, whether the demons be of indigenous or European origin and identification. The Vincentian and Korean phenomena are clearly similar. In fact, Zaleski (1987) shows that shamanistic events are common in the history of Christianity. All of this highlights the provisional nature of analytical categories in the light of ethnographic data.

3. This idea appears to be counter to recent work that explains religious experience as the embodiment of social experience and cultural memory (e.g., Csordas 1994a; Stoller 1995). Csordas (1994b:269) explains "embodiment" as "a methodological standpoint in which bodily experience is understood to be the existential ground of culture and self." However, Csordas' concept of embodiment emphasizes the impact of culture on the body nearly to the exclusion of the impact of the body on culture. Both are equally important in the Converted experience. Additionally, shamanic travels of the sort the Converted and other shamans do are a kind of "disembodiment" of experience: the shamans leaving their physical bodies for useful experiences. The metaphors of social realities are likewise placed in a remote (shamanic) world. Among the Converted, both embodiment and disembodiment are experienced to some extent. Because the placing of social reality in the body as well as the distancing of it from the body occur in shamanic cultures, embodiment may not be the best way to approach the subject.

4. There may be a question of the validity of the self-reported experiences of the Converted. However, the Converted are remarkably candid when they do not have the expected experience, even though it may lead to some surprisingly direct scorn. In only a few cases did I detect some Converted construing their experience to be the expected one after it was first described as something else (cf. Devereaux 1970:vii).

5. I am using the term "spontaneous shamanism" here to refer to cultures (subcultures) centered around shaman-like experiences. The cases I describe in this section do not have the integration with a local community that is usually associated with shamanism, although it is important to note once again that the experts disagree on just what constitutes shamanism (see Atkinson 1992). Whether these experiences are really shamanism or not is not as important as the comparison of like things.

6. Monroe refers to his experiences as out-of-body experiences (OOBE). An appropriate way to look at the difference between out-of-body-experiences (e.g., Gabbard and Twemlow 1984; Irwin 1985) and the sort of shamanic travel practiced by the Converted, is that shamanic travel is socialized while out-of-body experiences are those of more or less isolated individuals.

9: Converted Cosmology

1. We should recognize, however, that cultural material may be retained just as well for no good reason (Edgerton 1992). Likewise, the image may remain while the meaning changes. In Haitian Vodou, the center pole is the pathway by which Damballah (the snake god) enters the hounfour (K. Brown 1991:274). This same Fon image (Williams 1970) is found in St. Vincent. Many center poles in Converted churches have a snake painted on them. One night, I commented to a leader that I had not noticed a snake on the center poles of most churches. He replied, "Maybe they all have a snake, and you just didn't see it" (the implication being that those with spiritual eyes would see the snake on every center pole). A Converted teacher told me on another occasion that the center pole in Zion (the spiritual city) has a snake design on it. The snake on the pole in the Converted churches is said to represent Christ in John 3:14. Christ said, "And as Moses lifted up the serpent in the wilderness, even so must the Son of man be lifted up, That whosoever believeth in him should not perish, but have eternal life." Christ is referring to Numbers 21:8, where Moses was commanded by God to make an image of a serpent and "set it upon a pole."

2. In 1803, Dr. David Collins, a Vincentian planter wrote a book about slave management. He based his observations on over 20 years' residence in St. Vincent (Sheridan 1985:32). Collins is one of the best sources of information about slave life in the British West Indies. He mentioned "Coromantins" (Akan), "Phantees" (Fanti), "Mandingos" (Mandinga), and those from "Senegal" and "the Congo." He claimed that "Ebbos" and "Ebbo-bees" (Ibo and Ibibio) were the "greater part of the cargoes carried from the coast of Africa to the British Islands . . ." (Collins 1803:42). He reported that those from "the kingdom of Gaboon" usually

died on the journey over, but apparently some survived. He wrote that the "Whidaws and Papaws" were the best workers but that "Aradas" and those from "Judda" were better still (these last four were under Dahomean control at the time). It is likely that individuals from all of those nations were present in St. Vincent at the turn of the nineteenth century.

3. The Nine Mornings is mentioned by only one anthropologist (Jackson 1972:217) out of the many who have written ethnographic accounts of St. Vincent (Betley 1976; Abrahams 1983; Glesne 1985; Gullick 1985; Rubenstein 1987; Gearing 1988; Fraser 1979; V. Young 1993). Yet, it is a prominent part of Vincentian discourse throughout the year. When I arrived in April, Vincentians were still wearing their t-shirts from the Nine Mornings. Many old people told me stories about the Nine Mornings from when they were children. Perhaps it is an urban phenomenon. The other researchers did their work in areas relatively far from the capital (although Jackson, who did note the festival, did hers in Chateaubelair, a town on the Leeward coast).

4. The Christmas celebration is only one possible source. Undoubtedly, Converted practices are derived from a number of historical influences. One may be the tea parties introduced by the eighteenth-century Methodists as a way to civilize the Africans they had converted (Abrahams 1977). Sacred songs were sung and testimonials given, and afterward food was served. Many Converted services follow that same order.

10: Comparative History of the Converted Religion

1. Cox (1994) provides a comprehensive history of the development and passage of the law.

2. Most of the information about Christianity in St. Vincent comes out of the efforts of the Methodist missionaries to establish their own legitimacy (Burnet, n.d.; Coke 1810; Watson 1817; Moister 1866), but also from others (Collins 1803; St. Vincent 1823; Stephen 1824; Warner 1831; Coleridge 1832; Anderson 1938; Pitt 1955).

3. Jamaican Pukkumina "labouring" seems also to be identical to the Number One doption (Seaga 1982:7). Both may bear some relation to the African American "ring shout" that Stuckey (1987) suggests has a Kongo connection. Bilby and Bunseki (1983) situate the source of most of Kumina and Pukkumina practice in Kongo culture. It would appear that Converted doption had its roots there as well. The association of specific doptions with certain cities, though, seems to be completely Vincentian.

4. Additionally, the concept of "conversion" was seen in some islands as a protection against obeah (Smith 1953:70).

5. Duke, Johnson, and Duke. (1995:154, table 2) list St. Vincent as having the highest annual conversion rate (between denominations) from 1970 to 1980 of any Caribbean country except Suriname. St. Vincent's rate for that time period was 8,899 per million. Trinidad and Tobago, tied for third place, had only 5,403 per million—a significant difference. The high rate of conversion in St. Vincent, especially to Pentecostal-type religions, undoubtedly contributes to the distress some Converted feel vis-à-vis Pentecostals. However, the unusual legal history of Converted religion, changes in census questionnaires, and the practice of multiple denominational affiliations for individuals probably had a lot to do with the high figure for St. Vincent (ibid., 162).

6. Converted people told me that these were impolite terms, but it is possible that they are simply descriptive. The Plymouth Brethren, who have over a thousand adherents in St. Vincent, were known to some of my respondents only as "Long Sleeve for God."

7. Grenada, situated between St. Vincent and Trinidad, followed with its own law against Spiritual Baptists on March 21, 1927—*No. 11 of 1927, The Public Meetings ("Shakerism") Prohibition Ordinance* (Grenada 1928). It is nearly identical to the *1912 "Shakerism" Prohibition Ordinance* of St. Vincent. Apparently, by referring to Shakerism, the Spiritual Baptists in Grenada in the 1920s had more of an influence from St. Vincent than is visible today. On

my visit to Grenada in 1995, I noticed that although Vincentian Converted traditions had some presence, the Trinidadian traditions prevailed and the Spiritual Baptists were generally known as "Shouters," the Trinidadian term. Smith (1963:7) reports that the law in Grenada was sporadically enforced in the 1950s. The ordinance has never been repealed and appears as Chapter 266 of the revised laws of 1990 (Grenada 1992; UWI 1996). Although the law is still in effect, it seems to be no longer enforced. At a Spiritual Baptist convention I attended in Grenada in June 1995, a *marching* was preceded by the Grenadian Royal Police marching band.

8. This was clearly wrong, but Converted officials as well as government officials continued to refer to the 1951 date throughout the period of my fieldwork. The celebration of a National Spiritual Baptist Day in St. Vincent was only a few years old at the time of my research and had been patterned on the Trinidadian celebration.

9. "Sus orígenes se remontan a los esfuerzos misionales de parte de los Baptistas norteamericanos que proselitizataron en el área del Caribe."

10. Spiritual Baptists influence other religions as well, especially Shango (Houk 1995). Littlewood (1993a) has made an excellent study of a religion in Trinidad (the Earth People) that is the result of a combination of Spiritual Baptist and other philosophies.

11. Even though some authors (e.g., Moore 1965; Baer 1984) dwell on the topic of syncretism in Black religion, I think it is important to stress that all Christian religions are syncretic. The syncretism need not be with explicitly religious systems. For instance, a syncretism of Pentecostal, Southern Baptist, and American business techniques is apparent in the style of Christianity offered by televangelist and former presidential candidate Pat Robertson of the Christian Broadcasting Network (and his theological business college, Founder's University).

12. Sources on the Indian Shakers are: Gunther 1949; Smith 1954; Barnett 1957; Miller 1988; Ruby and Brown 1996.

11: Going to Brooklyn

1. Migration in the Caribbean has been a major topic of study for social scientists. The main sources I rely on for this discussion of Vincentian migration and employment are: Marshall 1984; Gearing 1992; Miller 1992; Thomas-Hope 1992; Basch, Shiller, and Blanc 1994; *The Vincentian* (newspaper), St. Vincent, June 2, 1995, p. 19; Watkins-Owens 1996:52–53.

2. It is difficult to estimate the number of Converted in New York at any one time since the Vincentian population in New York includes a large number of visitors who may stay a few weeks or a few months. My figure is based on those who regularly attended Converted churches during my field work in Brooklyn. I did meet some people who consider themselves Converted but attend Pentecostal churches in Brooklyn. Also, some Vincentians in New York attend Trinidadian Spiritual Baptist churches.

Ministers, in addition, sometimes inflate the membership numbers for their churches, including not only active members but all those who have baptized or mourned with the church. One Converted minister told me that he had 200 members in his church, but when he showed me one day a list of the members, there were only 32 names. Some of those on his list told me their membership was in another church but that they attended both. The smaller number is more in line with congregation size in St. Vincent (and with what I observed in that church). Converted tell me that with very large numbers (over 100), it is difficult to do the spiritual work.

3. The service in Brooklyn is nearly the same as in St. Vincent. Although the Converted practice shamanistic techniques, they are also Christians. Most Converted do not travel in the spiritual world on a daily basis and few mourn more than a few times in their life. The praise (the standard liturgy) is the main ritual the Converted use to sustain their faith.

————. 1989. *The art and politics of Wana shamanship*. Berkeley: University of California Press.

————. 1992. Shamanisms today. *Annual Review of Anthropology* 21:307–330.

Austin, Roy L. 1989. Family environment, educational aspiration and performance in St. Vincent. *The Review of Black Political Economy* 17 (3):101–122.

————. 1996. A Parkboy remembers colts, products of a subculture of sport. In *The social roles of sport in Caribbean societies*. Michael A. Malec, ed., pp. 154–171. Luxembourg: Gordon and Breach.

Baer, Hans A. 1984. *The Black spiritual movement: A religious response to racism*. Knoxville: University of Tennessee Press.

Balandier, Georges. 1970. *Political anthropology*. New York: Random House.

Banks, E. P. 1955. Island Carib folk tales. *Caribbean Quarterly* 4 (1):32–39.

Barnett, H. G. 1957. *Indian Shakers: A messianic cult of the Pacific Northwest*. Carbondale: Southern Illinois University Press.

Barrett, Dierdre. 1993. The "Committee of Sleep:" A study of dream incubation for problem solving. *Dreaming* 3 (2):115–122.

Barrett, Leonard E. 1974. *Soul-force: African heritage in Afro-American religion*. Garden City, NY: Anchor Press/Doubleday.

Basch, Linda. 1987. The Vincentians and Grenadians: The role of voluntary associations in immigrant adaptation to New York City. In *New immigrants in New York*. Nancy Foner, ed., pp. 159–194. New York: Columbia University Press.

Basch, Linda, Nina Glick Shiller, and Cristina Szanton Blanc. 1994. *Nations unbound: Transnational projects, postcolonial predicaments, and deterritorialized nation states*. Langhorne, PA: Gordon and Breach.

Basilov, V. N. 1976. Shamanism in Central Asia. In *The realm of the extra-human: Agents and audiences*. Agehananda Bharati, ed., pp. 150–157. The Hague: Mouton.

————. 1984. The *Chiltan* spirits. In *Shamanism in Eurasia*, pt. 2. Mihály Hoppál, ed., pp. 253–261. Gottingen: Editions Herodot.

————. 1992. Islamic Shamanism among Central Asian peoples. *Diogenes* 158:5–18.

Bastide, Roger. 1978. *African religions in Brazil: Toward a sociology of the interpretation of civilizations*. Baltimore and London: The Johns Hopkins University Press.

Bateson, Mary Catherine. 1994. *Peripheral visions: Learning along the way*. New York: HarperCollins.

Beck, Jane C. 1979. *To the windward of the land: The occult world of Alexander Charles*. Bloomington and London: Indiana University Press.

————. 1985. Hilda, woman of dreams. In *By land and by sea: Studies in the folklore of work and leisure*. Roger D. Abrahams, Kenneth S. Goldstein, and Wayland D. Hand, eds. Hatboro, PA: Legacy Books.

Beckett, Jeremy. 1993. Walter Newton's history of the world—or Australia. *American Anthropologist* 20 (4):675–695.

Beckwith, Martha Warren. 1923. Some religious cults in Jamaica. *The American Journal of Psychology* 34:32–45.

Bednarik, Robert G. 1990. On neuropsychiatry and shamanism in rock art. *Current Anthropology* 31 (1):77–84.

Beidelman, T. O. 1986. *Moral imagination in Kaguru modes of thought*. Bloomington: Indiana University Press.

Bell, Hesketh J. [1888] 1970. *Obeah: Witchcraft in the West Indies*. Westport, CT: Negro Universities Press.

Berger, Teresa. 1995. *Theology in hymns? A study of the relationship of doxology and theology according to* A collection of hymns for the use of the people called Methodists (1780), Timothy E. Kimbrough, trans. Nashville, TN: Kingswood Books.

Besson, Jean and Barry Chevannes. 1996. The continuity-creativity debate: The case of Revival. *New West Indian Guide* 70 (3/4):209–228.

Betley, Brian James. 1976. Stratification and strategies: A study of adaptation and mobility in a Vincentian town. Ph.D. diss. University of California, Los Angeles.

Bett, Henry. 1946. *The hymns of Methodism*. London: Epworth Press.

Bhabha, Homi. 1984. Of mimicry and man: The ambivalence of colonial discourse. October 28:125–133.

Bilby, Kenneth M. 1985. The Caribbean as a musical region. In *Caribbean contours*. Sidney Mintz and Richard Price, eds., pp. 181–218. Baltimore: The Johns Hopkins University Press.

Bilby, Kenneth M., and Fu Kiau Kia Bunseki. 1983. *Kumina: A Kongo-based tradition in the New World*. Bruxelles: Centre d'Etude et de Documentation Africaines.

Bisnauth, Dale. 1989. *History of religions in the Caribbean*. Kingston, Jamaica: Kingston Publishers, Ltd.

Black, Clinton V. 1989. *Pirates of the West Indies*. Cambridge: Cambridge University Press.

Bloothooft, Gerrit, Eldrid Bringmann, Marieke van Cappellen, Jolanda B. van Luipen, and Koen P. Thomassen. 1992. Acoustics and perception of overtone singing. *The Journal of the Acoustical Society of America* 92 (4):1827–1836.

Boddy, Janice. 1989. *Wombs and alien spirits: Women, men, and the Zar cult in Northern Sudan*. Madison: University of Wisconsin Press.

———. 1994. Spirit possession revisited: Beyond instrumentality. *Annual Review of Anthropology* 23:407–434.

Book of Common Prayer. [1549] 1948. Greenwich, CT: Seabury Press.

Boucher, Philip P. 1992. *Cannibal encounters: Europeans and island Caribs, 1492–1763*. Baltimore and London: The Johns Hopkins University Press.

Bourdieu, Pierre. 1977. *Outline of a theory of practice*. R. Nice, trans. Cambridge: Cambridge University Press.

———. 1990. *The logic of practice*. Cambridge: Polity Press.

Bourguignon, Erika. 1970. Ritual dissociation and possession belief in Caribbean Negro religion. In *Afro-American anthropology: Contemporary perspectives*, Norman E. Whitten, Jr. and John F. Szwed, eds., pp. 87–101. New York: Free Press.

———, ed. 1973. *Religion, altered states of consciousness, and social change*. Columbus: Ohio State University

Brathwaite, Edward Kamau. 1982a. *Kumina: The spirit of African survival in Jamaica*. Savacou Working Paper 4. Mona, Jamaica: Savacou.

———. 1982b. *Native language poetry*. Savacou Working Paper 5. Mona, Jamaica: Savacou.

Brittain, Ann W. 1991. Anticipated child loss to migration and sustained high fertility in an East Caribbean population. *Social Biology* 38 (1/2):94–112.

Brown, Audrey Lawson. 1994. Afro-Baptist women's church and family roles: Transmitting Afro-centric cultural values. *Anthropological Quarterly* 67 (4):173–186.

Brown, Donald E. 1991. *Human universals*. Philadelphia: Temple University Press.

Brown, Karen McCarthy. 1991. *Mama Lola: A Vodou priestess in Brooklyn*. Berkeley and Los Angeles: University of California Press.

Bruckner, Pascal. 1986. *The tears of the White man: Compassion as contempt*. William Bear, trans. New York: Free Press.

Bryce-Laporte, R. S. 1970. Crisis, contraculture, and religion among West Indians in the Panama Canal Zone. In *Afro-American anthropology: Contemporary perspectives*. Norman E. Whitten, Jr. and John F. Szwed, eds., pp. 103–118. New York: Free Press.

Bunyan, John. [1648] 1979. *The Pilgrim's Progress*. London: HarperCollins.

Burnet, Rev. Amos. [1924] n.d. *The isles of the western sea: The story of Methodist missions in the West Indies and Central America*. London: Wesleyan Methodist Missionary Society.

Byrne, Joycelin. 1969. Population Growth in St. Vincent. *Social and Economic Studies* 18 (2): 152–188.

Campbell, Joseph. [1949] 1968. *The hero with a thousand faces*, 2nd ed. Princeton, NJ: Princeton University Press.

Castaneda, Carlos. 1968. *The teachings of Don Juan: A Yaqui way of knowledge*. Berkeley: University of California Press.

de Certeau, Michel. 1984. *The practice of everyday life*. Steven Rendall, trans. Berkeley: University of California Press.

Chaney, Elsa M. 1987. The context of Caribbean migration. In *Caribbean life in New York City: Sociocultural dimensions*. Constance R. Sutton and Elsa M. Chaney, eds., pp. 3–14. New York: Center for Migration Studies of New York.

Chaumeil, Jean Pierre. 1992. Un Nouveau Testament pour un troisième millénaire: La religion du Daime au Brésil. *Cahiers d'Etudes Africaines* 32 (1):151–155.

Chevannes, Barry. 1978. Revivalism: A disappearing religion. *Caribbean Quarterly* 24:1–17.

Ciski, Robert. 1975. The Vincentian Portuguese: A study in ethnic group adaptation. Ph.D. diss. University of Massachusetts, Amherst.

Coke, Thomas. 1810. *History of the West Indies*. Vol. 2. London: A. Paris.

Coleridge, H. N. 1832. *Six months in the West Indies in 1825*, 3d ed. London: John Moray.

Collins, David [A Professional Planter]. 1803. *Practical rules for the management and medical treatment of Negro slaves in the sugar colonies*. London: J. Barfield, Printer.

Comaroff, Jean. 1985. *Body of power, spirit of resistance: The culture and history of a South African people*. Chicago and London: The University of Chicago Press.

Camaroff, Jean, and John Comaroff. 1991. *Of revelation and revolution: Christianity, colonialism, and consciousness in South Africa*. Chicago: University of Chicago Press.

Cosentino, Donald J. 1995. Imagine heaven. In *Sacred arts of Haitian Vodou*. Donald J. Cosentino, ed., pp. 25–55. Los Angeles: UCLA Fowler Museum of Cultural History.

———. 1996. Lavilokan. *African Arts* 29 (2):22–29.

Courlander, Harold. [1963] 1992. *Negro folk music, U.S.A.* New York: Dover.

———. [1976] 1996. *A treasury of Afro-American folklore*. New York: Marlowe.

Cox, Edward L. 1994. Religious intolerance and persecution: The Shakers of St. Vincent, 1900–1934. *Journal of Caribbean History* 28 (2):208–243.

Cox, Harvey. 1995. *Fire from heaven: The rise of Pentecostal spirituality and the reshaping of religion in the Twenty-First Century*. Reading, MA: Addison-Wesley.

Crawford, M. H., and A. G. Comuzzie. 1989. Genetic and morphological variation in the Black Carib populations of St. Vincent and Livingstone, Guatemala. *Collegium Anthropologica* 13 (1):51–61.

Creel, Margaret Washington. 1988. *"A peculiar people:" Slave religion and community-culture among the Gullahs*. New York: New York University Press.

Crowley, Daniel J. 1957. Song and dance of St. Lucia. *Ethnomusicology* 1 (9):4–14.

———. 1958. La Rose and La Marguerite Societies in St. Lucia. *Journal of American Folklore* 71:541–552.

Csordas, Thomas J. 1994a. *The sacred self: A cultural phenomenology of charismatic healing*. Berkeley: University of California Press.

———. 1994b. Words from the holy people: A case study in cultural phenomenology. In *Embodiment and experience: The existential ground of culture and self*. Thomas J. Csordas, ed., pp. 269–290. Cambridge: Cambridge University Press.

Cytowic, Richard E. 1989. *Synesthesia: A union of the senses*. New York: Springer-Verlag.

———. 1993. *The man who tasted shapes*. New York: Putnam.

Dalphinis, Morgan. 1985. *Caribbean and African languages: Social history, language, literature and education*. London: Karia.

Davy, John. [1854] 1971. *The West Indies before and since slave emancipation: Comprising the Windward and Leeward Islands' military command.* London: Frank Cass.

Dentan, Robert K. 1968. *The Semai: A nonviolent people of Malaysia.* New York: Holt, Rinehart and Winston.

———. 1988. Lucidity, sex, and horror in Senoi dreamwork. In *Conscious mind, sleeping brain: Perspectives on lucid dreaming.* Jayne Grackenbach and Stephen LaBerge, eds., pp. 37–63. New York: Plenum.

———. 1995. Bad day at Bukit Pekan. *American Anthropologist* 97:225–250.

Desch, Thomas J. Obi. 1994. Knocking and kicking, Ladya and Capoeira: Resistance and religion in the African martial arts of the Black Atlantic. Master's thesis, African Area Studies. University of California, Los Angeles.

Devereaux, G. 1970. Introduction to *The dream in primitive cultures*, by Jackson Steward Lincoln. New York: Johnson Reprint.

Diamond, Stanley. 1996. Dahomey: The development of a proto-state: An essay in historical reconstruction. *Dialectical Anthropology* 21 (2):121–216.

Dirks, Robert. 1987. *The Black Saturnalia: Conflict and its ritual expression on British West Indian slave plantations.* Gainsville: University of Florida Press.

Dobbin, Jay D. 1986. *The Jombee dance of Montserrat: A study of trance ritual in the West Indies.* Columbus: Ohio State University Press.

Domhoff, G. William. 1985. *The mystique of dreams: A search for Utopia through Senoi dream theory.* Berkeley: University of California Press.

Douglas, Mary. 1970. *Natural symbols: Explorations in cosmology.* New York: Pantheon Books.

Driver, Tom F. 1991. *The magic of ritual: Our need for liberating rites that transform our lives and our communities.* New York: Harper Collins.

Drury, Neville. 1982. *The shaman and the magician.* London: Routledge and Kegan Paul.

Dugan, Kathleen Margaret. 1985. *The vision quest of the Plains Indians: Its spiritual significance.* Lewiston, New York: Edwin Mellen Press.

Duke, James T., Barry L. Johnson, and James B. Duke. 1995. The world context of religious change in the Caribbean. *Social and Economic Studies* 44 (2/3):143–166.

du Tertre, Jean Baptist. [1667] 1978. *Histoire generale des Antilles habitées par les Français.* Vol. 1. Paris: E. Kolodziej.

Edgerton, Robert B. 1985. *Rules, exceptions, and social order.* Berkeley: University of California Press.

———. 1992. *Sick societies.* Berkeley and Los Angeles: University of California Press.

EIU (Economist Intelligence Unit). 1996. *EIU country, report, Windward and Leeward Islands,* 2d quarter.

Eliade, Mircea. 1958. *Yoga: Immortality and freedom.* Willard R. Trask, trans. New York: Pantheon Books.

———. 1964. *Shamanism: Archaic techniques of ecstasy.* London: Routledge and Kegan Paul.

———. 1982. *Ordeal by labyrinth: Conversations with Claude-Henri Rocquet.* Chicago, IL: University of Chicago Press.

Ember, Carol R., and Melvin Ember. 1996. *Cultural anthropology,* 8th ed. Upper Saddle River, NJ: Prentice Hall.

Empson, Jacob. 1993. *Sleep and dreaming,* 2d rev. ed. Hemel Hempstead, Herfordshire, U.K.: Harvester Wheatsheaf.

Entiope, Gabriel. 1987. Musique, danse dans le Vecu de l'Eclave Caribeen (approche historique). In *Social and festive space in the Caribbean, comparative studies on the plural societies in the Caribbean.* Vol. 2. Masao Yamaguchi and Masao Naito, eds., pp. 253–297. Tokyo: ILCAA.

Epstein, Benjamin. 1996. My lunch with Castaneda. *Psychology Today* 29 (2):30–34.

Errington, Frederick. 1974. Indigenous ideas of order, time, and transition in a New Guinea cargo movement. *American Ethnologist* 1 (2):255–267.

Fabian, Johannes. 1986. *Language and colonial power*. Berkeley: University of California Press.

Fayer, Joan M., and Joan F. McMurray. 1994. Shakespeare in Carriacou. *Caribbean Studies* 27 (3/4):242–254.

Ferguson, Moira. 1993. *Colonialism and gender relations from Mary Wollstonecraft to Jamaica Kincaid: East Caribbean Connections*. New York: Columbia University Press.

Festinger, Leon. 1957. *A theory of cognitive dissonance*. Stanford, CA: Stanford University Press.

Fisher, L. E. 1985. *Colonial madness: Mental health in the Barbadian social order*. New Brunswick, NJ: Rutgers University Press.

Foucault, Michel. 1980. *Power/knowledge: Selected interviews and other writings, 1972–1977*. Colin Gordon, ed. New York: Pantheon.

Foulkes, David. 1993. Data constraints on theorizing about dream function. In *The functions of dreaming*. Alan Moffitt, Milton Kramer, and Robert Hoffman, eds., pp. 11–20. Albany: State University of New York Press.

Fraser, Adrian. 1995. Transcripts from *From whence we came*. NBC Radio, St. Vincent and the Grenadines, 18 April–23 May.

Fraser, Grace Morth. 1979. The disputing process in St. Vincent. Ph.D. diss., University of Massachusetts, Amherst.

Fraser, Thomas M., Jr., ed. 1973. *Windward road: Contributions to the anthropology of St. Vincent*. Amherst: University of Massachusetts, Department of Anthropology.

———. 1975. Class and the changing bases of elite support in St. Vincent, West Indies. *Ethnology* 14:197–209.

Gabbard, Glen G., and Stewart W. Twemlow. 1984. *With eyes of the mind: An empirical analysis of out-of-body states*. New York: Praeger.

Gearing, Margaret Jean. 1988. The reproduction of labor in a migrating society: Gender, kinship, and household in St. Vincent, West Indies. Ph.D. diss. University of Florida, Gainesville.

———. 1992. Family planning in St. Vincent, West Indies: A population history perspective. *Social Science and Medicine* 35 (10):1273–1282.

Gell, Alfred. 1980. The gods at play: Vertigo and possession in Muria religion. *Man* n.s., 1: 219–248.

Glazier, Stephen D. 1980. Heterodoxy and heteropraxy in the Spiritual Baptist faith. *The Journal of the Interdenominational Theological Center* 8:89–101.

———. 1983. *Marchin' the pilgrims home: Leadership and decision-making in an Afro-Caribbean faith*. Westport, CT: Greenwood.

———. 1984. Organizatión social y económica de los Baptistas Espirituales con atención especial a sus misiones en Venezuela. *Montalban* 15:153–189.

———. 1985a. Mourning in the Afro-Baptist traditions: A comparative study of religion in the American South and in Trinidad. *Southern Quarterly* 23 (3):141–156.

———. 1985b. Religion and social justice: Caribbean perspectives. *Phylon* 46 (4):283–285.

———. 1985c. Syncretism and separation: Ritual change in an Afro-Caribbean faith. *Journal of American Folklore* 98 (387):49–62.

———. 1986. Prophecy and ecstasy: Religion and politics in the Caribbean. In *Prophetic religions and politics: Religion and the political order*. Vol. 1. Jeffrey K. Hadden and Anson Sharpe, eds., pp. 430–447. New York: Paragon House.

———. 1988. Worldwide missions of Trinidad's Spiritual Baptists. *The National Geographical Journal of India* 34 (1):75–78.

———. 1992. Pilgrimages in the Caribbean: A comparison of cases from Haiti and Trinidad. In *Sacred journeys: The athropology of pilgrimage*. Alan Morinis, ed., pp. 135–147. Westport, CT: Greenwood.

———. 1993. Funerals and mourning in the Spiritual Baptist and Shango traditions. *Caribbean Quarterly* 39 (3/4):1–11.

————. 1997. Embedded truths: Creativity and context in Spiritual Baptist music. *Latin American Music Review* 18 (1):44–56.

Glesne, Corrine Elaine. 1985. Strugglin', but no slavin': Agriculture, education, and rural young Vincentians. Ph.D. diss. University of Illinois at Urbana-Champaign.

Godelier, Maurice. 1986. *The making of great men: Male domination and power among the New Guinea Baruya.* Rupert Swyer, trans. Cambridge: Cambridge University Press.

Goldwasser, Michele Annette. 1996. The Rainbow Madonna of Trinidad: A study in the dynamics of belief in Trinidadian religious life. Ph.D. diss. University of California, Los Angeles.

Gonzalez, Nancie L. 1991. Prospero, Caliban and Black Sambo: Colonial views of the other in the Caribbean. Department of Spanish and Portuguese, University of Maryland, College Park. Working Papers, no. 11.

Goodman, Felicitas. 1990. *Where the spirits ride the wind: Trance journeys and other ecstatic experiences.* Bloomington: Indiana University Press.

Grackenbach, Jayne and Stephen LaBerge, eds. 1988. *Conscious mind, sleeping brain: Perspectives on lucid dreaming.* New York: Plenum.

Grenada. 1928. *Ordinances for the year 1927.* St. Georges, Grenada: Government Printing Office.

Grenada. 1992. *The Revised Laws of Grenada: The Statues in Force on the 31st December, 1990,* rev. ed. Portsmouth: Grosvenor Press (Portsmouth).

Griffith, Ezra E. H. and George E. Mahy. 1984. Psychological benefits of Spiritual Baptist "mourning."*American Journal of Psychiatry* 141 (6):769–773.

————. 1985. Spiritual Baptist mourning: A model of contemplative meditation. In *Psychiatry: The state of the art,* Vol. 8. P. Pichot, P. Berner, R. Wolf, and K. Thau, eds., pp. 685–690. New York: Plenum.

Griffith, Ezra E. H., George E. Mahy, and John L. Young. 1986. Psychological benefits of Spiritual Baptist "mourning," II: An empirical assessment. *American Journal of Psychiatry* 143 (2):226–229.

Grimes, Ronald L. 1990. *Ritual criticism: Case studies in its practice, essays on its theory.* Columbia: University of South Carolina Press.

Grossman, Lawrence S. 1993. The political economy of banana exports and local food production in St. Vincent, Eastern Caribbean. *Annals of the Association of American Geographers* 83 (2):347–367.

————. 1994. British aid and Windward bananas: The case of St. Vincent and the Grenadines. *Social and Economic Studies* 43 (1):151–179.

Guha, Ranajit, ed. 1987. *Subaltern Studies V.* Delhi: Oxford University Press.

Guibault, Jocelyne. 1985. A St. Lucian *Kwadril* evening. *Latin American Music Review* 6 (1): 31–47.

————. 1987. Oral and literate strategies in performances: The La Rose and La Marguerite organizations in St. Lucia. *Yearbook for Traditional Music* 19:97–115.

Gullick, Charles (C.J.M.R.). 1971. Shakers and ecstasy. *New Fire* [Oxford] 9:7–11.

————. 1985. *Myths of a minority: The changing traditions of the Vincentian Caribs.* Assen, Netherlands: Van Gorcum.

Gunther, Erna. 1949. The Shaker religion of the Northwest. In *Indians of the urban Northwest.* Mariam W. Smith, ed., pp. 37–76. New York: Columbia University Press.

Gupta, M. G. 1993. *Mystic symbolism in Ramayan, Mahabharat, and The Pilgrim's Progress.* Hirabagh Colony, Agra, India: MG.

Hackshaw, John Milton. 1992. *The Baptist denomination: 1816–1991.* Trinidad: Amphy and Bashua Jackson Memorial Society.

Hadley, C. V. D. [1949] 1973. Personality patterns, social class, and aggression in the British West Indies. In *Consequences of class and color: West Indian perspectives.* David Lowenthal and Lambros Comitas, eds., pp. 12–33. Garden City, NY: Anchor Books.

Halifax, Joan. 1979. *Shamanic voices: A survey of visionary narratives*. New York: E. P. Dutton.

Hamel, the Obeah man. 1827. 2 vols. London: Hunt and Clarke.

Harner, Michael. 1972. *The Jivaro: People of the sacred waterfall*. Garden City, NY: Doubleday.

———. 1980. *The way of the Shaman: A guide to power and healing*. San Francisco: Harper and Row.

Harris, Marvin. 1991. *Cultural Anthropology*, 3d ed. New York: HarperCollins.

Hart, Mickey. 1990. *Drumming at the edge of magic: A journey into the spirit of percussion*. San Francisco: Harper San Francisco.

Harvey, John. 1995. *Men in black*. Chicago: University of Chicago Press.

Havilland, William A. 1996. *Cultural anthropology*, 8th ed. Fort Worth, TX: Harcourt Brace College.

Hazell, Brenda S. 1994. The impact of the Caribbean Baptist Fellowship on christian education ministries in the Windward Islands with implications for its future role. Ed.D. diss. New Orleans Baptist Theological Seminary.

Hedges, Ken. 1993. Origines chamaniques de L'Art rupestre dans l'Oest Américain. *L'Anthropologie (Paris)* 97 (4):675–691.

Henman, Anthony Richard. 1986. Uso del ayahuasca en un contexto autoritario: El caso del la *Uniao Do Vegetal* en Brasil. *América Indígena* 46 (1):219–234.

Henney, Jeanette H. 1968. Spirit possession belief and trance behavior in a religious group in St. Vincent, British West Indies. Ph.D. diss., Ohio State University, Columbia.

———. 1971. The Shakers of St. Vincent: A stable religion. In *Religion, altered states of consciousness, and social change*. Erika Bourguignon, ed., pp. 219–263. Columbus: Ohio State University Press.

———. 1974. Spirit possession belief and trance behavior in two fundamentalist groups in St. Vincent. In *Trance, healing and hallucination: Three field studies in religious experience*. Felicitas D. Goodman, Jeanette H. Henney, and Esther Pressel eds., pp. 6–111. New York: Wiley.

———. 1980. Sex and status: Women in St. Vincent. In *A world of women: Anthropological studies of women in the societies of the world*. Erika Bourguignon, ed., pp. 161–183. New York: Praeger.

Herdt, Gilbert. 1978. Selfhood and discourse in Sambia dream sharing. In *Dreaming: anthropological and psychological interpretations*. Barbara Babcock, ed., pp. 55–85. Cambridge: Cambridge University Press.

Herskovits, Melville J. 1958. *The myth of the Negro past*. Boston: Beacon.

———. 1966. *The New World Negro: Selected papers in Afroamerican studies*. Bloomington: University of Indiana Press.

Herskovits, Melville J., and Frances S. Herskovits. 1947. *Trinidad village*. New York: Knopf.

Hill, Donald R. 1977. The impact of migration on the metropolitan and folk society of Carriacou, Grenada. Anthropological Papers of the American Museum of Natural History. Vol. 54, pt. 2.

Hill, Jonathan. 1992. A musical aesthetic of ritual curing in the northwest Amazon. In *Portals of power: Shamanism in South America*. E. Jean Matteson Langdon, and Gerhard Baer, eds., pp. 175–210. Albuquerque: University of New Mexico Press.

———. 1993. *Keepers of the sacred chants: The poetics of ritual power in an Amazonian society*. Tucson: The University of Arizona Press.

Hollan, Douglas W. and Jane C. Wellencamp. 1994. *Contentment and suffering: Culture and experience in Toraja*. New York: Columbia University Press.

Houk, James T. 1992. The Orisha religion in Trinidad: A study of culture process and transformation. Ph.D. diss. Tulane University, New Orleans, LA.

———. 1993. The terminological shift from "Afro-American" to "African-American": Is the field of Afro-American anthropology being redefined? *Human Organization* 52 (3):325–329.

———. 1995. *Spirits, blood, and drums.* Philadelphia: Temple University Press.

Hourihan, John J. 1975. Rule in Hairoun: A study of the politics of power. Ph.D. diss. University of Massachusetts, Amherst.

Huggins, A. B. 1978. *The saga of the companies.* Princes Town, Trinidad: Twinluck Printing Works.

Hultkrantz, Ake. 1973. A definition of shamanism. *Temenos* 9:25–37.

———. 1978. Ecological and phenomenological aspects of shamanism. In *Shamanism in Siberia.* V. Dioszegi and M. Hoppal, eds. pp. 27–58. Budapest: Akademiai Kiado.

———. 1985. Comment on Noll. *Current Anthropology* 26 (4):453.

Hymns ancient and modern. 1916. London: Williams Clowes.

Iaconetti, Joan. 1994. Anchoring progress in tradition. *Americas* 46 (6):6–14.

Irwin, H. J. 1985. *Flight of the mind: A psychological study of the out-of-body experience.* Metuchen, NJ: Scarecrow Press.

Ishmael, Len. 1988. Informal sector factor mobilization: The process by which poor people shelter themselves and implications for policy focus on the Caribbean: St. Vincent and Dominica. Ph.D. diss. University of Pennsylvania, Philadelphia.

Jacobs, Claude F. 1989. Spirit guides and possession in the New Orleans Black spiritual churches. *Journal of American Folklore* 102:45–67.

Jacobs, C. M. 1996. *Joy comes in the morning: Elton George Griffith and the Shouter Baptists.* Port-of-Spain: Caribbean Historical Society.

Jackson, Jane. 1972. Social organization in St. Vincent. B.Litt. thesis. Oxford University, Cambridge.

James, William. [1902] 1982. *The varieties of religious experience.* New York: Penguin.

Jilek, Wolfgang. 1992. The renaissance of shamanic dance in Indian populations of North America. *Diogenes* 158:87–100.

John, Sir Rupert. 1979. *Pioneers in nation building in a Caribbean mini-state.* New York: United Nations Institute for Training and Research.

Kalweit, Holger. 1988. *Dreamtime and inner space: The world of the shaman.* Boston: Shambhala.

———. 1992. *Shamans, healers, and medicine men.* Boston and London: Shambhala.

Keesing, Roger. 1994. Colonial and counter-colonial discourse in Melanesia. *Critique of Anthropology* 14 (1):41–58.

Kingsley, Charles. 1910. *At last: A Christmas in the West Indies.* London: MacMillan.

Klingholz, F. 1993. Overtone singing: Productive mechanisms and acoustic data. *Journal of Voice* 7 (2):118–122.

Knab, Timothy J. 1995. *A war of witches: A journey into the underworld of the contemporary Aztecs.* San Francisco: Harper San Francisco.

Kortt, I. R. 1984. The shaman as social representative in the world beyond. In *Shamanism in Eurasia*, pt. 2. Mihaly Hoppal, ed. pp. 253–261. Gottingen: Editions Herodot.

Krippner, Stanley. 1985. Comment on noll. *Current Anthropology* 26 (4):453–445.

Kroll, Jerome, and Bernard Bachrach. 1982. Visions and psychopathology in the Middle Ages. *Journal of Nervous and Mental Disease* 170 (1):41–49.

Kurlansky, Mark. 1992. *A continent of islands: Searching for the Caribbean destiny.* Reading, MA: Addison-Wesley.

LaBarre, Weston. 1972. *The ghost dance: Origins of religion.* New York: Dell.

Labat, Jean-Baptiste. [1722] 1970. *The memoirs of Père Labat.* John Eaden, trans. London: Frank Cass.

LaBerge, Stephen. 1985. *Lucid dreaming.* Los Angeles: Jeremy P. Tarcher.

Laderman, Carol. 1991. *Taming of the wind of desire: Psychology, medicine, and aesthetics in Malay shamanistic performance*. Berkeley: University of California Press.

Laguerre, Michel S. 1980. *Voodoo heritage*. Beverly Hills, CA: Sage.

Lakoff, George, and Mark Johnson. 1980. *Metaphors we live by*. Chicago and London: University of Chicago Press.

Lan, David. 1985. *Guns and rain: Guerillas and spirit mediums in Zimbabwe*. Berkeley: University of California Press.

Landman, Bette Emeline. 1972. Household and community in Canouan, British West Indies. Ph.D. diss. Ohio State University, Columbia.

Lane, Belden C. 1988. *Landscapes of the sacred: Geography and narrative in American spirituality*. New York: Paulist.

Langdon, E. Jean Matteson. 1992. Introduction: Shamanism and anthropology. In *Portals of power: Shamanism in South America*. E. Jean Matteson Langdon and Gerhard Baer, eds., Albuquerque: University of New Mexico Press.

Lee, Richard B. 1993. *The Dobe Ju/hoansi*, 2d ed. Fort Worth, TX: Harcourt Brace College.

Lewis, Gordon K. 1968. *The growth of the Modern West Indies*. New York: Monthly Review.

Lewis, I. M. [1971]. 1989. *Ecstatic religion: A study of shamanism and spirit possession*, 2d ed. London: Routledge.

Lincoln, Eric C., and Lawrence H. Mamiya. 1990. *The Black church in the African American Experience*. Durham, NC: Duke University Press.

Lincoln, Jackson Steward. [1935] 1970. *The dream in primitive cultures*. New York and London: Johnson Reprint.

Littlewood, Roland. 1993a. Divine femininity among Trinidad's Earth People: Appropriation and reinterpretation in Spiritual Baptist visions. *Caribbean Quarterly* 39 (3/4):56–73.

———. 1993b. *Pathology and identity: The work of Mother Earth in Trinidad*. Cambridge: Cambridge University Press.

Lovelace, Earl. 1982. *The wine of astonishment*. London: Deutsch.

———. 1988. *A brief conversion and other stories*. Oxford: Heineman.

Lowenthal, David. 1967. Race and color in the West Indies. *Daedalus* 96:580–626.

Madden, R. R. 1835. *A twelvemonths residence in the West Indies*. London: James Cochrane.

Malm, Krister. 1983. An island carnival. (CD liner notes). Electra Entertainment. Nonesuch Records 72091.

Manning, R. O. 1976. Shamanism as a profession. In *The realm of the extra-human: Agents and audiences*. Agehananda Bharati, ed., pp. 73–94. The Hague: Mouton.

Manuel, Peter (with Kenneth Bilby and Michael Largey). 1995. *Caribbean currents: Caribbean music from rumba to reggae*. Philadelphia: Temple University Press.

Marshall, Dawn I. 1984. Vincentian contract labour migration to Barbados: The satisfaction of mutual needs? *Social and Economic Studies* 37 (3):63–92.

Marshall, Woodville K. 1983. 'Vox Populi': The St. Vincent riots and disturbances of 1862. In *Trade, government and society in Caribbean history, 1700–1920*. B. W. Higman, ed., pp. 85–115. Kingston, Jamaica: Heinemann Educational Books Caribbean.

———. 1991. Provision ground and plantation labour in Four Windward Islands: Competition for resources during slavery. In *The Slaves' economy: Independent production by slaves in the Americas*. Ira Berlin and Philip D. Morgan, eds. London: Frank Cass.

Martin, R. Montgomery. 1937. *The British colonial library*. Vol. 5. London: Whittaker.

May, L. Carlyle. 1956. A survey of glossolalia and related phenomena in non-Christian religions. *American Anthropologist* 58 (1):75–96.

Mayhew, Frank. 1953. My life. *Caribbean Quarterly* 3:13–23.

McCall, John C. 1996. Portrait of a brave woman. *American Anthropologist* 98 (1):127–136.

McDaniel, Lorna. 1995. Memory spirituals of the liberated American soldiers in Trinidad's "company villages." *Caribbean Quarterly* 41:38–58.

McManus, John, Charles D. Laughlin, and John Shearer. 1993. The functions of dreaming in the cycles of cognition: A biogenetic structural account. In *The functions of dreaming*. Alan Moffitt, Milton Kramer, and Robert Hoffman, eds., pp. 21–50. Albany: State University of New York Press.

Merrill, William. 1978. The Rarámuri stereotype of dreams. In *Dreaming: Anthropological and psychological interpretations*. Barbara Babcock, ed., pp. 194–219. Cambridge: Cambridge University Press.

Methodist Hymn Book. 1954. London: The Methodist Publishing House.

Michalon, Josy. 1987. *Le Ladjia: Origine et pratiques*. Paris: Editions Caribéennes.

Midgett, Douglas K. 1977. Performance roles and musical change in a Caribbean society. *Ethnomusicology* 21:55–73.

Miller, Elmer S. 1975. Shamans, power symbols, and change in Argentine Toba culture. *American Ethnologist* 2 (3):477–496.

Miller, Jay. 1988. Shamanic odyssey: The Lushootsheed Salish journey to the land of the dead. Ballena Press Anthropological Papers No. 32. Menlo Park, CA: Ballena.

Miller, Suellen. 1992. Nurse-midwifery in St. Vincent and the Grenadines. *Journal of Nurse-Midwifery* 37 (1):53–60.

Mills, Frank L. and S. B. Jones-Hendrickson (and Lessons by Bertram Eugene). 1984. *Christmas sports in St. Kitts-Nevis: Our neglected tradition*. n.p.

Mintz, S. W. 1985. From plantations to peasantries in the Caribbean. In *Caribbean contours*. Sidney W. Mintz and Sally Price, eds., pp. 127–154. Baltimore: The Johns Hopkins University Press.

Moister, William. 1866. *Memorials of missionary labours in Western Africa, the West Indies, and at the Cape of Good Hope*. London: William Nichols.

Monroe, Robert A. 1971. *Journeys out of the body*. New York: Doubleday.

———. 1985. *Far journeys*. New York: Doubleday.

———. 1994. *Ultimate journey*. New York: Doubleday.

Monteiro, Clodomir. 1988. Culto del Santo Daime: Chamanismo rural-urbano en Acre. In *Rituales y Fiestas de las Américas*. Elizabeth Reichel, ed., pp. 286–300. Bogota, Columbia: Editorial Presencia.

Moore, Joseph G. 1965. Religious syncretism in Jamaica. *Practical Anthropology* 12:63–70.

Morris, Calvin S. 1995. African Americans and Methodism. In *Directory of African American religious bodies*. Wendell J. Payne, ed., Washington, D.C.: Howard University Press.

Morrish, Ivor. 1982. *Obeah, Christ, and Rastaman: Jamaica and its religion*. Cambridge: James Clarke.

Morse, Melvin. 1994. *Parting visions: Uses and meanings of pre-death, psychic, and spiritual experiences*. New York: Villard Books.

Mumford, Stan Royal. 1989. *Himalayan dialogue: Tibetan lamas and Gurung shamans in Nepal*. Madison: University of Wisconsin Press.

Murphy, Joseph. 1994. *Working the Spirit: Ceremonies in the African diaspora*. Boston: Beacon.

Murphy, Michael. 1992. *The future of the body: Explorations into the future evolution of human nature*. Los Angeles: Jeremy P. Tarcher.

Nagashima, Nobuhiro. 1985. A note on Spiritual Baptism in Trinidad and Tobago. In *Comparative studies on the plural societies in the Caribbean*. Masao Yamaguchi and Masao Naito, eds., pp. 111–128. Tokyo: ILCAA.

Nanton, Philip. 1983. The changing pattern of state control in St. Vincent and the Grenadines. In *Crisis in the Caribbean*. Fitzroy Ambursley and Robin Cohen, eds., pp. 223–246. New York: Monthly Review.

Noll, Richard. 1985. Mental imagery cultivation as a cultural phenomenon: The role of visions in Shamanism. *Current Anthropology* 26 (4):443–461.

North, David S. and Judy A. Whitehead. 1990. *Policy recommendations for improving the utilization of emigrant resources in Eastern Caribbean nations*. Washington, D.C.: United

States, Commission for the Study of International Migration and Cooperative Economic Development.

Ober, Fred A. 1880. *Camps in the Caribbees: The adventures of a naturalist in the Lesser Antilles.* Boston: Lee and Shepard.

Olivier de Sardan, Jean Pierre. 1990. Les réel des autres. *Cahiers d'Études Africaines* 29:127–135.

Ong, Aihwa. 1987. *Spirits of resistance and capitalist discipline: Factory women in Malaysia.* Albany: State University of New York Press.

Parks, Alfrieta Velois. 1981. The conceptualization of kinship among the Spiritual Baptists of Trinidad. Ann Arbor, MI: University Microfilms, Int. Ph.D. diss. Princeton University, Princeton, NJ.

Persinger, Michael A. 1983. Religious and mystical experiences as artifacts of temporal lobe function: A general hypothesis. *Perceptual and Motor Skills* 57:1255–1262.

Pitt, E. A. 1955. Acculturative and synthetic aspects of religion and life in the island of St. Vincent and other predominantly Protestant islands and areas of the West Indies and the Caribbean. Acts of the fourth international congress of anthropological and ethnological sciences, 1952, pp. 385–390. Vienna: Verlag Adolf Holzhausens Nfg.

Pitts, Walter F. 1989. "If you caint get the boat, take a log:" Cultural reinterpretation in the Afro–Baptist ritual. *American Ethnologist* 16 (2):279–293.

———. 1991. Like a tree planted by the water: The musical cycle in the African-American Baptist ritual. *Journal of American Folklore* 104:318–340.

———. 1993. *Old ship of Zion: The Afro-Baptist ritual in the African diaspora.* New York: Oxford University Press.

Planson, Claude. 1974. *Vaudou: Un Initié Parle.* Paris: Jean Dullis Editeur.

Polk, Patrick. 1995. Sacred banners and the divine cavalry charge. In *Sacred arts of Haitian Vodou.* Donald J. Cosentino, ed., pp. 325–347. Los Angeles: UCLA Fowler Museum of Cultural History.

Pollack-Eltz, Angelina. 1970. Shango Kult und Shouter-Kirche auf Trinidad und Grenada. *Anthropos* 65 (5/6):814–832.

———. 1972. *Cultos Afroamericanos.* Caracas, Venezuela: Universidad Católica "Andrés Bello."

———. 1993. The Shango cult and other African rituals in Trinidad, Grenada, and Carriacou and their possible influence on the Spiritual Baptist faith. *Caribbean Quarterly* 39 (3/4):12–26.

Pollock, Donald. 1992. Culina Shamanism: Gender, power, and knowledge. In *Portals of power: Shamanism in South America.* E. Jean Matteson Langdon and Gerhard Baer, eds. pp. 25–40. Albuquerque: University of New Mexico Press.

Prakash, Gyan. 1992. Writing post-Orientalist histories of the Third World: Indian historiography is good to think. In *Colonialism and culture.* Nicholas B. Dirks, ed., pp. 353–388. Ann Arbor: University of Michigan Press.

Price, Neil. 1988. *Behind the planter's back: Lower class responses to marginality in Bequia Island, St. Vincent.* London: Macmillan Caribbean.

Price-Mars, Louis. 1980. Une nouvelle etape dans la réflexion sur les théolepsies en Haïti. *Ethnographie* 83 (3):283–290.

Proudfoot, Wayne. 1985. *Religious experience.* Berkeley: University of California Press.

Punnett, Betty Jane. 1984. Goal setting, need for achievement and motivation in a lesser developed country: An empirical study of their relationship. Ph.D. diss. New York University.

Purcell, Sheila, Alan Moffitt, and Robert Hofmann. 1993. Waking, dreaming, and self-regulation. In *The functions of dreaming.* Alan Moffitt, Milton Kramer, and Robert Hoffmann, eds., pp. 197–260. Albany: State University of New York Press.

Raboteau, Albert J. 1978. *Slave religion: The "invisible institution" in the antebellum South.* New York: Oxford University Press.

———. 1995. *A fire in the bones: Reflections on African-American religious history.* Boston: Beacon.

Reichel-Dolmatoff, G. 1975. *The shaman and the jaguar: A study of narcotic drugs among the Indians of Columbia.* Philadelphia: Temple University Press.

Richards, E. McL. 1965. Selavoy. *Flambeau (Kingstown, St. Vincent)*, no. 1, pp. 17–18. June.

Riguad, Milo. [1953] 1985. *Secrets of Voodoo.* San Francisco: City Lights.

Ripinsky-Naxon, Michael. 1993. *The nature of shamanism: Substance and function of a religious metaphor.* Albany, NY: State University of New York Press.

Rokeach, Milton. 1964. *The three Christs of Ypsilanti: A psychological study.* New York: Alfred A. Knopf.

Rorty, Richard. 1995. Ironists and metaphysicians. In *The truth about the truth: De-confusing and re-constructing the postmodern world.* Walter Truett Anderson, ed., pp. 100–106. New York: G. P. Putnam's Sons.

Roseman, Marina. 1984. The social structuring of sound: An example from the Temiar of peninsular Malaya. *Ethnomusicology* 28:411–445.

Ross, David. 1978. Dahomey. In *West African resistance: The military response to colonial occupation.* Michael Crowder, ed., pp. 144–169. London: Hutchinson.

Rubenstein, Hymie. 1976. Incest, effigy hanging, and biculturation in a West Indian village. *American Ethnologist* 3 (4):765–781.

———. 1987. *Coping with poverty: Adaptive strategies in a Caribbean village.* Boulder and London: Westview.

———. 1991. Household structure and class stratification in St. Vincent: A critical reply to Young. *Social and Economic Studies* 40 (3):187–197.

Ruby, Robert H., and John A. Brown. 1996. *John Slocum and the Indian Shaker Church.* Norman: University of Oklahoma Press.

Ryan, Cecil, and Cecil Blazer Williams. n.d. *From Charles to Mitchell*, pt. 1. Kingstown, St. Vincent: Projects Promotion.

Ryle, John. 1988. Miracles of the people: Attitudes to Catholicism in an Afro-Brazilian religious centre in Salvador da Bahia. In *Vernacular Christianity: Essays in the social anthropology of religion presented to Godfrey Lienhardt.* Wendy James and Douglas H. Johnson, eds. pp. 40–50. Oxford: JASO.

Said, Edward. 1978. *Orientalism.* New York: Random House.

St. Vincent. 1823. *The laws of the Island of Saint Vincent, and its dependencies from the beginning of the year 1810 to the end of 1821.* Alexander Cruikshank, comp. Kingstown, St. Vincent: Printed at the Gazette Office.

———. 1913. *Report of the chief of police for the year 1913.* n.p.: n.p.

———. 1917. *Report of the chief of police for the year 1916–1917.* n.p.: n.p.

———. 1927. *The laws of Saint Vincent: Containing the ordinances of the Colony in force on the 4th day of May, 1926*, rev. ed. Prepared by James Stanley Rae. London: Waterlow and Sons.

———. 1965. *Ordinances for the year 1965.* Kingstown: Government Printing Office.

———. 1970. *Digest of statistics, statistical unit, Saint Vincent and the Grenadines.* No. 20. Kingstown: Government Printing Office.

———. 1993. *1991—Population and housing census report.* Vol. 2. Kingstown: Statistical Office, Ministry of Finance and Planning.

Sanday, Peggy Reeves. 1981. *Female power and male dominance: On the origins of sexual inequality.* Cambridge: Cambridge University Press.

Sankey, Ira. [1874] n.d. *Sacred songs and solos: With standard hymns combined.* London: Morgan and Scott.

Sargant, William. 1974. *The mind possessed: A physiology of possession, mysticism, and faith healing*. New York: J. B. Lippincott.

Schoelcher, Victor. 1847. *Histoire de l'esclavage pendant les deux dernières anneés*. Paris: Pagnerre.

Schoen, Max. 1948. Conclusion: Art the healer. In *Music and medicine*. Dorothy M. Schullian and Max Schoen, eds., pp. 387–405. New York: Henry Schuman.

Scott, James. 1985. *Weapons of the weak: Everyday forms of peasant resistance*. New Haven, CT: Yale University Press.

Seaga, Edward. [1969]. 1982. *Revival cults in Jamaica*. Kingston: The Institute of Jamaica.

Shacochis, Bob. 1985. *Easy in the Islands*. New York: Crown.

———. 1993. *Swimming in the volcano*. New York: Charles Scribner's Sons.

Sheppard, Jill. 1974. Historical sketch of the poor Whites of Barbados: From indentured servants to "Red Legs." *Caribbean Studies* 14 (3):71–94.

Sheridan, Richard B. 1985. *Doctors and slaves: A medical and demographic history of slaves in the British West Indies, 1680–1834*. Cambridge: Cambridge University Press.

Sherrill, John L. 1964. *They speak with other tongues*. New York: McGraw-Hill.

Siikala, Anna-Leena. 1985. Comment on Noll. *Current Anthropology* 26 (4):455–456.

Silva, José and Philip Miele. 1977. *The Silva mind control method*. New York: Pocket Books.

Silvera, Makeda. 1989. *Silenced*. Toronto, Canada: Sister Vision.

Simpson, George Eaton. 1956. Jamaican revivalist cults. *Social and Economic Studies* 5 (4): 321–442.

———. 1966. Baptismal, "mourning," and "building" ceremonies of the Shouters in Trinidad. *Journal of American Folklore* 79:537–550.

———. 1980. *Religious. cults of the Caribbean: Trinidad, Jamaica and Haiti*, 3d ed., enlarged. Institute of Caribbean Studies, University of Puerto Rico, Rio Piedras.

Simpson, George Eaton and Peter B. Hammond. 1957. The African heritage in the Caribbean: Discussion. In *Caribbean studies: A symposium*. Vera Rubin, ed., pp. 46–53. Jamaica: Institute of Social and Economic Research, University of the West Indies.

Singer, Margaret Thaler (with Janja Lalich). 1995. *Cults in our midst*. San Francisco: Jossey-Bass.

Slater, Mariam. 1977. *The Caribbean family: Legitimacy in Martinique*. New York: St. Martin's Press.

Smith, Huston, Kenneth N. Stevens, and Raymond S. Tomlinson. 1967. On an unusual mode of chanting by certain Tibetan lamas. *Journal of the Acoustical Society of America* 41 (5):1262–1264.

Smith, Marian W. 1954. Shamanism in the Shaker religion of Northwest America. *Man* 54 (181):119–122.

Smith, Michael G. 1953. Some aspects of social structure in the British Caribbean about 1820. *Social and Economic Studies* 1 (4):53–79.

———. 1962. *Kinship and community in Carriacou*. New Haven, CT: Yale University Press.

———. 1963. *Dark puritan*. Kingston, Jamaica: Department of Extra-Mural Studies, University of the West Indies.

Sobel, Mechal. 1979. *Trabelin' on: The slave journey to an Afro-Baptist faith*. Westport, CT: Greenwood.

Sölle, Dorothea. 1989. *O Grün des Fingers Gottes: Die Meditationen der Hildegard von Bingen*. Wuppertal: P. Hammer.

Sparling, Catherine Wilcox. 1970. The historical geography of St. Vincent. M.A. thesis, Carleton University, Northfield, MN.

Spencer, Jon Michael. 1992. *Black hymnody: A hymnological history of the African-American church*. Knoxville: University of Tennessee Press.

Spickard, James. 1991. Experiencing religious rituals: A Schutzian analysis of Navajo ceremonies. *Sociological Analysis* 52 (2):191–204.

Spinelli, Joseph. 1973. Land use and population in St. Vincent, 1763–1960: A contribution to the study of the patterns of economic and demographic change in a small West Indian island. Ph.D. diss., University of Florida, Gainesville.

Spivak, Gyatri. 1988. Can the subaltern speak? In *Marxism and the interpretation of culture.* Cary Nelson and Lawrence Grossberg, eds., pp. 271–313. Urbana: University of Illinois Press.

Steele, Beverly A. 1996. Folk dance in Grenada. *Bulletin of Eastern Caribbean Affairs* 21 (1): 25–45.

Stephen, J. 1824. *The slavery of the British West Indian colonies delineated.* London: Joseph Butterworth and Son.

Stevenson, George John. 1883. *The Methodist hymn book: Illustrated with biography, history, incident, and anecdote.* London: S. W. Partridge.

Stewart, Harry. 1993. A case study of a methods program in English as a second language in St. Vincent, West Indies. Ph.D. diss., University of Alberta.

Stewart, Kilton. [1969] 1990. Dream theory in Malaya. In *Altered states of consciousness*, 3d ed. Charles Tart, ed., pp. 191–204. San Francisco: Harper.

Stoler, Ann. 1992. Rethinking colonial categories: European communities and the boundaries of rule. In *Colonialism and culture.* Nicholas B. Dirks, ed., pp. 319–351. Ann Arbor: University of Michigan Press.

Stoller, Paul. 1984. Sound in Songhay cultural experience. *American Ethnologist* 11 (3):559–570.

———. 1995. *Embodying colonial memories: Spirit possession, power, and the Hauka in West Africa.* New York: Routledge.

Stone, Linda. 1973. East Indian adaptations on St. Vincent: Richland Park. In *Windward Road: Contributions to the anthropology of St. Vincent.* Thomas Fraser, ed., pp. 148–155. Amherst: University of Massachusetts, Department of Anthropology.

Stuckey, Sterling. 1987. *Slave culture: Nationalist theory and the foundations of Black America.* New York: Oxford University Press.

Taussig, Michael. 1980. *The Devil and commodity fetishism in South America.* Chapel Hill: University of North Carolina Press.

———. 1982. Coming home: Ritual and labour migration in a Colombian town. Working Paper Series, No. 30. Montreal, Quebec: Centre for Developing-Area Studies, McGill University.

———. 1987. *Shamanism, colonialism, and the Wildman: A study in terror and healing.* Chicago: University of Chicago Press.

———. 1993. *Mimesis and alterity: A particular history of the senses.* New York: Routledge.

Taylor, Ian Anthony. 1993. The rite of mourning in the Spiritual Baptist Church with emphasis on the activity of the Spirit. *Caribbean Quarterly* 39 (3/4):26–41.

Tessoneau, Alex-Louise. 1983. "Le don reçu en songe:" La transmission du savoir dans les métiers traditionnels (Haïti). *L'Ethnographie* 79 (1):69–82.

Thomas, Eudora. 1987. *A history of the Shouter Baptists in Trinidad and Tobago.* Tacarigua, Trinidad: Calaloux.

Thomas, Nicholas. 1991. *Entangled objects: Exchange, material culture, and colonialism in the Pacific.* Cambridge: Harvard University Press.

———. 1992. The inversion of tradition. *American Ethnologist* 19 (2):213–232.

Thomas-Hope, Elizabeth M. 1992. *Explanation in Caribbean migration: Perception and the image: Jamaica, Barbados, St. Vincent.* London: Macmillan Caribbean.

Thompson, Robert Farris. [1983] 1984. *Flash of the Spirit: African and Afro-American art and philosophy.* New York: Vintage Books.

Thomsen, Thomas Carl. 1988. *Tales of Bequia.* Cross River, NY: Cross River Press.

Thornton, John. 1992. *Africa and Africans in the making of the Atlantic world, 1400–1680.* Cambridge: Cambridge University Press.

Toney, Joyce Roberta. 1986. The development of a culture of migration among a Caribbean people: St. Vincent and New York, 1838–1979. Ph.D. diss., Columbia University, New York.

Trigger, Bruce G. 1969. *The Huron: Farmers of the North*. New York: Holt, Rinehart and Winston.

Turner, Victor. 1969. *The ritual process: Structure and anti-structure*. London: Routledge and Kegan Paul.

Tylor, Clarence. 1994. *The Black churches of Brooklyn*. New York: Columbia University Press.

UWI (University of the West Indies, Faculty of Law). 1996. *Grenada: Consolidated index of statutes and subsidiary legislation to 1st January 1996*. Holmes Beach, FL: W. W. Gaunt.

van Capelleveen, Remco. 1993. "Peripheral" culture in the metropolis: West Indians in New York City. In *Alternative cultures in the Caribbean*. Thomas Bremer and Ulrich Fleischmann, eds. pp. 131–147. Frankfurt am Main: Vervuert Verlag.

Vetter, Michael. 1983. Overtones, voice, and tambura. (CD liner notes). Mainz, West Germany: Music Factory GmbH.

Wallace, Anthony F. C. 1966. *Religion: An anthropological view*. New York: Random House.

Wallerstein, Immanuel. 1974. *The modern world system 1*. New York: Academic.

———. 1980. *The modern world system 2*. New York: Academic.

Walsh, Roger N. 1990. *The spirit of shamanism*. Los Angeles: Jeremy P. Tarcher.

Ward, Colleen, and Michael Beaubrun. 1979. Trance induction and hallucination in Spiritual Baptist mourning. *The Journal of Psychological Anthropology* 2 (4):479–480.

Warner, Ashton. 1831. *Negro slavery described by a negro; being the narrative of Ashton Warner, a native of St. Vincent's*. S. Strickland, [comp.] London: Samuel Maunder, Newgate Street.

Watkins, Mary. 1976. *Waking dreams*. New York: Gordon and Breach.

Watkins-Owens, Irma. 1996. *Blood relations: Caribbean immigrants and the Harlem community, 1900–1930*. Bloomington: Indiana University Press.

Watson, Richard. 1817. *A defence of the Wesleyan and Methodist missions in the West Indies*. London: T. Cordeaux.

Wesselman, Hank. 1995. *Spiritwalker: Messages from the future*. New York: Bantam Books.

Williams, Brackette. 1984. "Ef me naa bin come me naa been know:" Informal social control and the Afro-Guyanese wake, 1900–1948. *Caribbean Quarterly* 30 (3–4):26–44.

Williams, Charles. 1982. The conversion ritual in a rural Black baptist church. In *Holding on to the land and the Lord: Kinship, ritual, land tenure, and social policy in the rural South*. Robert L. Hall and Carol B. Stack, eds., pp. 69–79. Athens: The University of Georgia Press.

Williams, Eric. 1962. *History of the people of Trinidad and Tobago*. Port-of-Spain, Trinidad: PNM.

Williams, Joseph J. [1932] 1970. *Voodoos and obeahs: Phases of West Indian witchcraft*. New York: AMS.

Williams, Mervyn Russell. 1985. Song from valley to mountain: Music and ritual among the Spiritual Baptists ("Shouters") of Trinidad. M.A. thesis, Indiana University.

Winkelman, Michael J. 1992. *Shamans, priests, and witches: A cross-cultural study of magico-religious practitioners*. Tempe: Arizona State University.

Winthrop, Robert H. 1991. *Dictionary of concepts in cultural anthropology*. New York: Greenwood.

The world almanac and book of facts 1994. 1993. Mahwah, NJ: World Almanac.

Worsley, Peter. 1957. *The trumpet shall sound: A study of 'cargo' cults in Melanesia*. London: MacGibbon and Kee.

Wright, Pablo G. 1992. Dream, shamanism, and power among the Toba of Formosa Province. In *Portals of power: Shamanism in South America*. E. Jean Matteson Langdon and Gerhard Baer, eds., pp. 149–172. Albuquerque: University of New Mexico Press.

Young, Robert. 1990. *White mythologies: Writing history and the West*. London: Routledge.

Young, Virginia Heyer. 1990. Household structure in a West Indian society. *Social and Economic Studies* 39 (3):147–180.

———. 1991. Vincentian domestic culture: Continued debate. *Social and Economic Studies* 40 (4):155–167.

———. 1993. *Becoming West Indian: Culture, self, and nation in St. Vincent*. Washington: Smithsonian Institution.

Zaleski, Carol. 1987. *Otherworld journeys: Accounts of near-death experience in Medieval and Modern times*. New York: Oxford University Press.

Zane, Wallace W. 1995. Ritual states of consciousness: A way of accounting for anomalies in the observation and explanation of spirit possession. *Anthropology of Consciousness* 6 (4): 18–29.

Index

Africa (spiritual city), 47, 48, 84–85, 93, 97, 99, 118
  dances, 61–2, 101
African American churches, 102, 142, 211, 214
  in Brooklyn, 173
  Holy Spirit possession in, 100
  singing in, 65, 209n7
African warrior (spiritual gift), 53, 39, 141–143, 201
airplanes
  in the spiritual world, 146
Akan, 213n2
Aladura, 156, 169
Alphabet. *See* doption
altar, 23, 45–46, 191
altered states of consciousness. *See* consciousness
Amazons. *See* Fon
America, the United States of, 8, 11, 80, 135, 146, 147, 164, 166, 172, 173, 174, 176
American films and television, 132
  possible influence on Converted cosmology, 61, 85, 132, 143
American Baptists. *See* Southern Baptists
Anglican church, 31, 32, 54, 97, 151, 152, 153, 154, 205

animals
  in the Spirit, 91
  See also dogs; snakes
anointing (ritual), 25, 34, 45, 66, 72–73, 189–190
Apaches. *See* Indian tribes
Apostolics, 32, 38, 62, 125
  Apostolic Faith Mission, 153
apron, 25, 49, 86, 166, 196
  See also uniform
Arabia (spiritual location), 82, 87
Archdiocese, Spiritual Baptist, 54, 153, 169, 203
Argüelles, José, 136, 137
assistant leader (spiritual gift). *See* leader
assistant mother (spiritual gift). *See* mother
assistant nurse (spiritual gift). *See* nurse
assistant pointer (spiritual gift). *See* pointer
Auld Lang Syne (musical tune), 64
axis mundi, 131

Babylon (spiritual location), 82
Bajans. *See* Whites.
bands (blindfolds), 26, 40, 36, 37, 45, 96–99, 107, 111, 112, 114, 157, 190, 192, 196–197, 203, 211n11
  placing on the pilgrim's head, 63, 66, 74–75

bands (blindfolds) *(continued)*
  preparation of, 35, 48, 50, 96–99, 117,
    140, 196–197, 305
  swaddling bands, 99
  treatment of after mourning, 67, 117
  in Trinidad, 157
  wearing of in nine days, 26, 67, 114, 117,
    147, 194
  See also banning
banning (ritual), 20, 34, 36, 50, 60, 66–76,
    79, 80, 87, 92, 96, 107–108, 108–109,
    155, 190, 196, 203, 209
  See also bands
baptism (ritual), 32, 34, 35–36, 37, 95, 147,
    157, 159, 172, 173, 190
Baptists. *See* Converted
Baptists, Southern. *See* Southern
    Baptists
Barbados, 6, 11, 81, 148, 152, 169
  See also Spiritual Baptists
bath. *See* spiritual bath
Believers. *See* Converted
bell, 46, 50, 75
bell ringer (spiritual gift), 40, 198
belt, 19, 50, 94
bench of repentance, 36
Bequia
  whaling, 205n5
Bethlehem (spiritual location), 86–87
Beulahland (spiritual location), 86–87
Bible, 16, 47, 50, 70, 95, 97
  proofs, 70, 197
  use as a musical instrument, 56, 208n3
bishops, 34, 49
Black Caribs. *See* Caribs
blindfolds. *See* bands
blowing (ritual), 190
boats. *See* ships
bones, 98, 140–141
  See also the Valley
Book of Common Prayer, 191
Book of Offices, 191, 202
Bramble Picker (saint), 90–91
Britain. *See* Great Britain
Brooklyn, New York, 4, 80, 126–129, 164–
    175, 176
Brother Cutter (saint), 90–91, 108

Buddhism, 169
  statue of Buddha, 171

calabash, 46, 47, 85
calendar, 47
calypsos, 8, 17, 144, 211n8
Canaan (spiritual city), 85–86
candlelighting (ritual), 190–191
candles, 47–48, 50, 76, 116, 127
  candle wax, 69, 71, 74, 96–99
Candomblé, 146, 210n7
canons, 34
captain (spiritual gift), 40, 59, 101, 102, 202
cargo cults, 40–41
Caribs, 5, 6, 61, 150–51, 205n1, 205n2,
    209n6
  See also Garifuna
carnal
  differentiation between carnal and
    spiritual, 33, 43
Carnival, 143
  Carnival bands, 143–144, 177
Castaneda, Carlos, 136
Catherine (saint), 89–90
Catholicism. *See* Roman Catholicism
cave art, 140–141
center pole, 23, 45, 81, 140, 141, 207n7,
    213n1
centurion, 54
chalk, 19, 50, 96
change
  in Converted religious practice, 174–
    175
chanting, 54–55, 68
  See also choruses; humming; hymns;
    singing; songs
China (spiritual city), 64, 85, 98
Chiptees (spiritual beings), 85
choruses, 53–54, 62, 209n9
  See also chanting; humming; hymns;
    singing; songs
Christ, Jesus. *See* Jesus
christening, 191
Christian Pilgrim. *See* Converted
Christian shamanism, 124–125, 178, 212n2
Christmas, 9, 144–145
  See also Nine Mornings

church building, 23, 45–49
Church of Christ, 153
Church of God (Cleveland, Tennessee),
    173
colonialism, 3, 4, 8–11, 64–65, 145–148,
    177
communion (ritual), 192
conch (musical instrument), 56, 152
Confucianism, 169
Congo. *See* Ki-Kongo
consciousness
    altered, 99–106, 123, 132–135, 140, 178,
        211, 212
    collective, 27–28
    on journeys, 27
    ritual states, 99–106
    of spiritual purpose, 27, 133–135
consecration (ritual), 46, 166–167, 191–192,
    207n8
conversion, 214n4, 214n5
Converted, 3, 11–12, 153–154
    African influence, 1, 9–11, 56, 57, 60,
        130, 141–143, 145
    denominations, 153
    history, 149–163
    music. *See* music
    numbers of adherents, 4, 147, 153, 166,
        215n2
    terms for in St. Vincent, 160, 153–154
    Vincentian attitudes toward, 9, 17–18, 22,
        125–129
Converted cosmology, 4, 15, 80–95, 139–
    148
    and British colonialism, 10, 137–138, 147,
        159–160, 177
cords, 49
courts, 23, 142
Creole, 205n3
crosses, 74, 94
cross-bearer (spiritual gift), 24, 199
crotons. *See* plants
crowning (ritual), 39, 192
crowns, 18, 94, 112

Dahomey. *See* Fon
Daime, 212n14
Damballah, 213n1

dances, 59–62, 64, 112
    Grenada, 61, 152
    of spiritual cities, 55
danger in the spiritual world, 20, 92–94
deacons, 34–49
death, 125–129
    See also memorials; the Valley
Desana, 210n3
Desert, the (spiritual location), 61, 112
dialect
    Vincentian dialect, 16
dike nwami (brave woman), 142
discipline, 93–94
diver (spiritual gift), 201–202
doctor (spiritual gift). *See* pointer
doctor's shop, 83, 94, 211n9
dogs, 20, 84, 92, 131, 210n3
    See also Valley dogs
Dominica
    Caribs of, 205n2
doption, 17, 58, 62, 68, 83–84, 93, 100–102,
    159, 167, 211n12
Dorsetshire Hill, 205n4
dragon. *See* plants
dream interpretation. *See* dreams
dreams, 62, 103, 132–135
    interpretation of, 38
    lan domi (skill-learning dreams), 95
    lucid dreams. *See* lucidity
    multi-state, 132–133
    pattern dreams, 132
    practical skills learned in, 95
dress. *See* uniform
drums, 152, 202n3
    in Trinidadian churches, 171, 208n2
    spiritual instrument, 54, 56
dying away, 58, 104, 212n15
dying off. *See* dying away

Earth People, the, 215n10
East Indians, 6, 61, 205n4
Egypt (spiritual location), 87
eidetic imagery. *See* phosphenes
embodiment, 213n3
England. *See* Great Britain
epilepsy
    in relation to ecstatic experience, 211n11

Established Church. *See* Anglican church

Ethiopians (spiritual beings), 85

ethnic identification, 6, 205n4
    the words White and Black, 16, 205n3

European
    control of Caribbean, 5, 8
    influence on Converted religion, 60–61,
        62–65

Evangelical Church of the West Indies,
    153

Ezekiel (saint), 83, 90

Fanti, 213n2

fasting (ritual), 105–106, 192

female warriors, 141–143
    See also Fon

fighting. *See* spiritual fighting

fire
    walking through, 196

firearms. *See* spiritual fighting

flag waver (spiritual gift), 199

flags, 46, 81, 83–86, 98–99, 159, 170
    Jolly Roger, 84, 137
    Union Jack, 86, 137

florist (spiritual gift), 198–199

flowers. *See* plants

Fon (Dahomey), 141, 213n1, 214n2
    Amazons, 141

forty days. *See* memorials

foundation, 67

foundation lesson. *See* foundation

France
    influence in St. Vincent, 5, 150

Freemasonry, 170

funeral (ritual), 192–193

gaol. *See* lock up

Garifuna, 5, 165, 209n6
    See also Caribs

garment. *See* uniform

gazing, 58, 104, 170

gentlemen, 18, 91

gifts
    giving of to pilgrim, 116
    See also spiritual gifts

glossolalia, 68, 84–85, 94, 150, 210n8
    xenoglossia, 210n8

goblet, 47

God, 88–89, 207n2, 210n5
    See also Jesus; Holy Spirit; Spirit

Goodman, Felicitas, 136–137

Gospel Hall, 153

gown. *See* uniform

Great Britain, 5, 137, 146
    See also colonialism

greeting (ritual), 67, 167

Grenada, 143, 157, 169, 173
    dancing, 61, 143, 152
    prohibition against Shakers, 214n7

Gypsies (spiritual beings), 88

hailings, 55, 62, 69

Hairoun, 4

Haiti
    skills learned in dreams, 95
    See also Vodou

hands,
    anointing of, 45, 73
    use of, 44–45

handshakes, 45, 158, 167

Harner, Michael, 136

headtie, 36, 49, 67, 113

headwrap, 49, 67

healing, 123
    See also pointer

Hell (spiritual location), 82

Hildegard, St., 140

Hinduism, 96, 157, 169

historical symbols. *See* metaphors

Holy Spirit, 33, 75, 79, 88–90, 94, 100,
    207n2, 210n5
    See also God; Jesus; Spirit

hospital, 2, 94
    in spiritual world, 18, 21, 81, 113
    See also doctor's shop

house blessing (ritual), 137, 193

house christening (ritual), 191

humming, 54, 56
    See also choruses; hymns; sankeys;
        singing; songs

hymns, 54, 209n8
    See also choruses; hymns; sankeys;
        singing; songs

hymn-lining, 57

hymnals, 54, 62, 167

Ibibio, 142–143, 213n2
Igbo, 142, 213n2
India (spiritual city), 20, 61, 85, 98
Indian Sea (spiritual location), 82, 87
Indian Shaker Church, 160–161, 176
Indian tribes (spiritual beings), 20, 61, 85,
    143
    Apaches, 85
    Wild Indians, 61
Indians from South Asia. *See* East Indians
inspector (spiritual gift), 40, 49, 201
Israel (spiritual city), 85

Jacob's City (spiritual city), 82
jail. *See* lock up
Jamaica, 147, 151, 158–159
    Jamaican Spiritual Baptist church
        (Brooklyn), 171
    See also Pukkumina; Revival
Jehovah's Witnesses, 32
Jericho (spiritual city), 84–85, 101, 210n4
Jerusalem (spiritual city), 86–87, 101, 112
Jesuits, 150
Jesus, 45, 88–89, 108, 209n2, 210n5
    See also God; Holy Spirit; Spirit
John the Baptist (saint), 89–90, 112
Jordanites (Guyana), 158–159, 172
journey. *See* spiritual journey
Jungle, the (spiritual location), 84

keys, 99, 128
    as songs, 52–53, 128
    spiritual tools, 69, 94
Ki-Kongo, 141, 152, 158–159, 213n2,
    214n3
king, 39
knight commander (spiritual gift), 39–40
Kongo. *See* Ki-Kongo

labouring. *See* Revival; Pukkumina
ladder, 98–99
ladies, 91
ladiya, 210n7
ladjia. *See* ladiya
Lakota
    vision quest, 132
languages, spiritual. *See* spiritual languages
lash, 93–94, 108–109, 152

laying down of the pilgrim. *See* banning
laying of cornerstone for a church (ritual),
    193
leader (spiritual gift), 57, 59, 167, 202
leadress (spiritual gift), 167, 202
Letters, the. *See* doption, types of
licks. *See* lash
light, 114
    seeing a bright light, 73, 108, 112, 141
liturgy. *See* opening of the service
lock up, 19, 70, 92–93
locked up. *See* lock up
lota, 47, 208n9
lucidity, 132–135
    in spiritual journeys, 104
    lucid dreams, 104, 132–135
luther. *See* lota

mandalas
    compared to Converted wheels, 140
Mandinga, 213n2
Mansren movement (Papua New Guinea),
    148
marching (ritual), 67, 115, 193, 215n7
Mary (saint), 90, 99
matron. *See* nurse
McIntosh, George, 155
meditation, 62, 103
memorials, 37–38, 125–129, 193–194
mercy seat. *See* bench of repentance
messenger (spiritual gift), 200
metaphors
    historical symbols, 141–143
    natural symbols, 131, 140–142
    orientational, 131
    See also keys; roads; schools; ships
Methodist church, 60, 63
    and origin of the Converted, 129, 152
    in St. Vincent, 151, 152–153
    missionaries, 151
    tea parties used in conversion, 214n4
Methodist Hymn Book, 54, 62–63, 167
Michael (saint), 90
migration, 7, 156, 164–166
mission (ritual), 194, 207n6
Monroe, Robert. A., 135–136, 176
Montserrat
    the Jombee dance of, 60

Mormons, 147
   missionaries in St. Vincent, 32, 154
mother (spiritual gift), 202–203
mother deaconess (spiritual gift). *See*
   mother
mother leadress (spiritual gift). *See* mother
Mount Zion (spiritual location), 83
mourner, 67–68
mourning (ritual), 24–28, 37, 89, 102–103,
   107–118, 154–155, 194
   and improvement in mental and physical
      health, 134, 212n17
   practical skills learned in the spiritual
      world, 21, 95
   preparation for, 66–76, 95–106
mourning room, 19, 76, 105, 107–108
Mt. Zion (spiritual location). *See* Mount
   Zion
music, 52–65
   the Bible as musical instrument, 56,
      208n3
   and captain, 59
   historical context of, 57, 62–65
   and leader, 57, 59
   musician (spiritual gift), 40, 94
   and pointer, 52, 58, 59
   spiritual musical instruments, 56, 99,
      208n2
   Vincentian attitudes toward, 52

names, 39, 90
   allegorical, 90–91
   avoided in St. Vincent, 20, 26–27
   terms of address for mourners, 24
National Spiritual Baptist Day, 156,
   215n8
Nations, the (spiritual city), 85
Nations of the Sea (spiritual location), 87
natural. *See* carnal
natural symbols. *See* metaphors
Nevis, 143
New Testament Church of God, 173
New York. *See* Brooklyn, New York
nine days (ritual), 67, 117, 147, 194
Nine Mornings (Christmas celebration), 144–
   145, 214n3
nine night (ritual). *See* memorials
North Pole (spiritual location), 82, 88

Nurse Dinah (saint), 90–91, 108
nurse (spiritual gift), 21, 109, 113, 147, 201
   nurse matron, 146

obeah, 103, 152, 171, 172, 214n4, 216n6
ocean. *See* sea
Ogun, 210n7
one year's memorial (ritual). *See* memorial
open air mission (ritual), 194–195
open air. *See* open air mission
opening of the service (ritual), 46, 66–68,
   195
Order of Morning Prayer, 167
Organization, Spiritual Baptist, 153
orientational metaphors. *See* metaphors
Orisha. *See* Shango
orthography
   of Vincentian and Converted words, 15–
   16, 211n12
out-of-body experiences, 102, 213n6
overtone singing. *See* singing

palm. *See* plants
pass. *See* password
password, 20, 76, 92, 108
pastors, 34, 49
pattern dreams. *See* dreams
Peace Corps, 154
pencil, 19, 50
Penitent, the. *See* Converted
Pentecostalism, 4, 138, 152–154, 173,
   210n8, 212n2
Pentecostal churches in St. Vincent, 62, 63,
   214n5
Philomene (saint), 89–90
phosphenes, 140–141
pilgrim. *See* mourner
Pilgrim Baptists. *See* Converted
pilgrim journey. *See* mourning
Pilgrim's Progress, The, 4, 50, 73, 83, 86, 94,
   95–96, 141
plants, 23, 48
   croton, 44
   dragon, 44
   evergreen, 46
   sago palm, 44
Plymouth Brethren, 214n6
poetic imagination, 189

pointer (spiritual gift), 19, 94, 104, 142, 203
   as doctor, 38, 203
   pointers' tools, 50, 94–95
pointing. *See* banning
pointing father. *See* pointer
pointing mother. *See* pointer
pointing parents, 18, 36
population
   of Converted in New York, 166, 215n2
   of Converted in St. Vincent, 4, 147, 153
   of St. Vincent, 6
   of Vincentians in New York, 165
   of West Indians in New York, 165, 168
Portuguese, 6, 205n4
praise (ritual), 195
prayers
   singing prayers (sing prays, sing prayers),
      55, 167
   while mourning, 92, 109
Presbyterians, 152, 160
proofs (ritual), 70, 197
Prosperity (spiritual city), 87
prover (spiritual gift), 202
proving, 43
Public Meetings ("Shakerism") Prohibition
   Ordinance (Grenada 1928), 214n7
Pukkumina, 158–59, 211n13, 214n3
   See also Revival
pygmies (spiritual beings). *See* Chiptees

queen, 39

reading, 103
Red Sea (spiritual location), 87
rejoicing. *See* doption
releasing (ritual), 114
repentance (ritual), 195
Revival (Jamaica), 61–62, 101, 158, 172
   See also Pukkumina
rising (ritual), 36, 75, 99, 110–112, 195–196
rising morning (ritual). *See* rising
rising night (ritual). *See* rising
ritual experience, 16
ritual offices. *See* spiritual gifts
ritual performance, 31, 34, 41–42, 57, 59
ritual reversal, 31, 39–42, 60–61, 138, 144–
      148, 177
ritual states of consciousness, 99–106

rituals, 34–38, 189–198
roads
   Converted metaphors of, 53, 59
Robertson, Pat, 215n11
robing (ritual), 196
rod, 49–50
Roman Catholicism, 62, 89, 150, 152, 170
Rose and Marguerite societies, 41, 177

sago palm. *See* plants
Sahara (spiritual location), 87
St. Lucia, 61–62, 157, 205n3, 210n3
   grundé singing, 208n4
   Rose and Marguerite societies, 41, 61–
      62
St. Vincent, 4–8, 205n6
   agricultural products, 5, 6–8, 145
   attitudes toward African traits, 9
   as a British colony, 40, 149
   and Christianity, 150–154
   fishing, 7
   history, 5, 150–155, 177
   physical description, 4–5, 64
   previous anthropological research, 11, 12
   religious laws, 149–163
   riots, 152, 177
   slave laws, 151–152
   tourism, 7–8
   whaling, 7
St. Vincent and the Grenadines. *See* St.
   Vincent
saints, 21, 89–91, 170–171
Salish (Northwest Coast), 160
   shamans, 160, 211n13, 211n14
Salvation Army, 153
Sambia, 132
sankeys, 54
   Sacred Songs and Solos, 54
Santeria, 172
sashes, 49, 112
Satan, 20, 89, 91, 115
schools, 19, 94–95, 113, 137–138
   Converted metaphors of, 37, 80, 98, 102
   Vincentian schools, 40, 96, 137–138
scissors, 208n10
scriptures, 44, 50
sea (spiritual location), 20, 87
Sea of Glass (spiritual location), 87

Sea of Tingeling (spiritual location), 87
sea shanteys, 209n9
sealing, 73–74, 196
seals, 36, 50, 94–95, 96–99, 139–141, 206n13
seeing, 43–44, 103
    See also spiritual eyes
seeking
    in African American churches, 211n14
Senoi Dream Theory, 133–135, 178
Seventh Day Adventists, 62, 153
Shakerism Prohibition Ordinance, 9, 149–150, 154–155, 156
    text of, 161–162
Shakers
    American (United Order of Believers), 160
    Northwest Coast (see Indian Shaker Church), 160–161
    Vincentian (Converted), 149–155, 160, 161–163
    See also Converted
shaking, 62, 100, 128
shamanism, 10, 42, 59, 105, 121–131, 160, 176–178, 206n10, 212n16, 213n5
shamanistic Christianity, 124–125, 178, 212n2
Shango, 89–90, 158, 169–171, 172–173, 215n10
Shango Baptist, 171, 174–175
shepherd (spiritual gift), 24, 200
shepherdess (spiritual gift), 200
ships
    Converted metaphors of, 52–53, 59, 83, 99, 101, 140
    in spiritual travels, 59, 80, 81, 94
Shouters (Trinidadian Spiritual Baptists), 156–158
Shouters Prohibition Ordinance (Trinidad), 156
shouting (ritual), 17–28, 75, 89, 115–117, 196
shuttling, 102
signing of bands. *See* bands
Silva Mind Control, 136
Silva, José, 136
sin, 43, 177
sing pray. *See* prayers

singing, 3, 31, 52–57
    overtone singing, 56–57, 208n4
    See also chanting; choruses; hymns; humming; songs
Sister Clearer (saint), 90–91, 108
skeletons, 20, 83–84
slavery
    in St. Vincent, 5–6, 144–145, 147, 150–152, 213n2
Slocum, John, 160–161
smoking, 197
snakes, 19, 20, 92, 112, 210n3, 213n1
soca, 144
Sodom (spiritual location), 82
soldiers, 40
    in the spiritual world, 81, 88, 112
songs, 83, 208n5
    from the spiritual lands, 55
    sources of, 57–58, 62–64, 91
Soufriere volcano, 158
soul flight, 123
soul loss, 92–93, 123
South Pole (spiritual location), 82, 88
Southern Baptists, 33, 154
speaking in church, 44, 58
Spirit, 18, 33–34, 45, 53, 101
    actions in, 92–95
    See also Holy Spirit
spirit possession, 13, 99–100, 104
spirits, 33, 43–44, 88–89, 91, 122–124, 126–129, 159–160, 170, 172–173
Spiritual Baptist Archdiocese. *See* Archdiocese, Spiritual Baptist
Spiritual Baptist Organization. *See* Organization, Spiritual Baptist
Spiritual Baptist Emancipation Day. *See* National Spiritual Baptist Day
Spiritual Baptists, 4, 11
    Barbados, 11, 206n11
    Grenadian, 11, 40, 147, 208n2
    New York City, 140, 157, 168–172
    numbers of adherents. *See* population.
    Tobago, 11, 169
    Trinidadian, 11, 40, 81, 101, 140, 147, 156–158, 208n2, 211n12, 216n5
    use of name by Vincentians, 15, 35, 156–158, 169–170, 216n6
    Vincentian. *See* Converted

spiritual bath, 152, 197
  for sickness, 32, 38
spiritual beings, 88–91
spiritual cities, 80–88
spiritual clothing. *See* uniform
spiritual eyes, 42–44
spiritual fighting, 43, 93, 112, 131, 210n7
spiritual flags. *See* flags
spiritual gifts, 38–42, 198–203
  in Trinidad, 40, 207n4
spiritual journeys, 18, 19–20, 79–106, 146
  collective, 101–2, 130–31
  See also mourning
spiritual lands. *See* spiritual cities
spiritual languages. *See* glossolalia
spiritual names. *See* spiritual gifts
spiritual schools, 81, 98
spiritual work, 31–51, 121–138
spiritual world. *See* Spirit
Spiritualist Churches in New Orleans,
  143
spontaneous shamanism, 135–137, 213n5
Stewart, Kilton, 133–135, 178
Streams of Power, 153
Subaltern Studies Group, 9
surveying. *See* consecration
surveyor (spiritual gift), 167, 200–201
sword fighting. *See* spiritual fighting
syncretism, 65, 169–170, 215n11
synesthesia, 102
Syria (spiritual location), 87

table, giving a. *See* thanksgiving
Taps (musical tune), 64
taria, 209n9
teacher (spiritual gift), 40, 203
Temiar, 58, 133–135, 138
thanksgiving (ritual), 39, 167–168, 197
Tibetan monks, 57, 208n4
Tobago, 214n5
  See also Spiritual Baptists
tracking, 91, 99, 104
traveling. *See* spiritual journey
Trinidad, 143, 173, 207n4, 214n5, 215n10
  attitudes toward Vincentians, 156–158,
    169
  See also Spiritual Baptists
trumpet blower (spiritual gift), 199–200

Tshidi Zionists, 148
Tuvan singing, 57, 208n4

uniform, 21, 24, 25, 48–49, 50, 67, 69

Valley dogs, 84, 210n3
Valley, the (spiritual city), 20, 25, 67, 83–
  84, 98, 101
Valley of Dry Bones. *See* the Valley
Valley of Peace (spiritual location), 82
Valley of St. Philomene (spiritual location),
  82
veils, 24
veves, 141
Victory (spiritual city), 37, 97, 99
Vincentian history. *See* St. Vincent
Vincentian society. *See* St. Vincent
Vincentian Spiritual Baptists. *See*
  Converted
visions, 103, 105, 167
Vodou, 89, 141, 159–160, 168, 172, 176,
  210n6, 213n1
  kanzo, 159
  Lavilokan, 159
  Nan Ginin, 159
voodoo. *See* obeah

wakes. *See* memorials
Wakuénai, 65
Wana (Sulawesi), 130–131, 211n13
warrior (spiritual gift). *See* African
  warrior
washing (ritual), 70–72, 198
watchman (spiritual gift), 21, 200
water, 46, 48, 50, 109, 114
water carrier (spiritual gift), 199
Wesley, Charles, 62–63, 88, 152, 210n8
Wesley, John, 63, 152, 210n8
Wesleyan Baptists. *See* Converted
Wesselman, Hank, 136–137, 176
West Indian United Order of Spiritual
  Baptists, 156
whaling
  in Bequia, 205n5
  in St. Vincent, 7
wheel, 69, 96, 98, 126–127
whipping. *See* lash

Whites in St. Vincent, 6, 205n4
Wicket Gate, 73, 108
Wilderness People, 152
words, 44
    giving a word to the pilgrim, 68–70, 108–
        109
work. *See* spiritual work

Yamana (South America), 129–130, 211n13
Yoruba, 156

Zion (spiritual city), 81, 82–83, 101, 213n1
    doctor's shop in, 83, 94, 211n9
Zion, Mount (spiritual location). *See* Mount
    Zion